Peter Porter Wiggins

The descendants of John Porter, of Windsor, Conn.,

In the line of his great, great grandson, Col. Joshua Porter, M.D., of Salisbury, Litchfield county, Conn., with some account of the families into which they married

Peter Porter Wiggins

The descendants of John Porter, of Windsor, Conn.,
In the line of his great, great grandson, Col. Joshua Porter, M.D., of Salisbury, Litchfield county, Conn., with some account of the families into which they married

ISBN/EAN: 9783337733421

Printed in Europe, USA, Canada, Australia, Japan

Cover: Foto ©ninafisch / pixelio.de

More available books at **www.hansebooks.com**

DESCENDANTS

OF

Col. Joshua Porter, M. D.

OF

SALISBURY,

CONN.

DESCENDANTS

OF

Col. Joshua Porter, M. D.

OF

SALISBURY,

CONN.

ERRATA.

—Page 3, 24th line from top, 1630 should be 1680.
—Page 6, 10th line from top, 1795 should be 1759.
—Page 7, 30th line from top, William should be Walter.
Page 26, 32d line from top, Boxbury should be Roxbury.
Page 27, 11th line from top, Springfield should be Sheffield.
Page 33, 8th line from top, Aigail should be Abigail.
Page 37, 36th line from top, 1820-5 should be 1720-5.
Page 41, last line, Kooker should be Hooker.
Page 55, 24th line from top, 1656 should be 1856.
Page 71, 37th line from top, Sovia should be Sophia.
Page 74, 1st line from top, Julia E. should be Julia K.

THE DESCENDANTS

OF

JOHN PORTER,

OF

WINDSOR, CONN.,

IN THE LINE OF HIS GREAT, GREAT GRANDSON,

Col. Joshua Porter, M. D.

OF

SALISBURY, LITCHFIELD COUNTY, CONN.,

WITH SOME ACCOUNT OF THE FAMILIES INTO
WHICH THEY MARRIED.

*"Children's children are the crown of old men;
and the glory of children are their fathers.—Prov. xvii-6.*

PRINTED FOR THE COMPILERS BY
GEORGE W. BALL,
SARATOGA SPRINGS, N. Y.
1882.

PREFACE.

SEVERAL years ago the compilers of the following pages, desiring to ascertain the ancestry of their great-grandfather, Col. Joshua Porter, of Salisbury, Conn., were led to the careful examination of various letters, documents and records in their own possession, as also the public records and local histories of the various New England towns to which the different branches of the family removed.

This project was, after considerable time and labor, completely accomplished, and the direct line traced to JOHN PORTER, of Windsor, Conn., 1639–40; but in so doing a vast amount of data was collected relating to other branches of the family, descendants of the same common ancestor. Many curious and interesting incidents and connections were found, and an extensive correspondence opened with persons bearing the Porter name, or descended therefrom, in this country.

The work so modestly begun has grown to large dimensions, both through their own interest and that of many other descendants of this family, so that at the present writing upwards of 15,000 names have been recorded.

Having proceeded thus far, it is now proposed to complete, so far as may be possible, the entire record of the descendants of JOHN PORTER, in the lines of all his children, and at some future time prepare the same for publication.

While much of the work is accomplished, the records of many families are far from complete; and of some no data whatever has been obtained.

PREFACE.

The purpose in publishing these few pages is two-fold: First, to fulfill the promise made to the descendants of Colonel Joshua Porter, and to present to them a complete record of their generations; and, second, to aid in bringing to a satisfactory and early conclusion the more extended work which the compilers have in preparation, by interesting those throughout the country, who may be able to trace their ancestry to some one in the earlier generations, given in the first pages of this pamphlet, and inducing their transmittal to the compilers.

To add to the interest of this record, and that it may not be merely a bare list of the generations of the main line, some account has been given of the families with which the Porters became allied by marriage, thus bringing before the reader a large amount of genealogical information and curious connections.

Little need be said concerning the accuracy of this record. No one who has undertaken any genealogical work can confidently guarantee entire accuracy, particularly in a first edition.

The compilers will be glad to receive at any time suggestions and corrections from any one having data bearing upon the subject; and their desire is that sufficient interest may be manifested by the different branches of the family, now so widely separated, that with their assistance they may be able to present a complete record of the descendants of their general ancestor, JOHN PORTER.

To all who have assisted in the collection of data, and they are too numerous to be here specified, the compilers tender their hearty thanks.

HENRY P. ANDREWS.
P. PORTER WIGGINS.

SARATOGA SPRINGS, N. Y., June, 1882.

John Porter.

(1.)

Among the early settlers of New England, in the great tide of emigration from England, subsequent to the granting of the charter for the Colony of Massachusetts Bay, in 1628,—came JOHN PORTER.

The records in England give his descent, in the sixteenth generation, from *William de la Grande*, a Norman Knight, who came in the army of the Norman Duke, at the conquest, A. D. 1066, and that he acquired lands, at, or near, Kenilworth, in Warwickshire. His son, Ralph, (or Roger) became "Grand Porteur" to Henry 1st A. D. 1120–1140, from which he derived the name *Porter*.

[The Windsor Church was formed in Plymouth, Eng., in March, 1630, by people from Devon, Dorset, Somerset, and Warwickshires; the reverends John Maverick being ordained as pastor and John Warham, as teacher.

In 1630 they came to New England, settling at Dorchester, Mass., on the first settlement of that town. In the summer of 1635, the arrivals having been numerous, and the settlement "somewhat "crowded, and hearing ye fame of ye Quinnitukut River," a company was formed to make a settlement there, and on the 15th of October they took their departure, carrying with them their church organization, under the Rev. John Warham; the Rev. Mr. Maverick remaining at Dorchester.

Trumbull says: "The journey from Massachusetts was made in "about fourteen days' time, the distance being more than one hundred "miles, and through a trackless wilderness. They had no guide but their compass, and made their way over mountains, through swamps, thickets, and rivers, which were not passable but with the greatest difficulty. They had no cover but the heavens, nor any lodgings but those which simple nature afforded them. They drove with them one hundred and sixty head of cattle, and subsisted on the way, in a great measure, on the milk of their kine. They were nearly a fortnight on their journey."

"This adventure was the more remarkable, as many of the company were persons of figure, who had lived in England, in honor, affluence, and delicacy, and were entire strangers to fatigue and danger." (See Appendix "A.")

This company reached the Connecticut river at a place called, by the natives, Matteneaug, but to which the settlers gave the name of *Windsor*, many of them being natives of the place of that name in England.

In 1639 the Rev. Ephraim Hewitt, of Wraxhall, in Kenilworth, Eng., was called to assist Mr. Warham, and it is probable that John Porter accompanied him, as at about that date his name first appears upon the public records.]

John Porter's residence in Windsor appears to have been located near the "Little River," at its junction with the Connecticut, between the residences of George Phelps and Joseph Loomis, and nearly opposite those of Henry Wolcott and Matthew Allyn.

He was for that period a man of considerable substance, as appears by his will, printed in the public records of Connecticut.

He died in Windsor, April 22, 1648 ; his wife *Rose*, surviving him but a few weeks, and dying May 12th, of the same year.

Their children were [being of the second generation :]

2. John Porter, b. in England, m. Mary Stanley, of Hartford, Conn.
3. James Porter, b. in England, m. Sarah Tudor, of Windsor, Conn.
4. Sarah Porter, b. in England, m. Joseph Judson, of Stratford, Conn.
5. Anna Porter, b. in England, m. William Gaylord, of Windsor, Conn.
6. Samuel Porter, b. in England, m. Anna Stanley, of Hartford, Conn.
7. Rebecca Porter, b. in England, probably never married.
8. Mary Porter, b. in England, m. Samuel Grant, of Windsor, Conn.

9. Rose Porter, b. in England, probably never married.
10. Joseph Porter, b. in England, probably never married.
11. Nathaniel Porter, b. in Windsor, July 19, 1640, m. Anna Groves, of Stratford, Conn.
12. Hannah Porter, b. in Windsor, September 4, 1642, m. John Coleman, of Deerfield, Mass.

[6.] SAMUEL PORTER, married (about) 1659, *Anna* (or Hannah) *Stanley*, daughter of Thomas Stanley, who came from London, Eng., in 1634, in the ship "Planter," and in 1635 removed to Hartford, Conn., on the first settlement of that place. He removed to Hadley, Mass., in 1659, where he died September 6, 1689. His wife, *Anna*, died December 18, 1708.

Their children were [being of the third generation :]

13. Samuel Porter, b. April 6, 1660, m. Joanna Cooke, of Hadley.
14. Thomas Porter, b. April 17, 1663, d. May 27, 1668.
15. Hezekiah Porter, b. January 7, 1665, m. first, Hannah Coles, second, Esther Dickinson.
16. John Porter, b. December 12, 1666, m. first, Mary Butler, second, Sarah Church.
17. Hannah Porter, b. Oct. 18, 1668, m. John Brown, of Middletown, Conn.
18. Mehitabel Porter, b. Sept. 15. 1673, m. Nathaniel Goodwin, of Hartford, Conn.
19. Experience Porter, b. Aug. 5, 1676, m. Abigail Williams, of Roxbury, Mass.
20. Ichabod Porter, b. June 17, 1678, m. Dorcas Marsh, of Hatfield, Mass.
21. Nathaniel Porter, b. Nov. 15, 1680, m. Mehitabel Buell, of Killingworth, Conn.
22. Thomas S. Porter, b. April 1, 1683, m. Thankful Babcock, of Coventry, Conn.

[21.] NATHANIEL PORTER, married in Lebanon, Conn., November 18, 1701, *Mehitabel Buell*, born August 22, 1682, daughter of *Samuel Buell*, of Killingworth, Conn., and his wife, *Deborah Griswold*, born June 28, 1646, daughter of *Edward Griswold*, of Windsor, Conn., and sister of Capt. *Peter Buell*, who married Martha Huntington, widow of Noah Grant. (See Col. Joshua Porter, 26.)

Their only child [being of the fourth generation :]

23. Nathaniel Buell Porter, born April 29, 1704, married Eunice Horton.

The mother, Mehitabel, died soon after the birth of her only child; and the father, Nathaniel, joined the army in the expedition intended for the conquest of Canada, in 1709, and was killed (or died) at Fort Anne, in (now) Washington county, N. Y. The orphan child was adopted and reared by his maternal grandfather, Samuel Buell, of Killingworth, Conn.

[WILLIAM BUELL, born in Chesterton, Huntingdonshire, Eng., (about) 1610, emigrated to America, (about) 1630, and settled first in Dorchester, Mass., removing thence, in 1635-6, to Windsor, Conn., where he died November 13, 1681.

Second Generation.—*Samuel Buell*, born September 2, 1641, married as above, November 13, 1662, Deborah Griswold.

Eunice Horton, was daughter of *Joshua Horton*, and his wife, *Eunice Youngs*, daughter of Col. *John Youngs*, of Southold, Long Island, N. Y., who was son of *Rev. John Youngs.*

This REV. JOHN YOUNGS was Rector of St. Margaret's Church, in London, England. Having fallen under the displeasure of the imperious *Laud*, then Archbishop of London, he was deprived of his benefice, and imprisoned in the Tower, "in order for the stake and faggot." Through "high influence at court" he made his escape into Holland. Thence, with a number of families of his congregation, who had followed his fortunes, he came to New Haven, Conn. Here the "Puritans," or "Separatists," violently opposed the establishment of the church in that colony. The Duke of York, who held from the crown a grant of Long Island (then called "New Yorkshire,") relieved him from further embarrassment, by inviting him to establish his church in that territory, and they accordingly removed to Southold, in October, 1640, where he died in 1672, aged 74 years. (See Appendix "B.")

That *Joshua Horton*, who married *Eunice Youngs*, was a descendant of JOSEPH HORTON, born in Leicestershire, Eng., whose son *Barnabas Horton* came to New England in the ship "Swallow," about 1635, removed to New Haven, Conn., about 1638, and, in 1640, was of the company which made the settlement at Southold, Long Island, with Rev. John Youngs.]

[23.] NATHANIEL BUELL PORTER, married, in Lebanon, Conn., November 17, 1724, *Eunice Horton*. He lived in Lebanon, Conn., where he was a merchant and farmer. He died in Boston, Mass, November 4, 1739, while there "in the transaction of his business."

Their children were [being of the fifth generation :]

24. Mehitabel Porter, b. Sept. 26, 1725, m. Bezaleel Hyde, of Lenox, Mass.
25. Nathaniel Porter, b. August 15, 1727, m. Zerviah Wadsworth, of Hartford, Conn.
26. Joshua Porter, b. June 26, 1730, m. Abigail Buell, of Coventry, Conn.
27. Eunice Porter, b. ———, 1733, m. Jonathan Lee, of Lebanon, Conn.

[24.] MEHITABEL PORTER, married at Lebanon, Conn., January 13, 1743, *Bezaleel Hyde*, born in Norwich, Conn., May 29, 1719. She died in Lebanon, Conn., April 10, 1791. He died April 4, 1801.

[WILLIAM HYDE, came from England, it is believed, in the company with Rev. Thomas Hooker, who settled at Hartford, Conn., 1636.

Second Generation.—*Samuel Hyde*, born in Hartford (about) 1637, married June, 1659, *Jane Lee*, sister of THOMAS LEE, who came from England, with his mother and sisters, Phœbe and Jane, about 1640, removed to Saybrook, and thence to Lyme, Conn.

Third Generation.—Samuel Hyde, born in Norwich, Conn., May, 1665, married December 10, 1690. *Elizabeth Calkins*, born April, 1673, daughter of *John Calkins*, of Norwich, Conn., and his wife, *Sarah Royce*, who came from England in 1631, with her father, ROBERT ROYCE, and settled in Lyme, Conn.

Fourth Generation.—*Daniel Hyde*, born in Windham, Conn., August 16, 1694, married *Abigail Wattels*. He lived in Norwich, Conn., and died Dec. 26, 1770.

Fifth Generation.—*Bezaleel Hyde*, born in Norwich, Conn., May 29, 1719, married *Mehitabel Porter*]

Their children were, [being of the sixth generation :]

28. Nathaniel Hyde, b. in Lebanon, 1743, m. Lucretia Johnson.
29. Joshua Hyde, b. in Lebanon, 1745, m. Esther Evett.
30. Oliver C. Hyde, b. in Lebanon, 1747, m. Mary Lee.
31. Mehitabel Hyde, b. in Lebanon, 1748, m. Eliphalet Phelps.
32. Eunice Hyde, b. in Lebanon, 1750, m. Elisha Hutchinson.
33. Lucretia Hyde, b. in Lebanon, 1752, m. Josiah Buell.

[25.] NATHANIEL PORTER, M. D., married *Zerviah Wadsworth*, daughter of ―――― Wadsworth, of Hartford, Conn., a descendant probably of *Joseph Wadsworth* and his wife *Elizabeth*, daughter of *Bartholomew Barnard*. Joseph Wadsworth, born 1643, was son of WILLIAM WADSWORTH, who came with his family, in 1632, from England to Cambridge, Mass., and who removed to Hartford, Conn., in the "great exodus," in 1636.

BARTHOLOMEW BARNARD, born in England, about 1620, came from Coventry, Warwickshire, England., in 1635, with his brother, *Francis Barnard*, and settled in Hartford, Conn. (See Augusta Porter, 57.) Bartholomew Barnard married, 1647, *Sarah Birchard*, born in England, 1626, who came in 1635, aged nine years, with her father,

THOMAS BIRCHARD, in the ship "Truelove," from London, England, and removed to Hartford, Conn.

Their children were [being of the sixth generation :]
34. Nathaniel Porter, b. in Hartford, June 4, 1755.
35. John Porter, b. in Hartford, October 27, 1757, m. Mary Williams.
36. Henry Chester Porter, b. in Hartford, February 17, 1760, m.
37. Charles Leonard Porter, b. in Hartford, October 5, 1761.
38. Sophia Porter, b. in Hartford, 1763, m. ———— Clarke.
39. Emily W. Porter, b. in Lebanon, 1765, m. Rev. Walter King.

[26.] Colonel JOSHUA PORTER, married May 14, 1795, [1759] Abigail Buell, (46,) born February 28, 1734, daughter of Capt. *Peter Buell*, of Coventry, Conn., who was son of *Samuel Buell*, of Killingworth, Conn., and his wife, *Deborah Griswold*, born June 26, 1646, daughter of EDWARD GRISWOLD, of Windsor, Conn., who came from England. And *Samuel Buell*, born September 2, 1641, was eldest child of WILLIAM BUELL, who was born in Chesterton, Huntingdonshire, England, about 1610, who came to New England in 1630, and settled in Windsor, Conn., in 1635–6, where he died November 23, 1661.

[Capt. PETER BUELL, married January 27, 1729. *Martha Huntington*, born December 9, 1696, who was then the widow of *Noah Grant*. She was daughter of *John Huntington*, of Norwich, Conn., and his wife, *Abigail*, daughter of *Samuel Lothrop*.

(*John Huntington*, born 1660, was son of *Christopher Huntington*, born in Norwich, England, whose father SIMON HUNTINGTON, died on the passage from England. (His widow married Thomas Stoughton, who was one of the company which had come in the ship "Mary and John" in 1630, and who removed to Windsor, Conn.) *Martha Huntington* married first June 12, 1717, *Noah Grant*, born October 16, 1693, son of *Samuel Grant*, born April 26, 1659, and his wife, *Grace Minor*.)

Samuel Filley, born September 24, 1643, son of WILLIAM FILLEY, who came from England and settled in Windsor, Conn., married, October 29, 1663, *Anna Gillite*, born December 29, 1639, daughter of JONATHAN GILLETTE, who came from England with Rev. John Warham, and removed to Windsor in 1635.

Third Generation, Anna Filley, born August 16, 1664, married December 1, 1683, *Samuel Grant*. She died April 18, 1686, when he married, second, April 11, 1688, *Grace Minor*.

(*Richard Boothe*, born in Cheshire, England, 1601, son of WILLIAM BOOTHE, of Dunham-Massey, in Cheshire, England, who came to New England, and settled in Stratford, Conn., in 1640. He married *Elizabeth Hawley*, sister of JOSEPH HAWLEY, who came from England to Stratford, Conn.

Second Generation, Elizabeth Boothe, born September, 1641, married in Stratford, Conn., October 19, 1658, *John Minor*.

(*Thomas Minor*, son of WILLIAM MINOR, of Chew-Magna, in Somersetshire, England, came to New England in 1632, removed to New London, Conn. He married, April 23, 1634, *Grace Palmer*, daughter of WALTER PALMER, from England.

Second Generation, John Minor, born August 30, 1635, removed to Stratford, Conn., was the first town clerk and representative, 1667 to 1676. He married *Elizabeth Boothe*.

Third Generation, Grace Minor, born January 15, 1670, married *Samuel Grant*.)

Samuel Grant was son of *Samuel Grant, Sr.*, who married, May 26, 1658, *Mary Porter*, (8) daughter of JOHN PORTER (1) from England.

(*Samuel Grant, Sr.*, was the son of MATTHEW GRANT, who was one of the company who came from England, in the ship "Mary and John," in 1630, and who removed to Windsor in October, 1635, and made the settlement at that place.

Samuel Lothrop, born in England, came to New England previous to 1640. He removed in 1668 to New London, Conn., where he married Abigail ———.

He was son of Rev. JOHN LOTHROP, who graduated at Oxford University, England, and was settled as a minister in Edgerton, Kent, England, and afterwards in London.

He was imprisoned by Archbishop Laud for non-conformity, and sentenced to the stake. Escaping from prison, he embarked for New England, arriving at Dorchester, Mass., September 27, 1634, and rejoined his wife and family, who had preceded him. Settled in Barnstable, Mass., as pastor of the church, where he died November 8, 1653.)

(THOMAS MINOR, came to New England in 1630. He was son of *William Minor* of Chew-Magna, in Somersetshire, England. He removed to Charlestown, Mass., in 1632; thence in 1645 to New London, Conn. He married, April 23, 1624, —1634 *Grace Palmer*, daughter of W~~ILLIAM~~ PALMER [WALTER], who came from England, in the ship "Fortune," to Plymouth in 1621, and settled at Duxbury, Mass.

His son (third generation) *John Minor*, born August 30, 1635, removed to Stratford, Conn., where he was town clerk, and representative from 1667 to 1676. He married, October 19, 1658, *Elizabeth Boothe*, born September —, 1641, daughter of *Richard Boothe*, of Stratford, Conn., who married in 1640, *Elizabeth Hawley*, sister of JOSEPH HAWLEY, of Stratford, Conn. *Richard Boothe* was son of WILLIAM BOOTHE, of Dunham-Massey, in Cheshire, England.

Their daughter, (fourth generation) *Grace Minor*, born September 20, 1670, married, April 11, 1688, *Samuel Grant*, of Windsor, Conn.]

The children of *Noah Grant* and *Martha Huntington* were, [being of the sixth generation :]

40. Noah Grant, b. July 12, 1718, m. Susannah Delano.
41. Adoniram Grant, b. February 27, 1721, m. Mary West.
42. Solomon Grant, b. January 29, 1723, m. Eunice Meacham.
43. Martha Huntington Grant, b. June 29, 1726, m. Capt. Nathan Mather.

Noah Grant died in Tolland, Conn., October 16, 1727, when his widow, (*Martha Huntington,*) married, second, January 27, 1729, *Capt. Peter Buell,* of Coventry, Conn., son of Peter Buell and his wife Deborah, born June 26, 1646, daughter of *Edward Griswold*, of Windsor, Conn.

[That *Samuel Buell*, born in Windsor, September 2, 1641, removed in 1684 to Killingworth, Conn., where he died, July 11, 1720. He was the son of WILLIAM BUELL, (or as frequently written *Bewelle,*) who was born in Chesterton, in Huntingdonshire, England, about the year 1610, who emigrated to America in 1630, and settled in Dorchester, Mass., whence he removed in 1636, to Windsor, Conn., where he died November 13, 1681.

EDWARD GRISWOLD, born in England 1607, was the son of *Matthew Griswold*, of Malvern Hall, in Kenilworth, Warwickshire, England. He came to New England in 1639 with his brother *Matthew*, and in company with Rev. Ephraim Hewett, and settled in Windsor, Conn.

The children of Martha (Huntington) Grant and Peter Buell were :
44. Peter Buell, b. October 22, 1729.
45. Benjamin Buell, b. June 2, 1732.
46. Abigail Buell, b. February 22, 1734, m. Col. Joshua Porter.]

Col. JOSHUA PORTER, M. D., graduated at Yale College, 1754. He settled at Salisbury, Litchfield county, Conn., and was elected to the legislature of Connecticut for over forty sessions. He was judge of the Common Pleas thirteen years, and of the Court of Probate thirty-seven years.

In the War of the Revolution he commanded the Fourteenth Connecticut regiment, and with it was engaged in the battles of White Plains, Monmouth, Long Island, Saratoga, Etc. In the latter, his regiment formed part of the brigade of General Fellows. (See Doctor *Joshua Porter*, (47.)

He was also superintendent of the state iron works at Salisbury,

Conn., engaged in the manufacture of cannon, and munitions for the army in the war of the revolution.

Frequently on committees of the legislature, charged with duties in the prosecution of the war, the manufacture of gunpowder, &c., he was one of the most active men in the country, during the whole period of the critical existence of the new nation.

He married, May 14, 1759, *Abigail Buell* (46), daughter of Captain *Peter Buell*, of Coventry, Conn. [See appendix "C."]

Their children were [being of the sixth generation :]

47. Joshua Porter, b. May 1, 1760, m. first, Hannah Fellows, second, Thankful Smith.
48. Abigail Porter, b. October 21, 1763, m. Luther Stoddard.
49. Eunice Porter, b. September 10, 1766, m. first, John Bird, second, Joshua Stanton, third Albert Pawling.
50. Augustus Porter, b. January 18, 1769, m. Lavinia Steele.
51. Peter B. Porter, b. August 14, 1773, m. Lætitia Breckenridge.
52. Sally Porter, b. September 10, 1778, m. John M. Holley.

Col. Joshua Porter married, second, December 31, 1799, *Jerusha Burr*, daughter of Col. Burr, of Fairfield, Conn. She died February —, 1808, and he married, third, in August of the same year, *Lucy Ashley*, daughter of Col. *John Ashley*, of Sheffield, Mass. She was then the widow of Samuel Dutcher. She died August, 1815. Of these two marriages there was no issue. Col. Porter died at his residence in Salisbury, Conn., April 2, 1825, in the 96th year of his age, "in full possession of his faculties to the last week of his life."

[40.] Capt. NOAH GRANT married, in 1743, *Susannah Delano*, born June 28, 1724, daughter of *Jonathan Delano* of Tolland, Conn.

[JEAN DE LA NOYE, a Huguenot, left France and joined the Puritan brethren at Leyden, Holland, where he was admitted to the Walloon church, December 7, 1603, with his wife *Marie*.

Second Generation, Philip (de La Noye) *Delano*, born 1602, was baptized in the church at Leyden, December 7, 1603. He came with the Puritan emigrants in the ship "Fortune," to Dorchester, Mass., November 9, 1621, in company with John Winslow, Robert Cushman, John Adams, Jonathan Brewster, &c. He removed to Duxbury, Mass., where he married, December 19, 1634, *Esther Desborough*, a sister (probably) of Samuel Desborough, who came from London, England, son of James Desborough, of Elltisley, in Cambridgeshire, England.

Third Generation, Jonathan Delano, born 1648, married February 26, 1678, *Mercy Warren*, born February 20, 1658, daughter of *Nathaniel Warren*, of Plymouth, Mass., who married, 1645, *Sarah Walker*, who came from England, in the ship "Elizabeth," in 1638. *Nathaniel Warren* was son of RICHARD WARREN, who came in the ship "Mayflower," to Plymouth, Mass., in 1620, and died in 1628.

Fourth Generation, Jonathan Delano, born 1679, married January 12, 1699, *Hannah Doten*, daughter of *Thomas Doten*, who was son of EDWARD DOTEN, (or Dotey or D'Hote,) who came in the ship "Mayflower," in 1630, and who married, January 6, 1635, *Faith Clarke*, daughter of TRISTRAM CLARKE, who came from Ipswich, in Suffolk county, England, in the ship "Francis," in 1634, to Plymouth, Mass.

(That Edward Doten is noted as having been with Edward Leister engaged as principals in the first duel on record in America.)

Fifth Generation, Susannah Delano, born 1723, married *Noah Grant*.]

Capt. *Noah Grant* and his brother, *Capt. Solomon Grant*, (42) joined the Colonial forces in the "French war," and were both killed, in action, at Crown Point, September 20, 1755.

Their children were [being of the sixth generation :]
53. Noah Grant, b. July 4, 1744, m. Anna Buell.
54. Peter Grant, b. 1746.
55. Solomon Grant, b. 1748.
56. Susannah Grant, b. 1750.

[47.] Doct. JOSHUA PORTER, married April 1, 1785, *Hannah Fellows*, daughter of General John Fellows, of Sheffield, Mass.

[WILLIAM WHITING came from London, England, where he had been a merchant. He became associated with Lord Say-and-Sele, Lord Brooke, George Wyllys and others, in a patent for lands in Connecticut, and was one of the earliest settlers of Hartford, Conn., in 1636; treasurer of the Colony until his death, in 1647.

Second Generation, Joseph Whiting, born October 2, 1645, married October 5, 1669, *Mary Pynchon*, born October 28, 1650, daughter of *John Pynchon*, of Springfield, Mass., and his wife, *Amy*, daughter of *George Wylys*, of Hartford, Conn., who came from Fenny-Compton, in Warwickshire, England, in 1638, removed to Hartford, Conn., was deputy-governor in 1641; governor in 1642, and died March 9, 1645.

(NICHOLAS PYNCHON, born in Wales, before A. D. 1500, removed to London, where he was a merchant and, in 1532, lord mayor. He was succeeded by his son *John Pynchon*, whose son, *William Pynchon*, (being of the third generation,) became associated with the patentees in procuring the royal charter (dated March 4, 1629,) for the New England Colonies, and was named in that charter an "assistant" (or councillor). He came in the fleet with Winthrop, in 1630, and removed in 1636 to found the town of Springfield, Mass., so called from the place of his residence, Springfield, in Essex, England. His son, *John Pynchon*, fourth generation, accompanied him, and married *Amy Wyllys*.

Fifth Generation, *Mary Pynchon*, born October 28, 1650, married, October 5, 1669, *Joseph Whiting*.)

Third Generation, *Mary Whiting*, born August 19, 1672, married *John Ashley*.

(ROBERT ASHLEY came from England in 1630, and settled first in Roxbury, Mass. In 1636 he became connected with *William Pynchon* in making the settlement at Springfield, Mass., where he removed with his family.

Second Generation, *David Ashley*, born June 8, 1642, married, November 24, 1663, *Hannah Glover*, born May 5, 1646, daughter of HENRY GLOVER, who came from Ipswich, England, in the ship "Elizabeth," and removed to New Haven, Conn., and died 1689.

Third Generation, *John Ashley*, born —— 1670, married *Mary Whiting*.

Fourth Generation, *John Ashley*, born in Hartford, Conn., in 1709, graduated at Yale College 1730, admitted to the bar in 1732, removed to Sheffield, Berkshire county, where he was an extensive land proprietor, judge of the court, colonel of militia, &c. He married *Annetje* (Hannah) *Hoogebaum*, born in 1712, daughter of PIETER MEESE-HOOGEBAUM, who married, in Holland in 1693, JANNETJE (Jane) MULLER, and came to New Amsterdam (New York) and removed to Claverack, Columbia county, N. Y.

Fifth Generation, *Mary Ashley*, born —— 1739, married Gen. *John Fellows*.

(SAMUEL FELLOWS came from England (about 1638,) with his wife *Anna*, and settled in Salisbury, Essex county, Mass. He died March 6, 1698.

Second Generation, *Samuel Fellows*, born January 13, 1647, married, June 2, 1681, *Abigail Barnard*, daughter of JOHN BARNARD, who came from England, in 1630, with his wife *Phebe*, in the ship "Elizabeth," from Ipswich, England. He was a selectman in Watertown, Mass.

Second Generation, Col. *John Fellows*, born ——, married ——, *Huldah Ensign*, daughter of *David Ensign*, of Hartford, Conn., who was a descendant of JAMES ENSIGN, who came from England to Dorchester, Mass., in 1635, and in 1639 removed to Hartford, Conn. [See Appendix "D."]

Third Generation, Gen. *John Fellows*, born (about) 1730, married *Mary Ashley*.)

Sixth Generation, *Hannah Fellows*, born in Sheffield, Mass., —— 1765, married, April 14, 1785, Doct. *Joshua Porter*.

Their children were [being of the seventh generation :]
57. Augusta Porter, b. March 19, 1786, m. Robert F. Barnard.

58. Minerva Porter, b. September 26, 1787, d. at Saratoga Springs, April 16, 1864.
59. Frederick A. Porter, b. August 6, 1789, killed at Niagara June 21, 1808.
60. John F. Porter, b. October 25, 1791, lost at sea November 5, 1807.

Mrs. Hannah (Fellows) Porter, died in Salisbury, Conn., April 2, 1798.

Dr. Joshua Porter married, second, October 6, 1799, Thankful Smith, daughter of Capt. *Josiah Smith*, of Great Barrington, Berkshire county, Mass.

[SAMUEL SMITH, with his wife *Elizabeth*, came from Ipswich, county of Suffolk, England, in the ship "Elizabeth," arriving April 30, 1634, settled at Watertown, Mass. He removed, in 1636, to Weathersfield, Conn.; was representative from 1641 to 1658. Removed in 1659 to Hadley, Mass., where he was representative from 1661 to 1673, and died December —, 1680.

Second Generation, *John Smith*, born ——, 1637, was killed by Indians in Hatfield, Mass., May 30, 1676. He married, November 12, 1663, *Mary Partridge*, daughter of WILLIAM PARTRIDGE, who came from Berwick-upon-Tweed, Northumberland, England; settled in Hartford, Conn., whence he removed to Hadley, Mass.

Third Generation, *Benjamin Smith*, born ——, 1673, married March 14, 1700, *Ruth Bucke*, born ——, 1681, daughter of *Henry Bucke*, of Weathersfield, Conn., who married, October 31, 1660, *Elizabeth Churchill*, born May 15, 1642, daughter of JOSIAH CHURCHILL, who came from England, and was an early settler of Weathersfield, Conn. He married, in 1638, *Elizabeth Foote*, born in England, daughter of NATHANIEL FOOTE, who came from England with his wife *Elizabeth*, to Watertown, Mass., (about) 1634; removed to Weathersfield, Conn., 1636, and was representative 1641 to 1644. His wife, Elizabeth, was sister of JOHN DEMING, of Weathersfield, Conn. [See Abigail Porter (48) and Elizabeth Burrall, (108,)] 105

Fourth Generation, *Josiah Churchill Smith*, born January 31, 1709, married, September 4, 1740, *Mary Treat*, daughter of *Joseph Treat*, of Weathersfield, Conn., and his wife *Mary Robbins*.

(RICHARD TREAT came from England with his wife, *Joanna*, and was an early settler in Weathersfield, Conn. His name appears upon the Royal Charter of Connecticut, April 23, 1662. He died in 1669.

Second Generation, *James Treat*, born in England in 1634, married, January 25, 1665, *Rebecca Latimer*, born April 18, 1646, daughter of JOHN LATIMER, who came from England and settled in Weathersfield, Conn.

Third Generation, *Joseph Treat*, born ——, 1677, married, May 13, 1713, *Mary Robbins*, daughter of Capt. JOSHUA ROBBINS, of Weathersfield, Conn.

Fourth Generation, *Mary Treat*, born March 17, 1715, married *Josiah C. Smith*.)

Fifth Generation, Josiah Smith, born February 18, 1741, married ——, *Thankful* ——. He was a Captain and Quarter-master in the Continental Army in the War of the Revolution.

Sixth Generation, Thankful Smith, born ——, 1764, married Dr. *Joshua Porter*. She died at Saratoga Springs, N. Y., September 25, 1829.)]

Their only child [being of the seventh generation :]
61. Mary S. Porter, born February 17, 1801, married, first, Henry W. Andrews, (second, Peter V. Wiggins.)

Doct. Joshua Porter studied medicine and entered the army in the War of the Revolution as "Surgeon's Mate." While acting in that capacity he was severely wounded, taken prisoner, and confined on the prison ship "Jersey," at the Wallabout, (now the Navy Yard, N. Y.) until liberated on parole.

At the close of the war he commenced the practice of medicine at Litchfield, Conn., removing thence to Hudson, N. Y., and again to the town of Brutus, N. Y., and thence in 1817, to Saratoga Springs, N. Y., of which village he was the first president, on its incorporation, in 1825; his son-in-law, Peter V. Wiggins, being the first village clerk. He died at Saratoga Springs, October 26, 1831.

[48.] ABIGAIL PORTER, married ——, *Luther Stoddard*, born in Salisbury, Conn., March 31, 1746.

[JOHN STODDARD came from England about 1639, and removed to Weathersfield, Conn., previous to 1642, at which date he appears on the records as a juror. He was probably a brother of *Anthony Stoddard*, who came from England, in 1639, to Boston, Mass., whose son, Rev. *Solomon Stoddard*, of Northampton, Mass., married *Esther Warham*, daughter of Rev. JOHN WARHAM, of Windsor, Conn., she being then the widow of Rev. *Eleazer Mather*. He married, in 1642, *Mary Foote*, daughter of Nathaniel Foote. (See Dr. Joshua Porter, (47,) George W. Holley, (78,) and Elizabeth Burrall, (103.)

Second Generation, John Stoddard, born in Weathersfield, Conn., April 12, 1646, married, May 26, 1673, *Elizabeth Curtis*, born 1649. daughter of *Thomas Curtis*, an early settler of Weathersfield, Conn.

Third Generation, Josiah Stoddard, born in Weathersfield, Conn., February 22. 1674, married, November 19, 1696, *Sarah Camp*, born February 17, 1677, daughter of *John Camp*, of Hartford, Conn., whose wife, *Mary Sanford*, born April 18, 1650, was daughter of *Robert Sanford*, of Hartford, Conn., who married *Anna Adams*.

(JEREMY ADAMS came from England in 1632, and settled in Cambridge, Mass., removed to Braintree, Mass., and in 1636, to Hartford, Conn. He married Rebecca Greenhill, who came from Staplehurst, in county of Kent, England. His daughter, *Anna Adams*, married *Robert Sanford*.)

Fourth Generation, Ensign *Josiah Stoddard*, born in Weathersfield, Conn., December 21, 1716, removed to Salisbury, Conn., in 1743, where he married, November 7, 1743, *Sarah Roberts*, daughter of *John Roberts*, of Hartford, Conn. Josiah Stoddard was the first town clerk of Salisbury, and representative from 1757 to 1762, and died July 29, 1764.

Fifth Generation, *Luther Stoddard*, born in Salisbury, Conn., March 30, 1746, married *Abigail Porter*.

In 1776 Luther Stoddard raised one of the first companies of "Light Horse" in the War of the Revolution. With it, as its captain, he joined the regiment commanded by Col. Aaron Burr. After the defection of Burr, Capt. Stoddard became Major, and was in active service until the termination of the war.]

Their only child [being of the seventh generation :]

62. Abigail Porter Stoddard, b. September 30, 1783, m. William M. Burrall.

[49.] EUNICE PORTER married, first, October 6, 1789, *John Bird*. He was born in Bethlem, Litchfield county, Conn. Graduated at Yale College 1786, admitted to the bar and removed to Troy, N. Y., in 1791; member of the legislature of New York, at its sessions in New York city, 1796–7, and its first sessions after its removal to Albany, in 1798, 1799 and 1800. He was a member of that Congress which elected Jefferson president of the United States, of whom he was an active partizan, and an equally bitter opponent of the rival candidate, Aaron Burr. John Bird died February 2, 1806.

[THOMAS BIRD, born in England (about) 1595, came to New England, in 1635, and joined the church on its organization by Rev. Richard Mather, in Dorchester, Mass., in 1642; he died 1667. His wife, *Anne*, died 1673.

Second Generation, *James Bird*, born in England in 1632, married, March 31, 1657, *Lydia Steele*, born in England, daughter of John Steele.

JOHN STEELE came from Essex, England, to Cambridge, Mass., in 1632. In 1636 he was appointed, with William Pynchon, Roger Ludlow and others to "administer government over the Great Exodus to Connecticut." He was a representative and town clerk until his removal to Farmington, Conn., in 1645, where he died in 1708.

—*Second Generation*, *Lydia Steele*, born (about) 1637, married, March 31, 1657, *James Bird*.)

Third Generation, Thomas Bird, born (about) 1665, married, July 3, 1693, *Mary Woodford,* daughter of Joseph Woodford, of Farmington, Conn., whose wife was *Rebecca Newell,* daughter of *Thomas Newell,* of Farmington, who married *Rebecca Olmstead,* who with her brothers, Richard and John, came with their uncle, JAMES OLMSTEAD, from London, England, in the ship "Lion," to Boston, Mass., September 16, 1632, and removed to Hartford, Conn., in 1636, with the first settlers. Thomas Bird removed to Litchfield, Conn., where he died 1725.

Fourth Generation, John Bird, born in Litchfield, Conn., 1695, married, January 20, 1728, *Mary Atwood,* born April 20, 1705, daughter of *Jonathan Atwood* of Woodbury, Conn., born June 8, 1675, who married, November 5, 1701, *Sarah Terrill,* born March, 1684, daughter of *Roger Terrill,* one of the first settlers of Woodbury, Conn., whose wife was daughter of THOMAS UFFORD, who came from London, England, in the ship "Lion," to Boston, Mass., September 16, 1632, and removed with Pynchon, to Springfield, Mass., in 1636, and thence to Milford, Conn.

(*Jonathan Atwood,* born June 8, 1675, was son of Dr. THOMAS ATWOOD, who with his brother, Herman Atwood, came from Sanderstead, county of Surrey, England, in the ship "Abigail," from London, in 1635.)

Fifth Generation, Dr. *Seth Bird,* born in Litchfield, Conn., January 4, 1733, married, February 8, 1763, *Hannah Sheldon.*

(ISAAC SHELDON came from England to Dorchester, Mass., in 1634, removed to Windsor, Conn., in 1640, and thence in 1645 to Northampton, Mass. He married, in 1653, *Mary Woodford,* daughter of THOMAS WOODFORD, who came from England, in 1635, in the ship "William and Francis," to Dorchester, Mass. ; settled in Roxbury, Mass., removing to Hartford, Conn., and thence, in 1656, to Northampton, Mass, where he died March 6, 1667.

Second Generation, Isaac Sheldon, born ———, 1656, married, November 25, 1685, *Sarah Warner.*

—(ANDREW WARNER came from England and settled at Cambridge, Mass., in 1632. He removed to Hartford, Conn., "with the body of original proprietors," in 1636.

Second Generation, Daniel Warner, born (about 1638) married ———, 1662, *Mary* * * *

Third Generation, Sarah Warner, born June 24, 1667, married *Isaac Sheldon,*)

Third Generation, Isaac Sheldon, born August 26, 1686, married, ———, 1723, *Theoda Hunt.*

(THOMAS HOSMER, came from Hawkhurst, county Kent, England, to Cambridge, Mass., in 1632. He removed with Hooker and his company, in 1636, to Hartford, Conn, where he was a selectman, &c. He removed to Northampton, Mass., where he died April 12, 1687, aged 83.

Second Generation, Clemence Hosmer, born (about) 1642, married *Jonathan Hunt,* of Northampton, Mass., whose wife, *Mary Webster,* was a daughter of Gov. JOHN WEBSTER, of Hartford, Conn., who came from Warwickshire, England, to Hartford, Conn., 1636.

Third Generation, Jonathan Hunt, born January 20, 1666, in Northampton, Mass., married (about) 1693, *Martha Williams.*

(ROBERT WILLIAMS embarked in the ship "Thomas and John," at London, England, with his wife *Elizabeth Stratton,* June 6, 1635. He settled at Roxbury, Mass., where he died September 1, 1693.

Second Generation, Rev. *Samuel Williams,* born in England, 1632, married, March 2, 1654, *Theoda Parke,* born July 26, 1637, daughter of *William Parke,* who came with his father, ROBERT PARKE, from England, in the ship "Lion," to Boston, February —, 1631, and settled at Roxbury, Mass. William Parke, married, May 18, 1631, *Martha Ho'grave,* daughter of JOHN HOLGRAVE, of Salem, Mass.

Third Generation, Martha Williams, born May 19, 1671, married *Jonathan Hunt.*

Her brother, Rev. *John Williams,* of Deerfield, married Eunice Mather, and was known as the "Redeemed Captive," taken by Indians to Canada.

Her sister, *Deborah Williams,* married *Joseph Warren,* and was grandmother of Gen. *Joseph Warren,* killed at the battle of Bunker Hill.

Her sister, *Abigail Williams,* married Col. *Experience Porter,* brother of *Nathaniel Porter,* (21.)

Her brother, Rev. *Ebenezer Williams,* married *Penelope Chester,* daughter of Col. *John Chester,* of Weathersfield, Conn., and their sons Rev. *Chester Williams* and Col. *Ebenezer Williams,* married, respectively, *Sarah Porter* and *Jerusha Porter,* daughters of *Eleazer Porter,* of Hadley, Mass, who was son of *Samuel Porter,* of Hadley, son of *Samuel Porter,* (6.)

Sixth Generation, John Bird, born in Litchfield, Conn., ———. 1769, married, October 6, 1789, *Eunice Porter.*]

Their children were [being of the seventh generation ;]

63. John Herman Bird, b. August 12, 1790, (see appendix "E.")
64. Clarence Bird, b. April 18, 1793, died unmarried.
65. William A. Bird, b. March 23, 1797, m. Joanna Davis.
    Maria Bird, b. March 23, 1797, died ——.

Eunice (Bird) *Porter* married, second, October 6, 1803, Judge *Joshua Stanton,* of Burlington, Vt.

Their children were :

66. Abigail Porter Stanton, b. September 12, 1804, d. March 12, 1807.
67. Joshua Stanton, b. June 7, 1806, d. December 25, 1806.

[*Joshua Stanton* was a descendant of *Thomas Stanton*, of Stonington, Conn. He was educated at Harvard College, and became an expert in the language of the Indians, and served as interpreter. He married *Sarah Denison*, born March 20, 1642, daughter of GEORGE DENISON, who came with his father, WILLIAM DENISON, from England, in the ship "Lion," in 1631, and settled in Roxbury, Mass. He returned to England, in August, 1643, and served in the parliamentary army. He married in England *Anne*, daughter of JOHN BOURODELL, and came back to Roxbury, Mass., whence he removed to Stonington, Conn., and served in King Philip's war, and died in Hartford, Conn., October 23, 1694.

Thomas Stanton was son of THOMAS STANTON, who went from London to Virginia, in 1635, and thence to Hartford, Conn., where he was an original proprietor, in 1636. He married, in 1638, *Anne Lord*, daughter of THOMAS LORD, who came with his wife *Dorothy*, in the ship "Elizabeth and Ann," from London, England, in 1635, and settled at Hartford, Conn.]

Judge Stanton died at Salisbury, Conn., October 28, 1806.

Mrs. Eunice (Bird) Stanton, married, third, May 10, 1812, Col. *Albert Pawling*, born in Dutchess county, N. Y., son of Col. *Levi Pawling*, of the Army of the Revolution.

Col. Albert Pawling entered the service in the War of the Revolution as cornet of light horse, in the company raised by Capt. Stoddard. [See Abigail Porter (48).] He served as lieutenant in the regiment commanded by Col. James Clinton, in the expedition against Canada, in 1776, under Gen. George Clinton, when he was appointed "Brigade Major." In 1777, major in the regiment of Col. William Malcolm. Afterwards Colonel and Aid-de-camp on the staff of the commander-in-chief, Gen. GEORGE WASHINGTON. [See appendix F.]

Col. Pawling was the first mayor of Troy, N. Y., from 1816 to 1820. He died November 10, 1837. Mrs. Eunice Pawling died at the residence of her son, Col. William A. Bird, in Buffalo, N. Y.. March 15, 1848.

[50.] AUGUSTUS PORTER, married, first, March 10, 1796, *Lavinia Steele*, daughter of *Timothy Steele*, of Litchfield, Conn.

[RICHARD SEYMOUR, born in England, was an early settler in Hartford, Conn. He removed in 1652 to Norwalk, Conn., where he died November 23, 1655.

Second Generation, John Seymour, born in Hartford, Conn., (about) 1642, married *Mary Watson*, daughter of *John Watson*, of Hartford, and died in 1713.

Third Generation, Zechariah Seymour, born in Hartford, Conn., January 10, 1684, married November 24, 1709, *Hannah Olmstead*, daughter of *Thomas Olmstead*, of Hartford, and his wife Hannah Mix, born June 30, 1666, daughter of *Thomas Mix*, of New Haven, Conn., who married in 1649, *Rebecca Turner*, daughter of NATHANIEL TURNER, who came from England, in the fleet with John Winthrop, in 1630. He removed to New Haven, and was a captain in the fight with the Pequent Indians, in 1637, called the "great falls fight," and the locality since called "Turner's Falls." Capt. Turner removed again to Stamford, Conn., in 1640, being one of the original purchasers. He sailed for London, England, January, 1646, in a little vessel of eighty tons, with Capt. Lamberton, Thomas Gregson and others, of which nothing was ever heard until her "apparition was seen in the air." (See Mather's Magnalia.)

Fourth Generation, Zechariah Seymour, born September 24, 1710, married *Sarah Steele*, daughter of *James Steele* and *Sarah Barnard*.

(GEORGE STEELE came from England to Cambridge, Mass., in 1632. He removed to Hartford, Conn., in 1636, with Rev. Thomas Hooker and that company. He was a representative from 1637 to 1659, and died in 1660.

Second Generation, James Steele, born in England (about) 1620, married (probably) *Anne Bishop*, daughter of JOHN BISHOP, of Guilford, Conn.

Third Generation, James Steele, born ——, 1656, married, August 1, 1689, *Sarah Barnard*.)

(BARTHOLOMEW BARNARD, came from Coventry, Warwickshire, England, about 1638. (He was brother of Francis Barnard; see Augusta Porter, (57.) He removed to Hartford, Conn., where he married, October 25, 1647, *Sarah Birchard*, born in England, who came at the age of nine years, with her father, THOMAS BIRCHARD, in the ship "Truelove," from London, England, removed to Hartford, Conn., and thence to Saybrook, Conn., where he died in 1684.

Second Generation, Sarah Barnard, born ——, 1657, married 1689, *James Steele*.)

Fifth Generation, Sarah Seymour, born in Hartford, Conn., January 20, 1741, married *Timothy Steele*, of Litchfield, Conn., son of *Daniel Steele*, of Hartford, and his wife, *Mary Hopkins*, born January 30, 1705, daughter of *Ebenezer Hopkins*, of Hartford, who married, January 26, 1691, *Mary Butler*, daughter of *Samuel Butler*, of Weathersfield, Conn., who was son of RICHARD BUTLER, who came from England to Cambridge, Mass., in 1632, removed to Hartford, Conn., 1640-1, and died August 6, 1684.

Ebenezer Hopkins, was son of *Stephen Hopkins*, born ——, 1634, who married *Dorcas Bronson*, daughter of JOHN BRONSON, an early settler of Hartford, Conn., in 1639, who removed to Farmington, Conn., and died 1680.

Stephen Hopkins, born 1634, was son of JOHN HOPKINS, who came from England to Cambridge, Mass., with wife, *Jane*, in 1634, removed to Hartford, Conn., in 1638, where he was an original proprietor, and died in 1654.

Daniel Steele, born April 3, 1697, was son of *Samuel Steele*, of Hartford, Conn., born March 15, 1652, who married, September 16, 1680, *Mercy Bradford*, born at Boston, Mass., September 1, 1660, daughter of Col. *William Bradford*, who married *Alice Richards*. (See Henry P. Andrews, (95.)

Samuel Steele, born March 15, 1652, was son of *John Steele*, jr., of Farmington, Conn., born in England, who married, January 20, 1646, *Mary Warner*, born in England, daughter of ANDREW WARNER, who came from England in 1630, and settled in Cambridge, Mass., removed to Hartford, Conn., in 1636, and thence to Hadley, Mass., in 1659, where he died December 18, 1684. (See Eunice Porter, (49.)

John Steele, jr., born in England (about) 1618, came with his father, JOHN STEELE, (who was probably brother of GEORGE STEELE, before mentioned,) from England to Cambridge, Mass., in 1632. In 1636 he was appointed, with William Pynchon, Roger Ludlow and others, "to administer government over the great exodus to Connecticut," town clerk of Hartford, Conn., until his removal to Farmington, Conn., in 1645, where he died 1664. His wife, *Rachel*, died 1655.

Sixth Generation, Lavinia Steele, born (about) 1772, daughter of *Timothy Steele* and *Sarah Seymour*, married *Augustus Porter*.]

Judge Augustus Porter, went in 1789 to Canandaigua, N. Y., to make a survey of lands in (now) Wayne county, of which his father was in part proprietor, and soon after, with his brother, Gen. Peter B. Porter, became connected with the Holland Land Company of western New York and Ohio. He removed thence, in 1806, to Niagara Falls, N. Y., where they had purchased large tracts of land, including the islands in the rapids; and where he died June 10, 1849.

Their only child was [being of the seventh generation :]

68. Augustus Seymour Porter, b. January 18, 1798, m. Sarah G. Barnard, (93.)

Mrs. Lavinia Porter, died March 4, 1799. Augustus Porter married, second, January 24, 1801, *Jane Howell*, daughter of *Hezekiah Howell*, of Orange, N. Y.

[EDWARD HOWELL, of the manor of Westbury, Buckinghamshire, England, baptized July 22, 1584, son of Henry Howell; sold the estate in 1639, and came with his family to New England.

He settled at Lyme, Conn., but soon removed to Southampton, Long Island, of which he was one of the proprietors in the Indian deed of 1640. Magistrate 1647 to 1654, and died May, 1656.

Second Generation, *Richard Howell*, born ——, 1620, married *Elizabeth Halsey*, born in England, daughter of THOMAS HALSEY, who came from England to Lynn, Mass., in 1637, removed to Southampton, L. I., and died 1678.

Third Generation, *Hezekiah Howell*, born 1677, married, first, *Phebe Halsey*, second, Mary ——. He died in Blooming Grove, Orange county, N. Y., in 1795.

Fourth Generation, *Hezekiah Howell*, born May 6, 1709, married, December 11, 1735, *Susannah Sayre*, daughter of *Job Sayre*, of Southampton, L. I., a descendant of THOMAS SAYRE, who came from England to Lynn, Mass, in 1635. He became, in 1640, one of the purchasers of Southampton, L. I. Hezekiah Howell removed to Orange county, N. Y., about 1730, and settled at Blooming Grove.

Fifth Generation, *Hezekiah Howell*, born September 3, 1741, married *Joanna. Woodhull*, a descendant of RICHARD WOODHULL, of Brookhaven, L. I.

Sixth Generation, *Hezekiah Howell*, born ——, married ——.

Seventh Generation, *Jane Howell*, born April 22, 1779, married Augustus Porter.]

Their children were [being of the seventh generation :]
69. Albert Howell Porter, b. October 24, 1801, m. Julia Mathews.
70. Peter Buell Porter, b. March 17, 1806, d. June 15, 1871, unmarried.
71. Lavinia E. Porter, b. September 7, 1810, d. April 13, 1863, unmarried.
72. Nathaniel W. Porter, b. September 1, 1812, d. September 12, 1813.
73. Jane S. Porter, b. June 6, 1816, m. D. J. Townsend.

Mrs. Jane Howell Porter, died January 31, 1841.

[51.] PETER BUELL PORTER, graduated at Yale College in 1791. He studied law with Judge Reeve, in Litchfield, Conn. Removed to western New York in 1793. Member of Legislature in 1802, from Ontario county. Removed to Niagara Falls, N. Y. Elected to Congress 1808 to 1814.

As chairman of Committee on Foreign Relations, he was one of the most earnest advocates of the war with Great Britain, in 1812, and on its declaration resigned his seat, and repaired to New York, where he speedily recruited a brigade of volunteers, and was appointed brigadier general.

In the battle of Chippewa, sortie at Fort Erie, and battle of Lundy's Lane, he led his command of New York and Pennsylvania volunteers.

After the latter action he was brevetted major-general. At the termination of the war he was, on the reorganization of the army, appointed by President Madison commander-in-chief, which he declined.

He was secretary of war under President Madison. He married, September —, 1818, *Lætitia,* daughter of *John Breckinridge,* of Kentucky, and his wife *Mary Hopkins Cabell.*

[ALEXANDER BRECKINRIDGE, born in Scotland, removed to the north of Ireland, whence he came with his family, among the early emigrants to Virginia, about the year 1700, and settled first at the west foot of the Blue Ridge, in Virginia, in what was afterwards Augusta county.

Second Generation, Col. *Robert Breckinridge,* of Botetourt county, Va., born (about) 1725, married, July 10, 1758. *Lætitia Preston.*

(JOHN PRESTON was born in the city of Londonderry, Ireland. His father and three uncles were Englishmen, who served in the army of King William III., at the siege of Londonderry, in 1698.

The wife of *John Preston* was *Elizabeth Paton,* a sister of Col. *James Patton,* (or Paton) of Donegal, Ireland, who for several years commanded a ship in the Virginia trade, and was a man of property and influence. He obtained a grant from the governor of Virginia, for himself and associates, of over one hundred thousand acres of land, above the Blue Ridge, much of which became the property of his descendants. Col. Patton was killed by Indians, at Smithville, Va., in 1752. John Preston's first residence in Virginia was at Spring Hill, in Augusta county, but about the year 1743 he purchased a tract near Staunton, where he died, and was interred at the Tinkling Spring church, where Col. Robert Breckinridge was also buried.

Among the descendants of John Preston were: Governor McDowell of Virginia, Jessie Benton, daughter of Thomas H. Benton and wife of John C. Fremont, Harrietta Preston, wife of Gen. Albert Sidney Johnston, Wiliam Preston, minister to Spain and major-general in the Confederate army, Brigadier-General R. L. Gibson of the Confederate army, Col. James P. Preston of the United States army, Lætitia Preston, wife of John B. Floyd, secretary of war under President Buchanan, Anne Preston, grandmother of Francis P. Blair and mother of Montgomery Blair, postmaster-general, Thomas F. Marshall of Kentucky, Mary W. Preston, wife of Judge Thomas T. Crittendon of Kentucky, Margaret Howard, wife of Robert Wickliffe of Kentucky, &c.)

Third Generation, John Breckinridge, born ——, married ——, *Mary Hopkins Cabell.*

He was United States Senator, Attorney-General United States under President Jefferson, died 1806. His children were :
- a. Lætitia Preston Breckinridge, married Gen. Peter B. Porter.
- b. Joseph C. Breckinridge, secretary of state of Kentucky.
- c. Mary A. Breckinridge, married David Castleman of Kentucky.
- d. John Breckinridge, married Margaret Miller.
- e. Rev. Robert J. Breckinridge, married Sophonisha Preston.
- f. Rev. William L. Breckinridge, married Frances C. Provost.]

The children of Gen. P. B. Porter were [being of the seventh generation :]

74. Elizabeth L. Porter, b. April 19, 1823, d. unmarried January 28. 1876.
75. Peter A. Porter, b. July 14. 1827, m. Mary C. P. Breckinridge.

[52.] SALLY PORTER, married, March 9, 1800, *John Milton Holley*, of Salisbury, Litchfield county, Conn.

[JOHN HALLEY came from London, England, settled in Stamford, Conn.

Second Generation, John Holley, married *Waitstill Webb*, a descendant of RICHARD WEBB, who came from England, in 1630, to Cambridge, Mass., and who removed, in June, 1636, with Gov. John Haynes, Rev. Thomas Hooker and his congregation, to Hartford, Conn., on its first settlement.

Third Generation, John Holley, born ———, married *Sarah Lord*, a descendant of WILLIAM LORD, born in England in 1623, who came from England with his father, *Thomas Lord*, in the ship "Elizabeth and Anne," April 29, 1635, to Cambridge, Mass., and removed to Hartford, Conn., in 1636, with Rev. Thomas Hooker, &c., and thence to Saybrook, Conn.

Fourth Generation, Luther Holley, born in Sharon, Conn., June 12, 1751, married, October 1, 1775, *Sarah Dakin*, of Duchess county, N. Y.

Fifth Generation, John Milton Holley, born September 7, 1777, married *Sally Porter*.]

John M. Holley died March 12, 1826. Mrs. Sally (Porter) Holley died November 4, 1836.

Their children were [being of the seventh generation :]

76. Maria Holley, b. February 17, 1802, d. December 4, 1820, unmarried.
77. John M. Holley, b. November 10, 1803, m. Mary Kirkland.
78. Alexander H. Holley, b. August 12, 1804, m. first, Jane M. Lyman, second, Marcia Coffing, third, Sarah C. Day.
  Mary Anne Holley, b. April 18, 1806, d. December 20, 1812.
79. Harriet Holley, b. April 8. 1808, m. W. P. Burrall, (106.)

80. George W. Holley, b. February 17, 1810, m. Caroline E. Church.
81. Sally Porter Holley, b. September 10, 1811, m. Samuel S. Robbins.
82. Mary Anne Holley, b. May 13, 1813, m. Moses Lyman.

[53.] NOAH GRANT married ———, 1777, *Anna Buell*, then the widow of ——— *Richardson*.

[WILLIAM BUELL, born in Chesterton, Huntingdonshire, England, (about) 1610, came to New England (about) 1630, to Dorchester, Mass. He removed thence, in 1636, to Windsor, Conn., where he died November 13, 1681.

Second Generation, *Samuel Buell*, born in Windsor, September 2, 1641, married, November 13, 1662, *Deborah Griswold*, born June 26, 1646, daughter of *Edward Griswold*, of Windsor. (See Col. Joshua Porter, (26.)

Third Generation, *William Buell*, born in Windsor, ———, 1676, lived in Killingworth, Conn. He married in Hartford, Conn., in 1705, *Elizabeth Collins*, daughter of Rev. *Joseph Collins*, of Hartford., who was a son of HENRY COLLINS, who came with his wife *Anne*, in the ship "Abigail," in 1635, from England.

(WILLIAM WHITING, an early settler of Hartford, Conn., in 1636, had been a merchant in London, England. He became associated with Lord Say-and-Sele, Lord Brooke, George Wyllys and others in a patent for lands in New England, in 1632, Thomas Wiggins being their agent.

"He was one of the most respectable of the settlers of 1636 ; one of the civil "and religious fathers of Connecticut ; a man of wealth and education, and "styled in the records 'William Whiting, gentleman.'"

He was chosen one of the magistrates in 1641, treasurer of the colony until his death in July, 1647. (See Dr. Joshua Porter, (47.)

Second Generation, *John Whiting*, born ———, 1635, graduated at Harvard College in 1653, and was settled as minister in Salem, Mass. He removed to Hartford, Conn., and was ordained pastor of the church, in 1660.

He married, in 1653, *Sybil Collins*, daughter of EDWARD COLLINS, who with his wife, *Martha*, came from England, in 1636, and settled in Cambridge, Mass., where he was a deacon of the first church, and he purchased of Gov. Craddock a "plantation," at Medford, Mass., and died in Charleston, Mass., April--, 1689, aged 86.

Third Generation, *Sybil Whiting*, born ———, 1654, married Rev. *Joseph Collins*, of Hartford, Conn., son of HENRY COLLINS, who came from England, in the ship "Abigail," in 1635, with his wife, Ann.

Fourth Generation, *Elizabeth Collins*, born (about) 1680, married *William Buell*.)

Fourth Generation, *Abel Buell*, born June 5, 1714, married, April 9, 1734, *Mehitabel Dewey*, born June 29, 1706, daughter of *Josiah Dewey*, of Lebanon,

Conn., who was son of *Josiah Dewey*, born October 10, 1641, who married, November 6, 1662, *Hepzibah Lyman*, daughter of RICHARD LYMAN, from England. (See Mary A. Holley, (82.)

Josiah Dewey, married, November 6, 1662, *Hepzibah Ford*, daughter of THOMAS FORD, who came from England to Dorchester, Mass., in the ship "Mary and John," in 1630. (See Augusta Porter, (57.)

Josiah Dewey was son of THOMAS DEWEY, who came from England to Dorchester, Mass., in 1633, and removed to Windsor, Conn., in 1635, with Rev. John Warham, and the original settlers, and who married, March 22, 1638, *Frances Clark.*)

Fifth Generation, Anna Buell, born in Lebanon, Conn., August 17, 1738, married in Coventry, Conn., ———, 1777, Noah Grant.)

On the reception of the news of the battle of Lexington, April, 1775, Noah Grant joined a company in Tolland, Conn., which marched to Boston, and took part in subsequent operations. He soon became captain, and served to the end of the War of the Revolution. His wife, Anna Buell, died in Coventry, Conn., ———, 1789. He removed, with his children to Westmoreland county, Pennsylvania, where he married, second, March 3, 1792, *Rachel Kelley.*

Their children were [being of the seventh generation:]

83. Solomon Grant, b. ———, 1778.
84. Peter Grant, b. ———, 1780.
85. Susannah Grant, b. December 7, 1792.
86. Jesse R. Grant, b. January 23, 1794, married Harriet Simpson.
87. Margaret Grant, b. October 23, 1795.
88. Noah Grant, b. November 1, 1797.
89. John Grant, b. June 2, 1799.
90. Roswell Grant, b. January 10, 1802.
91. Rachel Grant, b. September 19, 1803.

[57.] AUGUSTA PORTER, married, November 6, 1806, *Robert Foster Barnard*, counsellor-at-law, of Berkshire county, Mass.

[FRANCIS BARNARD, born in Coventry, Warwickshire, England, in 1616, came in the ship "Truelove," from London, England, in 1636, to Dorchester, Mass. He was cousin of John Barnard of Coventry, England, who had come to New England, in 1634, in the ship "Francis," and had settled in Hadley, Mass., and who dying without children, gave his property to his "kinsman" Francis.

Francis Barnard settled in Hartford, Conn., in 1644. He married, in 1645, *Hannah Marvyn*, born in England, who came with her brothers MATTHEW and REGINALD MARVYN, in the ship "Increase," from London, England, in 1635, and who removed in 1638 to Hartford, Conn. Matthew Marvyn removed in 1653 to Norwalk, Conn., where he died. Francis Barnard died February 3, 1698, aged 81.

Second Generation, Joseph Barnard, born ———, 1646, married, June 13, 1675, *Sarah Strong*, born in Windsor, Conn., ———, 1656, daughter of Elder *John Strong*.

(Elder JOHN STRONG, born in Taunton, Somersetshire, England, in 1626, was son of *Henry Strong*, of Taunton, who was son of *Richard Strong*, born in Caernavonshire, North Wales, about 1580, who removed to Taunton. He sailed for New England, in the ship "Mary and John," with Rev. John Warham, Captain John Mason, Roger Ludlow and others, March 20, 1630, arriving at Nantasket, (Hull,) Mass., May 30. He married, December 30, 1630, *Abigail Ford*, daughter of THOMAS FORD, who had been fellow passengers from England. They removed to Windsor, Conn, on the settlement of that place, in 1635, and thence to Northampton, Mass., where he died, April 14, 1699, aged 94.

Second Generation, Sarah Strong, born ———, 1656, in Windsor, married *Joseph Barnard*.) Joseph Barnard removed to Deerfield, Mass., where he was killed in the attack by the Indians, September 6, 1695.

Third Generation, Ebenezer Barnard, born March 13, 1676, married, September 29, 1715, *Elizabeth Foster*. He lived in Roxbury and Deerfield, Mass.

(HOPESTILL FOSTER came from London, England, with his wife, *Patience*, and children, in the ship "Elizabeth," to Dorchester, Mass., April 7, 1635.

He was of the family of Fosters, of Bamborough Castle in Northumberland, Wardens of the Marches.

> "There was mounting 'mong Graemes of the Netherby clan,
> Fosters, Fenwicks and Musgraves, they rode and they ran."
>
> SIR WALTER SCOTT.

He was Freeman of the Colony 1639, Ancient and Honorable Artillery Company 1641, Selectman 1645.

Second Generation, Hopestill Foster, born in England, in 1621, was captain of the A. and H. Artillery Company. He married *Mary*, daughter of JAMES BATES, who had been fellow passengers from England to Dorchester, Mass., whence they removed to Hingham, Mass.

Third Generation, James Foster, born April 13, 1651, married, September 27, 1674, *Anna Lane*, ———, born 1654, daughter of JOB LANE, of Malden, Mass., whose wife, *Anna Reyner*, was daughter of Rev. JOHN REYNER, from England. (See Henry P. Andrews, (95.)

Fourth Generation, Elizabeth Foster, born ———, 1686, married *Ebenezer Barnard*.)

Fourth Generation, Abner Barnard, born January 13, 1713, married June 1, 1749, *Rachel Catlin*. They lived in Northampton, Mass.

(JOHN CATLIN went from England to Barbadoes, where he was a proprietor in the Parish of St. Michaels. He removed thence to Virginia, and again to Weathersfield, Conn, He was a trader between those places. His wife, *Isabel Ward*, was sister (probably of *Lawrence Ward*, who settled in New Haven, Conn., in 1639, and who removed to New Jersey, and died in 1671.)

John Catlin died in Weathersfield, Conn., about 1644, when his estate was there appraised.

Second Generation, John Catlin, born (about) 1640, lived in Weathersfield, Conn., in 1662, at which date he married *Mary Baldwin*, born ———, 1645, daughter of *Joseph Baldwin*, of Milford, Conn., who married as his second wife, *Isabel*, widow of *John Catlin*, sr. This John Catlin, sr., lived in Bradford, Conn., in 1665. He removed to Newark, N. J., about 1670, thence to Hadley, Mass., in 1682, and again to Deerfield, Mass., whence he was killed in the attack on that place by the Indians, February 29, 1704, with his children, Elizabeth and Joseph, the other children, John and Ruth, being carried into captivity.

Third Generation, Joseph Catlin, born (about) 1673, married, June 6, 1701, *Hannah Sheldon*, and was killed as before stated.

(ISAAC SHELDON came from England to Dorchester, Mass., and removed to Windsor, Conn., in 1640, He married, in 1653, *Mary Woodford*, daughter of THOMAS WOODFORD, who came from England, in the ship "William and Francis," June 5, 1632, removed to Hartford, Conn., and thence to Northampton, Mass. (See Eunice Porter, (49.)

Second Generation, Hannah Sheldon, born June 29, 1670, married *Joseph Catlin*.)

Fourth Generation, John Catlin, born ———, 1704, (posthumous,) married, June 15, 1727, *Mary Munn*, born ———, 1709, a descendant of *Benjamin Munn*, of Hartford, Conn., who removed to Springfield, Mass., where he married *Abigail Burt*, daughter of HENRY BURT, who came from England to Roxbury, Mass., with his wife, *Ulalie*, and removed to Springfield, Mass., in 1640.

Fifth Generation, Rachel Catlin, born ———, 1728, married, June 1, 1749, *Abner Barnard*.)

Fifth Generation, Doct. *Sylvester Barnard*, born in Deerfield, Mass., ———1759, married ———, Sally Grosse, a descendant of *Edmund Grosse*, of Boston, Mass., who married, February 19, 1695, *Dorothy Belcher*, born October 23, 1673, daughter of *Josiah Belcher*, of Boston, Mass., who married, March 3, 1655, *Ranis Rainsford*, born June 10, 1638, daughter of EDWARD RAINSFORD, of Boston, Mass., who came from England in the ship "Abigail," June, 1635.

Josiah Belcher, born ——, 1635, was son of GREGORY BELCHER, who came to New England, in 1634, with his wife, *Catherine*, and settled in Braintree, Mass., where he was one of the founders of the church, and died June 21, 1659.

Edmund Grosse, born in Boston, Mass., March 9, 1656, was son of CLEMENT GROSSE, who came to New England in 1635, and settled in Boston.)

Doct. Sylvester Barnard died April 14, 1817, Mrs. Sally Barnard, died September 12, 1796.

Sixth Generation, Col. *Robert Foster Barnard*, born August 14, 1784, married, November 1, 1806, *Augusta Porter*.]

Robert F. Barnard died in New York city December 9, 1850, Mrs. Augusta (Porter) Barnard died in Springfield, Mass., ——, 1833.

Their children were [being of the eighth generation :]

92. Sarah G. Barnard, b. June 19, 1807, m. A. S. Porter, (66.)
93. Frederick A. P. Barnard, b. May 5, 1809, m. Margaret McMurray.
94. John G. Barnard, b. May 19, 1815, m. first, Jane E. Brand, second, Anna E. (Hall) Boyd.

[61.] MARY PORTER, married, first, June 21, 1821, *Henry Walton Andrews*.

(WILLIAMS ANDREWS, born in Hemsworth, in the west riding of Yorkshire, England, came from England, in the ship "James," April 6, 1635, and settled in Cambridge, Mass. He removed in April, 1637, with Gov. Theophilus Eaton, Rev. John Davenport, and their associates, to New Haven, Conn. He was "captain of the Trained band, and an active man in the colony." He was one of the founders of the church, and died January 3, 1664.

Second Generation, *Samuel Andrews*, born ——, 1633, married, ——, 1661, *Elizabeth Peck*, only daughter of WILLIAM PECK, who came from England with Eaton, Davenport, &c., in the ship "Hector," to Boston, Mass., July 26, 1637, from London, Eng., where he had been a merchant, and settled in New Haven, Conn.

Third Generation, *William Andrews*, born February 9, 1665, married, ——, 1690, *Mary St. John*, born ——, 1668, daughter (probably) of *Samuel St. John*, of Norwalk, Conn., who married, September —, 1663, *Elizabeth Hayte*, daughter of *Walter Hayte*. Samuel St. John was son of MATTHEW ST. JOHN, who came from England to Dorchester, Mass., in 1634, removed to Windsor, Conn., in 1638, and thence to Norwalk, where he died in 1669.

Fourth Generation, *William Andrews*, born April 10, 1698, married, ——, *Mary Seymour*.

(RICHARD SEYMOUR came from England and settled in Hartford, Conn., in 1639. He removed to Farmington, Conn., and thence to Norwalk. Conn., where he died November 25, 1655.

28

Second Generation, John Seymour, born in Hartford, Conn., (about) 1642, married *Mary Watson*, daughter of JOHN WATSON, who came to Hartford from Cambridge, Mass., having been a passenger, with William Wadsworth, John White, William Goodwin and others, in the ship "Lion," from England, September 16, 1632. He was an elder in the church of which Rev. Thomas Hooker was pastor, and with his family, accompanied him, on their removal to Hartford, in 1636.

Third Generation, Thomas Seymour, born March 12, 1663, married *Ruth Norton*, born May 1, 1675, daughter of Thomas Norton.

(THOMAS NORTON came from England, and with his wife, *Grace*, were early settlers of Guilford, Conn., where he signed the first compact, June 1, 1639. He died in 1648.

Second Generation, Thomas Norton, born April 18, 1646, married, May 8, 1671, *Elizabeth Mason*.

(Capt. JOHN MASON came from England to Dorchester, Mass., in the company with John Winthrop, in 1632. He removed to Windsor, Conn., in 1636, with Rev. John Warham and that company. He had served in the Netherlands, under Sir Thomas Fairfax, and in 1637 was commissioned to command an expedition against the Pequots, whom, in a series of campaigns, he entirely destroyed. He was "Major of the Connecticut forces," until his death at Norwich, Conn., in 1672.

His second wife, the mother of his children, was *Anne Peck*, to whom he was married, July, 1639.

(Rev. ROBERT PECK, born at Beccles, county of Suffolk, England, graduated at Magdalen College, Oxford, England. in 1599, He was minister over the church at Hingham, in Norfolk, England, 1605 to 1623. He came to Dorchester, Mass., in the ship "Diligent," in 1638, and on November 28, of the same year, was appointed teacher in the church at Hingham, Mass.

He remained until the dissolution of the "Long Parliament," when he returned (October 27, 1641,) to his rectorship at Hingham, England. His daughter, *Anne Peck*, married Capt. *John Mason*.)

Second Generation, Elizabeth Mason, born August —, 1654, married, May 8, 1671, *Thomas Norton*, son of THOMAS NORTON, who came from England with his wife, *Grace*, and in 1639 was one of the founders of Guilford, Conn., being a native of Guilford, in Surrey, England.

Third Generation, Ruth Norton, born May 1, 1675, married *Thomas Seymour*.

Fourth Generation, Mary Seymour, born November 3, 1703, married *William Andrews*.)

Fifth Generation, Ashbel Andrews, born June 10, 1730, married (about) 1758, *Mary Dudley*, a descendant of WILLIAM DUDLEY, who was born at Ockley, in the county of Surrey, England, who came to New England, and in 1639, removed, with Col. George Fenwick, Rev. Henry Whitfield and others to Guilford, Conn.

In 1764, Ashbel Andrews removed, with a company from Connecticut, and settled at Stillwater, on the Hudson river, in Saratoga county, N. Y.

Sixth Generation, Ashbel Andrews, born April 10, 1760, married *Mary White*, a descendant of Elder JOHN WHITE, who came in the ship "Lion," from London, England, to Dorchester, Mass., in 1632, and removed in 1636, with Gov. Theophilus Eaton, William Andrews and others, to Hartford, Conn.

Ashbel Andrews was judge of the county court, and died at Saratoga Springs, April 28, 1823.

Seventh Generation, Henry Walton Andrews, born May 10, 1794, married, June 21, 1821, *Mary Porter*.]

Their only child [being of the eighth generation :]
95. Henry P. Andrews, b. April 18, 1822, m. Maria L. Adams.

Henry W. Andrews was a merchant and planter in Augusta, Ga. He died at Saratoga Springs, March 10, 1822.

Mrs. Mary (Porter) Andrews married, second, October 16, 1826, *Peter V. Wiggins.*

[JOHN WIGGINS, born in England, in 1641, came to New England at an early date, and was among the first settlers of Rhode Island. He soon removed thence to Long Island, with the first settlers of Southold, where his name appears on the records with that of the minister, the Rev. John Youngs.

Second Generation, James Wiggins, born ———, 1672, married (about) 1698, *Anais Concklin*, daughter of *Jeremiah Concklin*, of Southold, L. I., whose wife was *Mary Gardner*, born August 30, 1638, daughter of LION GARDINER.

(LION GARDINER was a native of Scotland and had served in the English army, in the Netherlands, as an officer of engineers, under General Fairfax. His wife, *Mary Williamson*, was daughter of DERICKE WILLIAMSON, burgomaster of Worden, in Holland. He embarked at London, England, August 11, 1635, for New England, in the barque "Batchiler," a vessel of only twenty-five tons, sent by Lords Say-and-Sele, and Lord Brooke, bringing his wife, daughter Mary and two servants. In 1637 he had command of Saybrook fort at the time Capt. John Mason destroyed the Pequots, in the swamp at Fairfield, Conn. He acquired from the Indian proprietors the title to the island, since known as "Gardiner's Island." He died in 1663.)

Third Generation, Capt. *John Wiggins*, born ———, 1700, married ——, *Mary Corey*, daughter of *Abraham Corey*, of Southold, L. I., whose wife, *Margaret*, was daughter of GEOFFREY CHRISTOPHERS, who was born at Torbay, on the coast of Devonshire, England, and came with his wife, *Margaret*, and brother, Christopher Christophers, from England to Barbadoes, and thence to New London, Conn., in 1667, and again removed to Southold, 1676.

Capt. John Wiggins died December 18, 1767. Mrs. Mary (Corey) Wiggins died July 3, 1749.

Fourth Generation, David Wiggins, born ———, 1723, married, February 2, 1744, *Ruth Terry*, daughter of *Thomas Terry*, of Orient, L. I.

(THOMAS TERRY came from Barnet, county of Hereford, England in the ship "James," from London, in 1635, aged 28 years. His sister, Abigail Terry, married Selah Strong. (See Albert H. Porter, (67.)

Thomas Terry removed to Southold, L. I., about 1646.

Second Generation, Thomas Terry, born ———, married ———.

Third Generation, Ruth Terry, born ———, married David Wiggins.

Fifth Generation, David Wiggins, born ———, 1751, married, December 26, 1777, *Mary Vaill*, who was born November 21, 1754, daughter of *Peter Vaill*, of Orient, L. I., whose wife was *Martha Terry*, daughter of *Thomas Terry*.

(SAMUEL TERRY, born April, 1632, at Barnet-Chipping, county of Hereford, England, eleven miles from London, came in 1650 to Springfield, Mass., where he married, January 3, 1660, *Anna Lobdell*, sister of *Simon Lobdell*, of Hartford, Conn.

Second Generation, Samuel Terry, born July 18, 1661, married, May 17, 1682, *Hannah Morgan*, born February 11, 1656, daughter of MILES MORGAN, who came from Bristol, England, to New England, in 1636, removed to Springfield, Mass., and died May 28, 1699, and who married, (about) 1643, *Prudence Gilbert*, daughter of JOHN GILBERT, who came from England, in the ship "Mary and John," in 1630, to Dorchester, Mass., with his wife, *Winifred*, and removed in 1637, to Taunton, Mass., where he died in May, 1654.

Third Generation, Thomas Terry, born (about) 1680, married ———.

Fourth Generation, Martha Terry, born (about) 1725, married *Peter Vaill*.

JEREMIAH VAILL, born in England, came to Salem, Mass., (about) 1640. He removed soon after to Rhode Island, and thence to Southold, L. I.

Second Generation, Jeremiah Vaill, (baptized) December 30, 1649, married *Ann* ———.

Third Generation, Jeremiah Vaill, born (about) 1672, married, ———, 1698, *Elizabeth Youngs*, daughter of *Joseph Youngs*, of Southold, L. I., who was son of Rev. JOHN YOUNGS. (See Nathaniel Porter, (21.)

Fourth Generation, Peter Vaill, born March 22, 1722, married *Martha Terry*.

Fifth Generation, Mary Vaill, born November 21, 1755, married, December 26, 1777, *David Wiggins*.

Sixth Generation, Peter Vaill Wiggins, born June 23, 1793, married *Mary Porter.*]

Peter V. Wiggins was a merchant and banker at Saratoga Springs, where he died May 28, 1862. Mrs. Mary (Porter Andrews) Wiggins died at the residence of her son P. Porter Wiggins, Ausable Grove, Illinois, August 16, 1859.

Their children were [being of the eighth generation :]

96. Martha V. Wiggins, b. October 8, 1827, m. Cruger Walton.
97. Augusta P. Wiggins, b. October 29, 1829.
98. Mary E. Wiggins, b. June 19, 1831, d. October 6, 1853.
99. Ellen M. Wiggins, b. August 25, 1833, d. September 12, 1834.
100. Peter Porter Wiggins, b. May 8, 1835, m. S. Emily Burhans.
101. Frederick B. Wiggins, b. April 27, 1838, d. August 13, 1838.
102. William F. Wiggins, } b. August 5, 1841, { d. January 21, 1842.
103. John Wiggins,   { d. September 19, 1841.
104. John P. Wiggins, b. May 6, 1845, d. August 16, 1845.

[62.] ABIGAIL PORTER STODDARD, married, November 4, 1803, *William Morgan Burrall*, son of *William Burrall*, of Canaan, Conn.

[WILLIAM BURRALL came from England (about) 1715. He married *Mary* (or Joanna) daughter of *Jonas Westover*, of Windsor, Conn., a descendant of JONAS WESTOVER, who settled in Windsor, in 1639, removed to Killingworth, Conn., and died in 1702.

Second Generation, Col. *Charles Burrall,* born March 4, 1720, married *Abigail Kellogg,* daughter of *Stephen Kellogg,* of Westfield, Mass.

(JOSEPH KELLOGG came from England to Boston, Mass., removing thence, in 1651, to Farmington, Conn., and again to Hadley, Mass., in 1661-2. He was a selectman and lieutenant. In the "great falls fight," with the Pequots, in 1676, he led the men of Hadley. He married, May 9, 1667, *Abigail Terry,* born September 27, 1646, daughter of *Stephen Terry,* and died ——, 1707, aged 80.

(STEPHEN TERRY came from England, in the ship "Mary and John," to Dorchester, Mass. In July, 1635 "he partook of the spirit of migration," and removed with Rev. John Warham and that company to Windsor, Conn., where he was, with John Porter and others, in the "troop of horse.")

Second Generation, Stephen Kellogg, born ——, 1668, married Lydia ——.
Third Generation, Stephen Kellogg, born ——, 1694, married ——.
Fourth Generation, Abigail Kellogg, born ——, 1728, married Charles Burrall.)

Col. *Charles Burrall,* of Canaan, Conn., in August 1776, was appointed to the command of a regiment, in the brigade of Gen. James Wadsworth, and was in the command of Gen. George Washington, on Long Island and in New Jersey,

&c. He was also, with his regiment, at Ticonderoga, Crown Point and the battles of Saratoga, September and October, 1777. (See Col. Joshua Porter, (26.)

Third Generation, William Burrall, born July 18, 1749, married, October —, 1774, *Elizabeth Morgan*, born March 28, 1755, daughter of *Theophilus Morgan*.

(JAMES MORGAN, born in Llandaff, Glamorganshire, (Wales) England, in 1607, came from the port of Bristol, England, to New England, in 1636. He married, August 6, 1640, *Margery Hill*, sister (probably) of JOSEPH HILL, who came from Malden, county of Essex, England, in 1638, and settled in Charlestown, Mass,

Second Generation, Capt. *John Morgan*, born in Roxbury, Mass., March 30, 1645, married *Elizabeth Jones*, daughter of WILLIAM JONES, of New Haven, Conn., who came from London, England, to Boston, Mass., July 27, 1660, in the ship with the Regicides, Colonels Goffe and Whalley, and whose wife was *Hannah Eaton*, daughter of *Theophilus Eaton*, of New Haven, Conn.

(THEOPHILUS EATON, born in Stony Stratford, county of Bucks, England, was son of the minister of that parish. He married *Anne Morton*, daughter of THOMAS MORTON, Bishop of Chester, and came to Boston, Mass. He accompanied Rev. John Davenport, William Andrews and others in the settlement of New Haven, Conn., in 1639, and was chosen governor, annually, until his death, January 7, 1658, at the age of 67.)

Third Generation, Theophilus Morgan, born May 16, 1703, married, ——, 1729, *Elizabeth Sherman*.

(PELEG SHERMAN, an early settler of Portsmouth, R. I., married, July 25, 1657, *Elizabeth Lawton*, born (about) 1635, daughter of THOMAS LAWTON, of Portsmouth.

Second Generation, William Sherman, born October 3, 1659, married, May 12, 1681, *Martha Wilbor*, daughter of *William Wilbor*, who was son of SAMUEL WILBOR, who came from Doncaster, in Yorkshire, England, with his wife, *Anne Bradford*. He was of the company that came with William Coddington, Sir Richard Saltonstall and others, in the fleet with Winthrop, in 1629, and with Coddington, he removed in 1637, to Rhode Island.

Third Generation, Elizabeth Sherman, born ——, 1695, married *Theophilus Morgan*.)

Theophilus Morgan was a merchant in Berlin, Conn., and died November 22, 1766.

Fourth Generation, Theophilus Morgan, born January 26, 1732, married, December 7, 1752, *Rebecca Shipman*, of Boston, Mass. He lived in Killingworth, Conn., where he was a merchant, and died February 17, 1788.

Fifth Generation, Elizabeth Morgan, born March 28, 1755, married, October —, 1774, *William Burrall*.

Fourth Generation, William Morgan Burrall, born August —, 1779, married, November 4, 1803, *Abigail Porter Stoddard.*]

Their children were [being of the eighth generation :]
105. Elizabeth Burrall, b. December 22, 1804, m. Edmond S. Belden.
106. William P. Burrall, b. September 18, 1806, m. Harriet Holley (79.)
107. Edward Burrall, b. June 11, 1809, drowned June 22, 1814.
108. Abigail S. Burrall, b. April 22, 1811, d. March 25, 1813.

William Morgan Burrall, died November 21, 1856. Mrs. Aigail (Porter) Stoddard Burrall, died March 25, 1813.

[65.] WILLIAM AUGUSTUS BIRD, born at Salisbury, Conn., March 23, 1797, married, December 23, 1820, *Joanna Davis,* born July 12, 1802, daughter of Col. Thomas and Grace (Noble) Davis, of Troy, N. Y.

Thomas Davis, born March 4, 1772, was the son of William and Joanna Davis, of Philadelphia, Pa. He was married, April 2, 1797, to Grace Noble, born June 24, 1780, daughter of Abel and Anne Noble, of Belleville, Orange county, N. Y.

Thomas Davis died at Troy, N. Y., April 21, 1823. Mrs. Grace (Noble) Davis died November 29, 1813. William Davis, father of Thomas, died at Barbadoes Neck, N. J., March, 1813, and his wife, Joanna, died at the same place, March 2, 1797,

W. A. Bird removed at an early date to Erie county, N. Y. He was secretary and one of the surveyors in the commission to establish the boundaries between the United States and the British possessions, of which his uncle, Gen. Peter B. Porter, was a commissioner. He was an extensive land owner in Erie county, which he frequently represented in the legislature, president of the Erie County Savings Bank of Buffalo, and one of its prominent citizens. He died August 19, 1878.

Their children were [being of the eighth generation :]
109. John Herman Bird, b. September 3, 1821, m. Frances Blaney.
110. Maria Davis Bird, b. November 12, 1823, m. Thos. M. Foote, d. June 28, 1876.
111. Grace Eunice Bird, b. June 13, 1827, living in Buffalo, 1881.
112. William Augustus Bird, b. February 11, 1830, m. Mary M. Miller.

[68.] AUGUSTUS SEYMOUR PORTER, born January 18, 1798, at Canandaigua, N. Y., graduated at Union College 1818. He married, first,

July 25, 1822, *Sarah Augusta Mansfield*, a descendant of *Moses Mansfield*, of New Haven, Conn., a captain in the Indian wars, who was son of RICHARD MANSFIELD, who came from England, in 1638, and removed with his wife, *Gillian*, and family, to New Haven, Conn., about 1640, and died 1655.

Augustus S. Porter studied law with Judge Howell at Canandaigua, N. Y. He removed to Detroit, Mich., 1827. He was mayor of that city, and United States Senator 1839–45. He removed to Niagara Falls, N. Y., in 1847, and died there September 18, 1872.

Their only child [being of the eighth generation :]

113. Samuel Mansfield Porter, b. February 11, 1824, died in childhood.

Mrs. Sarah A. Porter died May 27, 1824. He married, second, September 24, 1832, in Sheffield, Mass., *Sarah G. Barnard*, (90.)

Their children were :

114. Jane Augusta Porter, b. July 7, 1833, unmarried in 1881.
115. Sarah Frederika Porter, b. November 17, 1836, m. Stephen E. Burrall.

[69.] ALBERT HOWELL PORTER, graduated at Union College 1820. He married, October 14, 1829, *Julia Mathews*, daughter of *Vincent Mathews*, and his wife, *Juliana Strong*.

[Elder JOHN STRONG, born in Taunton, Somersetshire, England, in 1605, sailed from England, in the ship "Mary and John," March 20, 1630, with John Warham and others, arriving at Nantasket. Mass., May 30, 1630. He removed, in 1635, to Windsor, Conn., and thence, in 1639, to Northampton, Mass., where he died November 28, 1676. He married, December 30, 1638, *Abigail Ford*, daughter of THOMAS FORD, who came from England in the ship "Mary and John," to Dorchester, Mass., in 1630, and removed to Windsor, Conn., in 1636.

Second Generation, *Thomas Strong*, born ———, 1633, married, October 10, 1671, *Rachel Holton*, born ———, 1651, daughter of WILLIAM HOLTON, who came from England, in the ship "Francis," in 1634, from Ipswich county, Suffolk, England, and was one of the original settlers of Hartford, Conn. (*Sarah Strong*, sister of Thomas, married *Joseph Barnard*. (See Augusta Porter, (57.)

Third Generation, *Selah Strong*, born December 23, 1680, married, June 23, 1702, *Abigail Terry*, daughter of THOMAS TERRY, who Embarked for New England in the ship "James," from Ipswich, England, July 13, 1635, and was an early settler of Hartford, Conn., whence he removed to Orient, Long Island, N. Y. His son, *Thomas Terry*, Jr., (brother of Abigail) had a daughter, *Ruth Terry*, who married *David Wiggins*. (See Mary Porter, (61.)

Fourth Generation, Selah Strong, Jr., born February 23, 1713, married *Hannah Woodhull,* daughter of *Nathaniel Woodhull,* of Brookhaven, L. I.

Fifth Generation, Maj. *Nathaniel Strong,* born November 18, 1737, married *Amy Brewster,* daughter of Rev. *Nathaniel Brewster,* of Brookhaven, L. I.

(Elder WILLIAM BREWSTER was born in 1563, at Scrooby, in Nottinghamshire, England, in the Manor Hall, belonging to the Archbishop of York; his father being a tenant of Bishop Sandys. The son was educated at Cambridge University, and was in the employment of the government, as post-master at Scrooby, where he married Mary ———. He went with *William Bradford,* afterwards governor of Plymouth colony, (see Henry P. Andrews, (95,) in 1607-8, to Holland, and was the ruling elder of the church at Leyden, of which Rev. John Robinson was teacher. He came thence in the ship "Mayflower," in December, 1620, to Plymouth, Mass.

Second Generation, Jonathan Brewster, born at Scrooby, came in the ship "Fortune," November 29, 1621. He married Lucretia ———. In 1636 he was in command of the trading post of the Plymouth colony on the Connecticut river, near Hartford. Removed to New London, Conn., in 1648, where he died.

Third Generation, Rev. *Nathaniel Brewster,* born ———, 1622, graduated at Harvard College 1642, and went to England, where he was a clergyman in Norfolk. Returning to America in 1662 he settled at Brookhaven, Long Island, N. Y., in 1665. He married *Sarah Ludlow,* daughter of *Roger Ludlow.*

(ROGER LUDLOW was chosen an "Assistant" in the last "General Court," held in London, England, February 10, 1630. He came from Plymouth, England, in May, 1630, in the ship "Mary and John," and was made deputy-governor in 1634. He removed, in 1635, to Windsor, Conn. He was a lawyer, and compiled a Code of Law for the United Colonies, captain in the Pequot war. He became dissatisfied, and in 1634 removed to Virginia, where he died. He married, in England, *Mary Endicott,* sister of Gov. JOHN ENDICOTT, who came from Weymouth, England, in the ship "Abigail," to Salem, Mass., September, 1628. He was one of the six original purchasers of the Massachusetts Bay, from the Plymouth Council, in England. Endicott was an assistant until 1635, when for his excess of zeal, in cutting the cross from the English ensign, he was "left out." In 1636 he commanded the expedition against the Pequots, and in 1641 was deputy governor, and in 1644 governor. He died March 15, 1655.

Second Generation, Sarah Ludlow, born ———, married Rev. *Nathaniel Brewster.*)

Sixth Generation, Juliana Strong, born ———, 1774, married, August 11, 1791, *Vincent Mathews.*

(PETER MATHEWS came from England with Col. Benjamin Fletcher, who was governor of New York 1691 to 1698, and who was probably his uncle, and who had reared him from childhood. Mathews was a captain in the colonial military force, and died in 1719.

Second Generation, Vincent Mathews, born ——, 1698, married ——, *Catryna Abeel*, born October 23, 1698, daughter of *Johannes Abeel*, who married, March 1694, *Catalina Sayles.*

Johannes Abeel was mayor of Albany, N. Y., 1694-5, and 1709-10, and died January 28, 1711.

Third Generation, James Mathews, born ——, 1736, married, February 18, 1762, *Hannah Strong*, born ——, 1742, sister of Maj. *Nathaniel Strong*, who married *Amy Brewster*, as before stated.

Fourth Generation, Gen. *Vincent Mathews*, born June 29, 1766, in Orange county, N. Y., married, August 11, 1791, his cousin, *Juliana Strong.*)

Fifth Generation, Julia Mathews, born April 16, 1808, married Albert H. Porter,]

Their children were [being of the eighth generation :]
116. Vincent M. Porter, b. August 25, 1831, d. May 30, 1838.
117. Julia M. Porter, b. May 23, 1835, m. John H. Osborne.
118. Albert A. Porter, b. May 4, 1837, m. Julia E. Jeffrey.
119. Vincent M. Porter, b. July 14, 1841, unmarried 1881.
120. Jane H. Porter, b. March 6, 1844, m. Arthur Robinson.

[73.] JANE S. PORTER, married, September 26, 1837, *Daniel J. Townsend.* Residence Niagara Falls, N. Y.

[*Richard, John* and HENRY TOWNSEND came to New England about 1638, and in 1655 were residents of Warwick, R. I. Richard married *Deliverance*, John married *Elizabeth*, and Henry married *Anna Cole*, daughters of ROBERT COLE, (or Coale,) who came in the fleet with John Winthrop, in August, 1630, and settled at Roxbury, Mass. Removed to Ipswich, Mass., and thence to Providence, R. I., where he was one of the founders of the Baptist church.

Henry Townsend and wife, *Anna*, removed to Oyster Bay, Long Island, N. Y., where, on September 16, 1681, he obtained a grant of the mill privilege, now (1881) the property of his g. g. g. g. g. grandson, Beekman H. Townsend.

Second Generation, Henry Townsend, born at Oyster Bay ——, married ——, *Deborah Underhill*, daughter of John Underhill, Jr., son of JOHN UNDERHILL, who with his wife, *Helena*, and children came with John Winthrop to New England, in 1630. Underhill had served as a captain in the English army in the Netherlands, under the Prince of Orange. He was a deputy in the first General Court of Conecticut, and served throughout the Pequot war. He removed to Long Island, N. Y., and died in 1671 or 2. Henry Townsend died about 1700.

Third Generation, Henry Townsend, born about 1660, married, ——, *Elizabeth Wright,* born November 18, 1667, daughter of *Joseph Wright,* of Weathersfield, Conn., who was son of THOMAS WRIGHT, from England, one of the early settlers of Weathersfield, in 1639.

Fourth Generation, Henry Townsend, born (about) 1690, married *Elizabeth Titus,* a descendant of *Samuel Titus,* who settled at Newtown, L. I., 1664.

Fifth Generation, Peter Townsend, born January 1, 1736, married, February 14, 1760, *Hannah Hawkhurst,* a descendant of CHRISTOPHER HAWKHURST, from England, who settled in Warwick, R. I., about 1650, and who removed to Long Island.

Sixth Generation, Isaac Townsend, born in Chester, N. Y., November 20, 1772, married Elizabeth Jackson, a descendant (probably) of ROBERT JACKSON, of Hempstead, L. I., 1665,

Seventh Generation, Daniel Jackson Townsend, born October 17, 1810, married *Jane S. Porter.*]

Their children were [being of the eighth generation :]
121. Augustus P. Townsend, b. July 13, 1838, d. March 8, 1840.
122. Elizabeth J. Townsend, b. March 14, 1840.
123. Jane H. Townsend, b. February 14, 1844, m. E. S. Wheeler.
124. Lavinia P. Townsend, b. January 17, 1849, m. Lauren W. Pettibone.

[75.] PETER AUGUSTUS PORTER, graduated at Harvard College in 1845, and at Heidelberg and Breslau, Germany, 1849. He married, first, March 30, 1852, his cousin *Mary Cabell Preston Breckinridge,* daughter of John Breckinridge (d.) and his wife, Margaret Miller.

[WILLIAM CABELL, born (about) 1640, at Warminster, near Salisbury, in Wiltshire, England, was a descendant of a family who were seated at Frome, in Dorsetshire, as early as the thirteenth century.

He was buried at Warminster, September 4, 1704. His wife, *Mary,* was buried December 5, 1704. He was a "dissenter," in faith, and it is a curious circumstance that the Puritans destroyed the colored glass in the church at Frome, save that representing the Cabell arms.

Second Generation, Nicholas Cabell, baptized May 29, 1667, at Warminster, England, married, November 19, 1697, at Frome-Selwood, Somersetshire, England, *Rachel Hooper.* He died July 30, 1730. She died October —, 1737.

Third Generation, William Cabell, born March 9, 1699, at Warminster, came to Virginia about 1820–5, when he married *Elizabeth Burke* (or Burks], daughter of *Samuel Burke,* a planter of Virginia. William Cabell died at Warminster, Nelson county, Va., April 19, 1774.

Fourth Generation, Col. *Joseph Cabell*, born September 8, 1732, in Goochland county, Va.

He was a justice, and represented Amherst and Buckingham counties in the House of Burgesses, and in the conventions of 1775-76.

He commanded a regiment in the war of the revolution, and was present at Yorktown and the surrender of Cornwallis.

He married *Mary Hopkins*, daughter of Dr. *Arthur Hopkins*, of "*Winton*," in Amherst, and "*Variety Shades*," and "*Sion Hill*," in Buckingham county, Va. Col. Joseph Cabell died March 1, 1798. Mrs. Mary Cabell died July 12, 1811.

Fifth Generation, Mary Hopkins Cabell, born (about) 1762, married, June 28, 1785, *John Breckinridge.*] (See Gen. Peter B. Porter, (51.)

Their only child [being of the eighth generation :]

125. Peter A. Porter, b. October 10, 1853, m. Alice A. Taylor.

Mrs. Mary (Breckinridge) Porter, died at Niagara Falls, N. Y., August 4, 1854. He married, second, in New York city, November 9, 1859, *Josephine M. Morris*, born July 31, 1832, daughter of *George W. Morris*, of Charleston, S. C. Their children were

126. Lætitia E. Porter, b. February 16, 1861, d. October 17, 1864.
127. George M. Porter, b. July 7, 1863.

Col. *Peter A. Porter* raised and commanded the first regiment of New York Heavy Artillery, in the war of the rebellion, and was killed at the front, while leading his command against the Confederate works, at the battle of Cold Harbor, June 3, 1864, pierced by five balls from the enemy's sharpshooters.

[77.] JOHN MILTON HOLLEY graduated at Yale College in 1822. He removed to Lyons, Wayne county, N. Y. He married, May 30, 1827, *Mary Kirkland*, born April 9, 1804, daughter of Gen. *Joseph Kirkland*, of Utica, N. Y., with whom he studied law.

[JOHN KIRKLAND, of London, England, came to New England, in 1635, when he became one of the first settlers of Saybrook, Conn.

Second Generation, John Kirkland, born (about) 1650, married, November 18, 1679, *Lydia Pratt*, born January 1, 1660, daughter of WILLIAM PRATT, from England, an early settler at Hartford, Conn., whose wife, *Elizabeth*, was daughter of JOHN CLARK, of Milford, Conn., who came from England, in 1630, and settled in Cambridge, Mass. He removed, with Rev. Thomas Hooker and that company, to Hartford, Conn., in 1636, and thence to Milford.

Third Generation, Daniel Kirkland, born June 17, 1701, married *Hannah Per-*

kins, born ——, 1701, daughter of *Jabez Perkins*, who married, June 30, 1698, *Hannah Lothrop*, daughter (probably) of *Samuel Lothrop*, of New London, Conn., who was son of Rev. JOHN LOTHROP, a minister in London, England, who had been imprisoned by Archbishop Laud, for non-conformity, and who on his liberation embarked for Boston, Mass., in 1634, and settled in Barnstable, Mass., where he died November 8, 1653.

(*Jabez Perkins*, of Norwich, Conn., born ——, 1669, was son of *Jacob Perkins*, of Ipswich, Mass., born in England in 1624, who was son of *John Perkins*, born in Newent, in Gloustershire, England, in 1590, who came to Boston, Mass., in 1631, with his wife, *Judith*, and children, removed to Ipswich in 1633, and died in 1654.)

Fourth Generation, Joseph Kirkland, born March 18, 1744, married (unknown.)

Fifth Generation, Joseph Kirkland, born ——, 1770, was the first mayor of Utica, N. Y. He married, 1795, *Sarah Backus*, a descendant of WILLIAM BACKUS, one of the early settlers of Saybrook, in 1639,

Sixth Generation, Mary Kirkland, born ———, 1804, married, May 30, 1827, John M. Holley.]

John M. Holley died in Jacksonville, Fla., March 8, 1848, while a representative in Congress from the 27th district of New York.

Their children were [being of the eighth generation :]
128. Henry K. Holley, b. March 16, 1828, d. July 8, 1854.
129. Sarah Holley, b. January 30, 1830, d. March 6, 1853.
130. Harriet L. Holley, b. November 23, 1831, married John T. Clark.
131. John M. Holley, b. March 28, 1835, d. June 1, 1836.
132. Sarah Holley, b. November 30, 1837, d. December 3, 1840.
133. Mary E. Holley, b. October 17, 1840, d. April 29, 1850.
134. Julia K. Holley, b. August 27, 1842, married Charles H. Roys.
135. John M. Holley, b. June 12, 1845, married Orilla A. King.

[78.] ALEXANDER H. HOLLEY, lieutenant-governor and governor of Connecticut, &c., married, first, October 4, 1831, *Jane M. Lyman*, born February 7, 1808, daughter of *Erastus Lyman*, of Goshen, Conn.

[RICHARD LYMAN, of Norton-Mandeville, parish of Ongar, county of Essex, England, came with his family, in the ship "Lion," from the port of Bristol, England, (with John Eliot, the famous apostle to the Indians,) arriving at Dorchester, Mass., November 3, 1631. He settled first in Roxbury, Mass. On the 15th October, 1635, with his family, he joined the company which made the first settlements on the Connecticut river, at Hartford, Windsor and Weathersfield,

Conn. He was one of the original proprietors at Hartford, where he died August, 1640. His wife, *Sarah*, dying soon after.

Second Generation, John Lyman, born in England, September —, 1623, married, June 12, 1655, *Dorcas Plumbe*, daughter of JOHN PLUMBE, from England to Weathersfield, in 1635.

John Lyman removed to Northampton, Mass., where he died August 20, 1690. As lieutenant, he led the Northampton men in the famous "Falls fight," with the Pequots, above Deerfield, Mass., May 18, 1678. He died August 20, 1690.

Third Generation, Moses Lyman, born February 20, 1662, married, April 18, 1666, *Ann* ———. He died February 28, 1701.

Fourth Generation, Moses Lyman, born February 27, 1689, married, December 18, 1712, *Mindwell Sheldon*, born March 22, 1693, daughter of *Isaac Sheldon*, of Hatfield, Mass., and his wife, *Sarah Warner*, born June 21, 1667, daughter of *Daniel Warner*, of Hartford, Conn.

(*Isaac Sheldon*, born in Windsor, Conn., September 4, 1656, was son of *Isaac Shelden*, of that place, who married, in 1653, *Mary*, daughter of *Thomas Woodford*, of Hartford, Conn. (See Eunice Porter, (49.)

(*Daniel Warner*, of that part of Hadley, Mass., which became Hatfield, was son of ANDREW WARNER, who came from England, and in 1632 removed from Dorchester to Cambridge, Mass., and thence with the original settlers to Hartford, Conn.)

Fifth Generation, Moses Lyman, born in Northampton, Mass., October 2, 1713, removed to Goshen, Conn., in 1739, and married, March 24, 1742, *Sarah Hayden*, born September 17, 1716, daughter of *Samuel Hayden*, of Windsor, Conn., whose wife was *Hannah Holcombe*, born ———, 1680, daughter of *Joshua Holcombe*, of Windsor, and his wife, *Ruth Sherwood*, daughter of THOMAS SHERWOOD, who came from England, in the ship "Francis," in 1634, from Ipswich, England, and settled in Stratford, Conn.

(*Joshua Holcomb*, born September 27, 1640, was son of THOMAS HOLCOMBE, who came from England to Dorchester, Mass., in 1633, and who removed with the congregation of Rev. John Warham, in 1635, to Windsor, Conn.

(*Samuel Hayden*, born February 22, 1679, was son of *Daniel Hayden*, of Windsor, Conn., born September 2, 1640, who married, March 12, 1674, *Hannah*, daughter of WILLIAM WILCOCKSON, who came from England in the ship "Planter," in 1636, and removed to Hartford, Conn. *Daniel Hayden* was eldest son of WILLIAM HAYDEN, who came from England, in 1630, and removed with Rev. Thomas Hooker and that company to Hartford, Conn., in June, 1636.

In 1642 he purchased lands in Windsor, Conn., to which place he removed. He served in the Pequot war, and died in Killingworth, Conn., in 1699.

Sixth Generation, Col. *Moses Lyman*, born March 20. 1743, married, ———, 1767,

Ruth Collins, daughter of *William Collins*, of Guilford, Conn., a descendant of WLLIAM COLLINS, from England, who lived in New London and New Haven, Conn.

Moses Lyman entered the army, on the first call for troops after the battle of Lexington. He commanded a regiment at the battle of Saratoga, and on the night of October 7, 1777, was detailed to watch the movements of Gen. Burgoyne, and was the first to give information of his retreat.

Gen. Gates made him bearer of dispatches to Gen. Washington, announcing the capitulation.

Seventh Generation, Moses Lyman, born April 16, 1768, married, January 21, 1796, *Elizabeth Buell*.

(WILLIAM BUELL, born in Chesterton, Huntingdonshire, England, (about) 1610, came to New England (about) 1630, and settled in Windsor, Conn., where he died November 13, 1681.

Second Generation, Samuel Buell, born September 2, 1641, married, November 13, 1662, *Deborah Griswold*, born June 28, 1646, daughter of MATTHEW GRISWOLD, of Windsor, Conn., who was born in Kenilworth, Warwickshire, England, and came to New England, with Rev. Ephraim Hewitt, in 1639, and who married *Anne Wolcott*, daughter of HENRY WOLCOTT.

(Henry Wolcott, born (about) 1578, at Wellington, in Somersetshire, England, where he held a commission from the government as justice, and had a large landed estate; came to Dorchester, Mass., in 1630, with his wife, *Elizabeth Saunders*, he was of the company which traversed the wilderness, in 1635, and made the settlement at Windsor, Conn. He died May 30, 1655. His widow, Elizabeth, died July 17, 1655, aged 73.)

Third Generation, Deacon *John Buell*, born in Killingworth, Conn., February 17, 1671, married, November 20, 1695, *Mary Loomis*, born October 2, 1680, daughter of *Thomas Loomis*, of Windsor, who married, January 2, 1680, *Hannah Porter*, born June 1, 1662, daughter of *John Porter*, (2) and *Mary Stanley*.

John Porter, born in England, in 1618, was son of JOHN PORTER, (1) from England.

Mary Stanley, was daughter of THOMAS STANLEY, and sister of *Anna Stanley*, who married *Samuel Porter*, (6.)

Fourth Generation, Solomon Buell, born in Lebanon, Conn., August 30, 1715, married, in Litchfield, Conn., January 19, 1738, *Eunice Griswold*, a descendant of MATTHEW GRISWOLD, from Kenilworth, England, before named.

Fifth Generation, Ira Buell, born in Litchfield, Conn., February 20, 1745, married, in Lyme, Conn., January 20, 1767, *Prudence Deming*, a descendant of *John Deming*, of Weathersfield, Conn., who married, September 20, 1657, *Mary Mygatt*, born ——, 1637, daughter of JOSEPH MYGATT, who came from England, in 1633, in the ship "Griffin," with Revs. Thomas Kooker, John Cotton, &c., and who removed in the "great migration," to Hartford, Conn., in 1636, where he died December 7, 1680, aged 84.

(John Deming, born September 9, 1838, was son of JOHN DEMING, who came from England, and in 1635 was one of the original settlers of Weathersfield, Conn , named in the charter of Connecticut; of 1662. His wife was *Honor Treat*, born (about) 1618, daughter of RICHARD TREAT, who came from England, with his wife, *Joanna*. (See Doct. Joshua Porter, (47.)

Sixth Generation, *Elizabeth Buell*, born in Litchfield, Conn., December 4, 1770, married *Moses Lyman*.

Seventh Generation, *Erastus Lyman*, born November 1, 1773, married, September 8, 1803, *Abigail Starr*.

(Doct. COMFORT STARR, of Asheford, county Kent, England, "Chirurgeon," warden of St. Mary's church, Asheford, came to New England, in the ship "Hercules," in 1635, with his wife, *Elizabeth*, and settled in Cambridge, Mass., where he died January 2, 1660. His wife died January 25, 1658.

Second Generation, Doct. *Thomas Starr*, born in England, was surgeon, in 1637, in the expedition against the Pequots. He lived in Duxbury, Scituate and Boston, Mass. His wife's name was *Rachel*. He died October 26, 1658.

Third Generation, *Comfort Starr*, born in Scituate, Mass., married, in Boston, *Marah Weld*, daughter of JOSEPH WELD, of Roxbury, Mass., who came from England, in 1635, and married, April 20, 1639, *Barbara Clap*, niece of Edward and Roger Clap, who were born at Salcombe-Regis, on the coast of Devonshire, England. Roger Clap came to New England, in the ship "Mary and John," from Plymouth, England, March 20, arriving at Nantasket May 30, 1630. Comfort Starr removed to New London, Conn., and thence, about 1674-5, to Middletown, Conn., where he died October 18, 1693.

Fourth Generation, *Joseph Starr*, born in Middletown, Conn., Septembar 23, 1676, married, June 24, 1697, *Abigail Baldwin*, daughter of *Samuel Baldwin*, of Milford, Conn., born 1645, who was son of *John Baldwin*, who settled in Milford, Conn., in 1639, son of SYLVESTER BALDWIN, born in St. Leonard's, parish of Aston-Clinton, county Bucks, England, who took passage in the ship "Martin," for New England, June, 1638, but died on the voyage, his widow, *Sarah*, marrying, in 1640, John Astwood, of Milford, Conn.

Fifth Generation, *Joseph Starr*, born September 6, 1698, married, (second wife) February 25, 1741, *Priscilla Roper*, a descendant of JOHN ROPER, who came with his wife, *Alice*, in 1637, from Buckingham, on the river Ouse, fifty-five miles from London, England, in the county of Norfolk. He settled in Dedham, Mass.

Sixth Generation, *Ephraim Starr*, born in Middletown, Conn., June 9, 1745, married, ——, 1776, *Hannah Beach*, born February 28, 1745, daughter of *Adna Beach*, and his wife, *Hannah Miles*. He died August 27, 1809.

(*Adna Beach*, was a descendant of RICHARD BEACH, who came from England, and was an early settler of New Haven, Conn., where he signed the compact, in 1639, and who married *Catherine*, widow of Andrew Hull.

Hannah Miles, was a descendant of *Samuel Miles*, born in Milford, Conn., April 12, 1640, who removed to New Haven, Conn., whose wife was *Hannah Wilmot*, born January 25, 1645, daughter of BENJAMIN WILMOT, Jr., who came with his father from England, and was in 1639, one of the signers of the compact, on the settlement of New Haven, Conn.)

Samuel Miles, was son of RICHARD MILES, from England, who settled at Milford, Conn., in 1639, removed to New Haven, Conn., in 1643, where he died January 7, 1667.

Seventh Generation, Abigail Starr, born January 24, 1778, married, September 6, 1803, *Erastus Lyman*.

Eighth Generation, Jane M. Lyman, born February 7, 1808, married *A. H. Holley*.]

Their only child [being of the eighth generation :]

136. Alexander L. Holley, born July 20, 1832, married Mary H. Slade.

Mrs. Jane M. Holley died September 18, 1832. A. H. Holley married, second, September 10, 1835, *Marcia Coffing*, daughter of *John C. Coffing*, of Salisbury, Conn. Their children were :

137. John Milton Holley, born ——
138. William R. Holley, born ——
139. John Coffing Holley, born December 20, 1837, married Lucinda Sterling.
140. George W. Holley, born July 29, 1839, died November 1, 1846.
141. Maria C. Holley, born July 26, 1842, married William B. Rudd.

Mrs. Marcia Holley died March 11, 1854. A. H. Holley married, third, November 11, 1856, *Sarah C. Day*, born September 23, 1814, daughter of *Thomas Day*, of Hartford, Conn.

[79.] HARRIETT HOLLEY married, May 9, 1831, *William Porter Burrall*, (106,) son of *William Morgan Burrall* and *Abigail Porter Stoddard*, (62.) W. P. Burrall graduated at Yale College in 1826, lawyer, state senator, mayor of Bridgeport, Conn., &c. He died March 2, 1874. Mrs. Harriett Burrall died December 30, 1876.

Their children were [being of the eighth generation :]

142. William Holley Burrall, b. May 29, 1832, civil engineer, Springfield, Mass.
143. John Milton Burral', b. August 30, 1834, m. Mary H. Dickinson.
144. Elizabeth M. Burrall, b. October 24, 1836, living in Springfield, Mass.

145. Sarah B. Burrall, b. September 14, 1838, m. H. H. Anderson.
147. Harriett H. Burrall, b. September 17, 1840, d. January 26, 1860.
147. Porter Burrall, b. July 26, 1843, died in childhood.
148. Porter S. Burrall, b. February 13, 1846, m. Anna E. Croome.

[80.] GEORGE W. HOLLEY, married, August 26, 1833, *Caroline E. Church*, residence Niagara Falls, N. Y. Author, member of legislature, &c.

[RICHARD CHURCH came from England to Plymouth, Mass., in 1630, in the fleet with John Winthrop and that company. He removed, in 1637, to Hartford, Conn., where he was an original proprietor. Thence he removed, in 1660, to Hadley, Mass., where he died December 16, 1667. His widow, *Anne*, died March 12, 1684, aged 83. He drew twelve acres of land, on the first allotment in Hartford, and sixty acres in East Hartford. His residence, in 1640, was on Burr street.

At a meeting in Hartford, April 18, 1659, he signed an agreement, with numbers of others, for the settlement of Hadley, Mass., to which place he removed in 1660, and where he died in 1667.

Second Generation, John Church, born ——, 1637, married, October 21, 1657, *Sarah Beckley*, daughter of RICHARD BECKLEY, who came from England, in 1638, and was one of the early settlers of Hartford and Weathersfield, Conn., and whose wife was *Rachel Deming*, daughter of JOHN DEMING, one of the first settlers of New Haven, Conn., and named in its charter; and whose wife was *Honor Treat*, daughter of RICHARD TREAT. (See Doct. Joshua Porter, (47.)

Third Generation, Samuel Church, born ——, 1676, married, ——, *Mary Churchill*, daughter of *Josiah Churchill*, of Weathersfield, Conn., whose wife was *Elizabeth Foote*, daughter of *Nathaniel Foote*, of Weathersfield, Conn. (See Doct. Joshua Porter, (47.)

(*Nathaniel Foote* married, in 1646, *Elizabeth Smith*, born in England, in 1627, daughter of SAMUEL SMITH, who came from Ipswich, England, in the ship "Elizabeth." (See Doct. Joshua Porter, (47.)

Fourth Generation, Samuel Church, born ——, married, January 2, 1745, *Sarah Porter*, daughter of *Nathaniel Porter*, of Hartford, Conn.

(JOHN PORTER, (1,) from England, with wife, *Rose*, to Windsor, Conn.

Second Generation, Nathaniel Porter, born July 19, 1640, married, —— 1664, *Anna Groves*, born (about) 1645, daughter of PHILIP GROVES, an early settler of Hartford, Conn., who came from Bristol, England, and who was a noted captain in "King Philip's war." Removed from Hartford to Stratford, Conn., and was representative, ruling elder, and died in 1673.

Third Generation, John Porter, born March 23, 1674, married, ——, *Abigail Eggleston*, born September 1, 1671, daughter of *James Eggleston*, of Windsor,

Conn., who was son of BIGOD EGGLESTON, who came from England to Dorchester, Mass., in 1630, removed to Windsor, Conn., in 1635, and died September 1, 1674, "ner 100 yer ould."

Fourth Generation, Sarah Porter, born December 1, 1720, in Hartford, Conn., married, June 2, 1745, *Samuel Church*.)

Fifth Generation, Nathaniel Church, born November 16, 1756, married *Lois Ensign*, daughter of Capt. *John Ensign*, a descendant of JAMES ENSIGN, from England, who, in 1639, was an early settler of Hartford, Conn., and died in 1671.

Gen. ROBERT SEDGWICK, came from England in the ship "Trulove," in 1635, with his wife *Joanna*. He had been, as is said, "nursed in London's artillery garden," and was one of the founders of the "Ancient and Honorable Artillery Company," of Boston, Mass,, in 1638. Its captain in 1640. Colonel of the Middlesex regiment, in 1643, and major-general of the Colonial forces. He was recalled to England by Oliver Cromwell, when protector, and sent with a military force to the West Indies, for the conquest of Jamaica, where he died May 24, 1656.

Second Generation, William Sedgwick, born in England (about) 1643, served in the English army. He married *Elizabeth Stone*, daughter of Rev. *Samuel Stone*.)

(Rev. SAMUEL STONE, born in Hertford, county of Herts, England, about twenty miles from London, graduated at Emanuel College, Oxford, England. He came to New England, with Revs. John Cotton, Thomas Hooker and others, in the ship "Griffin," arriving at Boston, Mass., September 4, 1633. He removed to Cambridge, Mass., and was teacher of the church of which Hooker was pastor. Removed thence with Hooker, Davenporte and others, in May, 1636, to Hartford, Conn., and founded the church at that place. In the Pequot war he was chaplain to the troops under Capt. John Mason. He married, in Boston, Mass., *Elizabeth Allen*, and died in Hartford, Conn., July 20, 1663.)

THOMAS ALLEN, born in Norwich, county of Norfolk, England, graduated at Caius College, Oxford, England, A. M. 1631. He married *Anne*, daughter of Rev. *Mr. Sadlier*, of Patcham, in the county of Sussex, England, and came to New England in 1638. He was colleague of Rev. Zachary Symmes, in the church at Charlestown, Mass., but returned in 1650, to Norwich, Egland. His daughter, *Elizabeth Allen*, married Rev. *Samuel Stone*.)

Second Generation, Elizabeth Stone, born ——, 1648, married *William Sedgwick*.

Third Generation, Samuel Sedgwick, born ——, 1667, married ——, 1689, *Mary Hopkins*, daughter of *Stephen Hopkins*, born ———, 1634, whose wife, *Dorcas Bronson*, born ——, 1641, was daughter of JOHN BRONSON, who came from England and removed in 1636 to Hartford and thence, in 1639, to Farmington, Conn.

(*Stephen Hopkins*, born (about) 1634, was son of JOHN HOPKINS, who came from England to Cambridge, Mass., in 1634, removed to Hartford, Conn., in 1636, and died in 1654.)

Fourth Generation, Ebenezer Sedgwick, born February 25, 1695, married, June 20, 1720, *Prudence Merrill*, born December 20, 1700, daughter of *Abraham Merrill*, of Hartford, Conn., who married *Abigail Webster*, daughter of JOHN WEBSTER, who came from Ipswich, England, in 1634, to New England, and settled in Ipswich, Mass. *Abraham Merrill*, born (about) 1660, was son of NATHANIEL MERRILL, who came from England and settled in Newbury, Mass., where he married *Susanna Jordan*, daughter of STEPHEN JORDAN, (or Jourdaine,) who came from England with his wife, *Susanna*, in the ship "Mary and John," in 1634, and settled in Ipswich, Mass.

Fifth Generation, Mary Sedgwick, born April 29, 1726, married, June 6, 1746, Capt. *John Ensign*, a descendant of JAMES ENSIGN, from England, in 1634, who removed from Cambridge, Mass., in 1639, to Hartford, Conn., where he died in 1671.

(JAMES ENSIGN came from England with Rev. Thomas Hooker, in 1634, to Cambridge, Mass., removing, in 1636, to Hartford, Conn. He died in 1671.

Second Generation, David Ensign, born ——, 1646, married, October 22, 1663, *Mehitable Gunn*, born July 28, 1644, daughter of THOMAS GUNN; who came from England to Dorchester, Mass., and removed thence to Windsor, Conn., in 1636, and again to Westfield, Mass, where he died February 26, 1681.

Third Generation, Thomas Ensign, born December 7, 1668, married *Hannah Shepard*, born January 29, 1672, daughter of *John Shepard*, of Hartford, Conn., who married, May 12, 1680, *Hannah Peck*, born ——, 1681, daughter of *Paul Peck*, of Hartford, Conn., who married, in 1665, *Elizabeth Baysey*, born August 24, 1645, daughter of *John Baysey*, of Hartford, Conn.

Paul Peck, born April 18, 1639. was son of PAUL PECK, an early settler of Hartford, Conn., in 1639, with his wife, *Martha*. He died December 23, 1696, aged 87.

John Shepard, born January 22, 1658, was son of JOHN SHEPARD, from England to Cambridge, who married, October 4, 1649, *Rebecca Greenhill*, daughter of *Samuel Greenhill*, of Cambridge, Mass.

Fourth Generation, John Ensign, born February 21, 1694, married, May 13, 1709, *Elizabeth Dickinson*, born (about) 1698, daughter of *Thomas Dickinson*, of Stratford, Conn.

Fifth Generation, John Ensign, born February —, 1723, married, June 6, 1746, *Mary Sedgwick*.)

Sixth Generation, Mary Ensign, born ———, married *Nathaniel Church*.)

Sixth Generation, Samuel Church, born February 4, 1785, graduated at Yale College, 1803. He married, November 1, 1806, *Cynthia Newell*, daughter of *Seth*

Newell, who was a descendant of *Thomas Newell*, of Farmington, Conn., whose wife was *Rebecca Olmstead*, who came from England, in the ship "Lion," September 16, 1632, with her uncles, JAMES and RICHARD OLMSTEAD, who removed to Hartford, Conn., in 1636, with the other proprietors.

Samuel Church was chief justice of Connecticut. He died September 13, 1851.

Seventh Generation, Caroline E. Church, born at Salisbury, Conn., January 6, 1810, married, August 26, 1833, *George W. Holley*.]

Their children were [being of the eighth generation :]

Porter Holley, b. May 2, 1844, d. August 17, 1844.
149. Porter Holley, b. August 8, 1845, d. April 14, 1846.
150. Edith Holley, b. April 17, 1847, d. February 4, 1859.
151. Elizabeth P. Holley, b. June 3, 1849, m. Irving P. Church.

[81.] SALLY PORTER HOLLEY, married, May 9, 1831, *Samuel S. Robbins*, a descendant of JOHN ROBBINS, from England, who was, in 1638, with his wife, *Mary*, an early settler of Weathersfield, Conn.

[*Sarah Porter*, (4,) daughter of JOHN PORTER, (1,) from England, married, October 24, 1644, *Joseph Judson*, born in England, who came with his father, WILLIAM JUDSON, from Yorkshire, England, to Concord, Mass., in 1634, removing thence, in 1639, to Hartford, Conn,, and again to Stratford, Conn.

Joseph Judson was a captain in "King Philip's war," and a representative from 1658 to 1667, when he removed to Woodbury, Conn., where he died October 8, 1691, aged 71. His widow, Mrs. *Sarah* (Porter) *Judson*, died March 19, 1696.

Second Generation, Ruth Judson, born October 27, 1664, married ———, 1688, Capt. *Samuel Welles*, born ———, 1661, son of *Thomas Welles*, who married, June 3, 1651, *Anna Tuttle*, who came at the age of eight years, with her father, RICHARD TUTTLE, from London, England, in 1635, in the ship "Planter."

(*Thomas Welles*, born in England, was son of THOMAS WELLES, who came from England in the ship "Susan and Ellen," in 1635, and was an original proprietor at Hartford and Weathersfield, Conn., in 1636. He was the second magistrate of the colony, May 1, 1637; governor, May, 1554, alternating each year with Fitz John Wintrhop, as governor and lieutenant-governor, until his death, January 14, 1660.)

Third Generation, Samuel Welles, born December 26, 1693, married, January 31, 1722, *Esther Ellsworth*, daughter of *John Ellsworth*, of Windsor, Conn., whose wife, *Esther White*, was daughter of *Daniel White*, of Hadley, Mass., who married, ———, 1661, *Sarah Crowe*, born March 1, 1647, daughter of JOHN CROWE, who came from England to Hartford, Conn., in 1637, and who married *Elizabeth Goodwin*, only child of WILLIAM GOODWIN, who came from England, in the ship "Lion," arriving at Boston, Mass., September 16, 1632. He (Goodwin) was a representative in the first general court, in Massachusetts, in 1634, and removed, with Rev. Thomas Hooker, to Hartford, Conn., in May, 1636, and thence to Hadley, Mass., in 1659. He was ruling elder in these places, and died March 11, 1673. His widow, *Susanna*, died May, 17, 1676. (See Moses Lyman, (159.)

(*John Ellsworth*, born October 7, 1671, was son of *Josias Ellsworth*, of Windsor, Conn., who married, November 16, 1654, *Elizabeth Holcombe*, daughter of THOMAS HOLCOMBE, who came from England, in 1633, and removed to Windsor, Conn., in 1636.)

(*Daniel White*, was son of Elder JOHN WHITE, born in England (about) 1600, who came to New England, in the ship "Lion," September 16, 1632, and settled in Cambridge, Mass. In June, 1636, with his family, he joined the company, with Rev. Messrs. Hooker and Stone and others, which traversed the "trackless wilderness" to Hartford, Conn., where he was an "original proprietor." His son, *Daniel White*, married *Sarah Crowe*.)

(JOHN ROBBINS, came from England, and in 1638 settled at Weathersfield, Conn. He was a representative in 1656 to 1659, and died in 1680.

Second Generation, John Robbins, born April 29, 1649, married *Mary* ——.

Third Generation, Samuel Robbins, born ——, 1680, married ——.

Fourth Generation, Samuel Robbins, born ——, 1719, married *Esther Welles*.)

(THOMAS WELLES, from England, before named.)

Second Generation, John Welles, born in England (about) 1620, cames with his father, and settled in Hartford, Conn. He was a representative, &c. He married, in 1647, *Elizabeth Curtis*, daughter (probably) of that "widow of WILLIAM CURTIS," who came from England, with her family, and settled in Stratford, Conn.

Third Generation, Robert Welles, born ——, 1651, married, June 9, 1675, *Elizabeth Goodrich*, born ——, 1658, daughter of WILLIAM GOODRICH, from England, who married, October 4, 1648, *Sarah Marvin*, born in England, who came at the age of three years, with her father, MATTHEW MARVIN, from England, in the ship "Increase," in 1635, and who removed to Hartford, Conn., in 1638, and thence, in 1653, to Norwalk, Conn.

Fourth Generation, Joseph Welles, born September 1, 1680, married, January 6, 1708, *Hannah Robbins*, daughter of *Joshua Robbins*, of Weathersfield, son of JOHN ROBBINS, from England, (before mentioned.)

Fifth Generation, Esther Welles, born May 1, 1716, married *Samuel Robbins*.)

Fifth Generation, Samuel Robbins, born ——, 1748, married Salome Lee.

(JOHN LEE, came from England in the ship "Francis," from Ipswich, England, April, 1634, in company with his uncle, William Westwood, and settled at Hartford, Conn. He removed to Farmington, Conn., and thence to Hadley, Mass., where he died. He married, in 1658, *Mary Hart*, born in 1638, daughter of STEPHEN HART, who was born in Braintree, county of Essex, England, and came to New England and settled in Cambridge, Mass., in 1632. He was a deacon in Rev. Thomas Hooker's church, and with him removed to Hartford, Conn., in 1636, and thence, in 1672, to Farmington, Conn.

Second Generation, David Lee, born ——, 1674, married, September 5, 1695, *Lydia Strong.*)

(Elder JOHN STRONG, from Taunton, England. (See Augusta Porter, (57.)

Second Generation, Jedediah Strong, born May 7, 1637, married, November 12, 1662, *Freedom Woodward,* born ——, 1642, daughter of Doct. HENRY WOODWARD, who came from England, in the ship "James," to Dorchester, Mass., in 1635, with his wife, *Elizabeth,* and who removed to Northampton, Mass., where he was accidentally killed April 7, 1685.

Third Generation, Lydia Strong, born November 9, 1675, married *David Lee.* They removed to Coventry, Conn., and thence to Lebanon, where he died in 1759.)

Third Generation, Jonathan Lee, born July 14, 1713, graduated at Yale College in 1742, became a minister and died in Salisbury, Conn., October 8, 1788, after a pastorate of forty-four years; married, October 3, 1744, *Elizabeth Metcalf,* daughter of Rev. *Joseph Metcalf,* minister at Falmouth, Mass., who was born April 11, 1682; graduated at Harvard College 1703.

(MICHAEL METCALF, born in Tatterford, county of Norfolk, England, in 1586, came with his wife, *Sarah,* and nine children, from Ipswich, England, in the ship "John and Dorothy," Capt. William Andrews, to Boston, Mass., in April, 1637. They settled at Dedham, Mass., where he died August 13, 1645.

Second Generation, Michael Metcalf, born in England, August 20, 1620, married, April 2, 1644, *Mary Fairbanks,* born April 18, 1622, daughter of JOHN FAIRBANKS, who came from England, with his father, Jonathan, and mother, Grace Fairbanks, in 1638, and settled in Dedham, Mass.

Third Generation, Jonathan Metcalf, born September 21. 1650, married, April 10, 1674, *Anna Kenrick,* born March 20, 1652, daughter of JOHN KENRICK, who came with Rev. Richard Mather, from England, in the ship "James," from Bristol, England, to Dorchester, Mass., arriving August 17, 1735. He lived in what is now Brookline, Mass., where his wife, *Anna,* died November 15, 1656. He died in Newton, Mass., August 29, 1686.

Fourth Generation, Joseph Metcalf, born April 11, 1682, was a minister at Falmouth, Mass.; graduated at Harvard College 1703. He married *Alice Adams,* daughter of Rev. *William Adams,* of Dedham, Mass. (See. H. P. Andrews, (95.)

Fifth Generation, Elizabeth Metcalf, born (about) 1718, married *Jonathan Lee.*)

Fourth Generation, Salome Lee, born December 1, 1754, married *Samuel Robbins.*

Sixth Generation, Samuel Robbins, born ——, 1774, married *Lucy Beebe,* of Canaan, Conn., a descendant of *James Beebe,* of Hadley, Mass., whose wife, *Mary,* was a daughter of Robert Boltwood, of Hadley, Mass.

Seventh Generation, Samuel S. Robbins, born June 2, 1804, married Sally P. Holley.)

Their children were [being of the eighth generation :]

152. Samuel Robbins, b. December 25, 1832, d. November 26, 1835.
153. Sally Holley Robbins, b. March 13, 1834, d. December 3, 1835.
154. Mary Ann Robbins, b. June 28, 1835, married Alonzo W. Church.
155. Samuel Robbins, b. March 25, 1837, d. September 8, 1855.
156. Milton Holley Robbins, b. September 2, married Anna E. Bostwick.
157. Lucy Maria Robbins, b. April 7, 1848.
158. Sarah Lucretia Robbins, b. June 11, 1854.

[82.] MARY ANNE HOLLEY, married May 6, 1834, *Moses Lyman,* of Goshen, Conn., iron manufacturer and merchant.

[RICHARD LYMAN, born at Norton-Mandeville, parish of Ongar, county of Essex, England, came with his family to New England, in the ship "Lion," arriving at Dorchester. Mass., November 3, 1631. (See A. H. Holley, (78.)

On the 15th of October, 1631, they joined a party of emigrants and went through the "wilderness," to settle on the Connecticut river. (See John Porter, (1.) An "original proprietor" at Hartford, Conn., where he died ——, 1640.

Second Generation, John Lyman, born in England, September —, 1613 ; came with his parents to New England. He married, June 12, 1655, *Dorcas Plumbe,* who came from England, with her father, JOHN PLUMBE, in 1635, to Dorchester, Mass., and removed to Weathersfield, Conn., in 1636, and thence to Branford, Conn. "Lieut." John Lyman had command of the Northampton men, in the famous "Falls Fight," with the Pequots, above Deerfield, Mass., May 18, 1676. He died in Northampton, Mass., August 20, 1690.

Third Generation, Moses Lyman, born February 20, 1663, married *Anne* ——, from Long Island, N. Y.

Fourth Generation, Capt. *Moses Lyman,* born February 27, 1689, married, December 13, 1712, *Mindwell Sheldon,* born March 23, 1693, daughter of *Isaac Sheldon,* of Windsor, Conn.

(ISAAC SHELDON came from England, and removed to Windsor, Conn., in 1640. He married, ——, 1653, *Mary Woodford,* daughter of THOMAS WOODFORD, who came from England, June 5, 1632, in the ship "William and Francis." (See Augusta Porter, (57.) He removed to Hartford, Conn., in 1636-7, and thence to Northampton, Mass., where he died March 6, 1667.

Second Generation, Isaac Sheldon, born September 4, 1656, married, November 25, 1685, *Sarah Warner,* born June 24, 1667, daughter of *Daniel Warner,* of

Hadley, Mass., son of ANDREW WARNER, who came from England to Cambridge, Mass., in 1632, and removed with the first settlers to Hartford, Conn., in 1636, and thence to Hadley, Mass., where he died December 18, 1684, aged 90.

Fifth Generation, Moses Lyman, born October 3, 1713, married, March 24, 1742, *Sarah Hayden*.

(WILLIAM HAYDEN, came from England, in the ship "Mary and John," in 1630, to Dorchester, Mass. He removed to Hartford, Conn., in 1635, and thence to Windsor, Conn. He served under Capt. John Mason in the "Pequot war," and died in Killingworth, Conn., September 27, 1699.

Second Generation, Daniel Hayden, born September 2, 1640, married, March 17, 1665, *Hannah Wilcoxon*, daughter of WILLIAM WILCOXON, who came from England, in the ship "Planter," in 1635, and removed to Hartford, Conn.

Third Generation, Samuel Hayden, born February 28, 1677, married, January 4, 1704, *Anna Holcombe*, born March 19, 1675, daughter of BENAJAH HOLCOMBE, who married in Windsor, Conn., April 11, 1667, *Sarah Eno*, born June 15, 1649, daughter of *James Eno*, of Windsor, who married, August 18, 1648, *Anna Bidwell*, daughter of John Bidwell, of Hartford, Conn.

Benajah Holcombe, born June 2, 1644, was son of THOMAS HOLCOMBE, who came from England to Dorchester, Mass., in 1633, removed to Windsor, Conn., and died September 6, 1657.

Fourth Generation, Sarah Hayden, born September 17, 1716, married *Moses Lyman*.)

Sixth Generation, Col. *Moses Lyman*, born March 20, 1743, married *Ruth Collins*, a descendant of EDWARD COLLINS, who came from London, England, in 1633, and settled in Medford, Mass., and died in Charlestown, Mass., April 9, 1689, aged 86. His daughter, Sybil Collins, married Rev. John Whiting. (See Noah Grant, (53.)

Col. Moses Lyman was early in the field, in the war of the revolution. He took part in the battles of Saratoga, and was bearer of despatches from General Gates to General Washington, announcing the capitulation of General Burgoyne. He died September 29, 1829.

Seventh Generation, Moses Lyman, born April 16, 1768, married, January 21, 1796, *Elizabeth Buell*.

(WILLIAM BUELL, from England. (See Nathaniel Porter, (21,)

Second Generation, Samuel Buell, born September 2, 1641, married, November 13, 1662, *Deborah Griswold*, born June 28, 1646, daughter of MATTHEW GRISWOLD, who came from Kenilworth, Warwickshire, England, with his brother *Edward*, 1639, in a vessel sent out by William Whiting, and removed with Rev. Ephraim Hewett to Windsor, Conn.

Matthew Griswold married, in 1645, *Anne Wolcott*, born (about) 1625, daughter of HENRY WOLCOTT, born in Wellington, Somersetshire, England (about) 1575, a magistrate of that county. He came to New England, in the ship "Mary and John," with the early settlers of Windsor, and with his wife, *Elizabeth Saunders*, and their children, made the advance into the "wilderness, and began the settlement at Windsor, Conn., in October, 1635. He died May 30, 1655.

Third Generation, Deacon *John Buell*, born in Killingworth, Conn., February 17, 1671, married in Windsor, Conn., November 20, 1695, *Mary Loomis*, born October 2, 1680, daughter of *Thomas Loomis*, of Windsor, who married, January 2, 1680, *Hannah Porter*, born June 1, 1662, daughter of *John Porter*, (2,) who married, ——, 1650, *Mary Stanley*, daughter of THOMAS STANLEY, who came to New England, in the ship "Planter," in 1635, and was among the first settlers of Hartford, Conn., in 1636, and who removed to Hadley, Mass., where he died January 30, 1663.

Fourth Generation, Solomon Buell, born August 30, 1715, in Lebanon, Conn., removed to Litchfield, Conn., married January 19, 1737, *Eunice Griswold*, born ——, 1720.

(EDWARD GRISWOLD, came with his brother, *Matthew*, from Kenilworth, England, and settled at Windsor, Conn. He died in Killingworth, Conn.

Second Generation, Joseph Griswold, born March 2, 1647, married, July 14, 1670, *Mary Gaylord*, born March 19, 1650, daughter of *Walter Gaylord*, who married, April —, 1648, *Mary Stebbins*, daughter of EDWARD STEBBINS, who came from England to Dorchester, Mass , removed to Cambridge in 1633, and thence in 1634 to Hartford, Conn. Joanna Gaylord, sister of *Mary*, married *John Porter*, son of *John Porter*, (2.)

(Deborah Griswold, born June 26, 1646, sister of *Joseph*, married Peter Buell, of Coventry, Conn. (See Col. Joshua Porter, (26.)

Third Generation, Matthew Griswold, born February 25, 1686, married, June 6, 1709, *Mary Phelps*.

(WILLIAM PHELPS came from England to Dorchester, Mass., in 1630, with Rev. John Warham, and removed to Windsor, Conn., in 1635. He was a member of the first court held in Connecticut, magistrate, representative, &c. He died July 14, 1672.

Second Generation, Timothy Phelps, born September 1, 1639, married, May 19, 1661, *Mary Griswold*, born October 5, 1644, daughter of EDWARD GRISWOLD, from England, before named, and died in 1719.

Third Generation, Joseph Phelps, born September 27, 1666, married, November 18, 1686, *Sarah Hosford*, born September 27, 1666, daughter of *John Hosford*, of Windsor, Conn., who married, November 5, 1657, *Philippa Thrall*, daughter of WILLIAM THRALL, of Windsor, who served in the Pequot war, and died August

3, 1678, John Hosford was son of WILLIAM HOSFORD, from England to Dorchester, Mass., 1630, who removed to Windsor, in 1638 9. Joseph Phelps removed to Hebron, Conn., where he died , 1716.

Fourth Generation, Mary Phelps, born June 8, 1689, married *Matthew Griswold.*)

Fourth Generation, Eunice Griswold, born ——, 1720, married *Solomon Buell.*

Fifth Generation, Ira Buell, born February 20, 1645, married, January 29, 1767, *Prudence Deming,* of Lyme, Conn., a descendant of JOHN DEMING, who came from England, and was one of the early settlers of Weathersfield, Conn., in 1636, and who married, in 1637, *Honor Treat,* daughter of RICHARD TREAT, who came from England and was, in 1636, one of the settlers of Weathersfield, and died in 1670. (See Doct. Joshua Porter, (47.)

Sixth Generation, Elizabeth Buell, born September 16, 1772, in Litchfield, Conn., married, January 21, 1796, *Moses Lyman.*

Eighth Generation, Moses Lyman, born October 1, 1810, married, May 6, 1834, *Mary Ann Holley.*]

Their children were [being of the eighth generation :]

159. Moses Lyman, b. August 20, 1836, m. Ellen A. Douglas.
160. Mary Lyman, b. August 15, 1839, m. Philip Wells.
161. Alice Lyman, b. May 15, 1845, m. J. T. Sawyer.
162. Richard Lyman, b. June 27, 1848, d. December 24, 1851.
163. Holley P. Lyman, b. January 22, 1855, d. December 5, 1865.

[86.] JESSE ROOT GRANT, married, June —, 1820, *Harriet Simpson,* born ——, 1798, daughter of *John Simpson,* of Montgomery county, Pa. He received his name from Hon. Jesse Root, L.L. D., Chief Justice of Connecticut, who was a colonel in the war of the revolution, with whom Capt. Noah Grant had served, and with whom he was subsequently on terms of intimate friendship.

Their children were [being of the eighth generation :]

164. Ulysses S. Grant, b. April 27, 1822, m. Julia B. Dent.
165. Samuel S. Grant, b. September 23, 1825.
166. Clany Grant, b. December 11, 1828
167. Virginia Grant, b. February 20, 1832.
168. Orville L. Grant, b. May 15, 1835.
169. Mary F. Grant, b. July 30, 1839.

[92.] FREDERICK A. P. BARNARD, (Rev.) graduated at Yale College in 1828 ; L.L. D., Yale College, 1859 ; D. D., University of Mississippi, 1860 ; L. H. D., University State of New York, 1872 ; Professor of

Mathematics and Natural Philosophy in University of Alabama, 1837 to 1854 ; University of Mississippi, 1854–56, and President and Chancellor of University of Mississippi, 1856–61 ; President of Columbia College, New York City, since 1864. United States Commissioner to Paris Exposition, 1867, and Assistant Commissioner-General, 1878 ; Officer of Legion of Honor of France, 1878.

He married, December 27, 1847, *Margaret MacMurray*, of Mississippi. They have no children.

[93.] SARAH G. BARNARD, married *A. S. Porter*, (66,) which see.

[94.] JOHN G. BARNARD, graduated at United States Military Academy, West Point, in 1833.

In charge of construction of fortifications in Louisiana, 1835 to 1852. Captain of Engineers on the staff of General Winfield Scott, in the war with Mexico ; battles of Chepultepec, Churubusco, Molino-del-Rey, City of Mexico, &c., major of engineers.

Chief engineer of the survey of the Isthmus of Tehuantepec, Mexico, 1850–51. Superintendent of construction of military works in California, in 1854. Superintendent of United States Military Academy, West Point, 1855–6.

Brigadier-general and chief engineer of the army of the Potomac, at Bull Run, Blackburn's Ford, siege of Richmond and Yorktown, and as chief engineer directed the defenses of Washington, D. C.

In the campaign of 1864–5, he served on the staff of Lieutenant-General *U. S. Grant*, (164,) as "Chief Engineer of the Armies in the field," until the surrender of General Lee at Appomattox Court House. Colonel of Engineers.

He was brevetted through several grades to that of "Brevet Major-General, United States Army, for gallant and meritorious services in the field."

He married, first, *Jane Elizabeth Brand*, born at St. Francisville, Louisiana, October 25, 1822, daughter of *William Brand*, of New Orleans, La., and his wife, *Jane Brouwer*.

Their children were [being of the ninth generation :]

Robert Foster, b. November 26, 1842, died ———

170. William Frederick Barnard, b. November 16, 1844, d. September 17, 1863.
171. Augustus Porter Barnard, b. May 30, 1847, civil engineer, New York city.
172. Robert Foster Barnard, b. June 10, 1850, d. February 23, 1853.

Mrs. Jane E. Barnard died in New York city, February 24, 1853.

J. G. Barnard married, second, at St. Mary's Church, Hartford county, Maryland, October 2, 1860, *Anna Eliza* (*Hall*) *Boyd*, daughter of Major *Henry Hall*, (son of Major *Benedict Edward Hall*, of Shandy Hall, Hartford county, Maryland,) and his wife, *Charlotte J. Ramsay.*

Their children were :

173. John Hall Barnard, b. July 5, 1861, midshipman United States Navy 1880.
174. Jane Brand Barnard, b. November 26, 1862.
175. Anna McHenry Barnard, b. June 26, 1866.

[95.] HENRY P. ANDREWS, Rensselaer Institute, Troy, N. Y. ; civil engineer in the service of the United States from 1844 to 1861, in Louisiana, Pennsylvania, New Jersey, Massachusetts and New York ; volunteer aid to Gen. Edmund P. Gaines, in the war with Mexico, in 1846 ; captain of Louisiana volunteers, and aid to Gen. P. F. Smith.

In 1851 he was attached to the expedition for the survey of the Isthmus of Tehuantepec, (Mexico,) of which Major J. G. Barnard (94) was chief engineer. In the service of the United States in construction of fortifications at the "Golden Gate," San Francisco, Cal., from 1853 to 1859.

Paymaster and major United States army from May, 1861.

He married, October 9, 1656, *Maria L. Adams*, born May 1, 1830, daughter of Doct. *Elijah Adams*, of Boston, Mass., whose wife, *Maria Stearnes*, was a descendant of *John Stearnes*, of Watertown, Mass., who married, in 1681, *Judith Lawrence*, born May 12, 1660, daughter of GEORGE LAWRENCE, of Watertown, Mass.

[*Elijah Adams* was a descendant of Rev. *William Adams*, of Dedham, Mass., born May 27, 1650, Harvard College in 1671, who was son of *William Adams*, Jr., who came from England, in 1635, in the ship "Elizabeth and Anne," with his father, WILLIAM ADAMS, who settled at Cambridge, Mass.

Rev. *William Adams* married, March 27, 1680, *Alice Bradford*, daughter of Col. *William Bradford*, whose wife, *Alice Richards*, was daughter of THOMAS RICHARDS, who came from England in the ship "Mary and John," to Dorchester, Mass., in 1630, and settled in Dedham, Mass.

Col. *William Bradford*, born June 17, 1624, deputy-governor of Plymouth Plantation, was son of WILLIAM BRADFORD, who was born at Austerfield, in Yorkshire, England, March 19, 1590, who came from England, in the ship "Mayflower," in 1620, with his wife, *Dorothy May*, to whom he was married in Leyden, Holland, and was drowned at Cape Cod, December 7, 1620, before the landing at Plymouth. He married, second, August 24, 1623, *Alice Reyner*, (then widow of Edward Southworth,) sister of Rev. John Reyner, who was born at Gildersome, near Leeds, in the west riding of Yorkshire, England.

(John Reyner, graduated at Magdalen College, Oxford, England, A. B. in 1623, and came with his family and sister to New England. He was for eighteen years minister at Plymouth, Mass., and died in Dover, Mass., in 1669. (See Augusta Porter, (57.)

John Stearnes, born January 24, 1657, was son of CHARLES STEARNES, from England to Watertown, Mass., who married, June 22, 1654, *Rebecca Gibson*, daughter of JOHN GIBSON, of Cambridge, Mass., from England, 1634.

Mrs. Maria L. Andrews died in New York city, April 18, 1873.

Their children were [being of the ninth generation :]

176. Charles Adams Andrews, b. December 18, 1857, died in childhood.
177. Harry Seymour Andrews, b. January 10, 1861, died in childhood.

[96.] MARTHA V. WIGGINS, married, June 13, 1848, *Cruger Walton*, born in New York City, November 8, 1809, son of *Henry Walton*, born October 8, 1768, of New York City, Ballston and Saratoga Springs, who married, February 15, 1800, his second wife, Mrs. *Yates*, (Matilda Caroline Cruger,) daughter of Henry Cruger, Jr., of New York City, and widow of —— *Yates*.

[*Henry Walton* was son of *Jacob Walton*, Jr,, of New York City, whose wife, *Polly Cruger*, was daughter of *Henry Cruger*, Sr.

Jacob Walton, Jr., was son of *Jacob Walton*, Sr., and his wife, *Maria Beekman*, daughter of *Gerard Beekman* and *Magdalen Abeel*, and *Jacob Walton*, Sr., was brother of *William Walton*, who built and occupied the "Walton House," in Pearl street, New York city.

They were sons of WILLIAM WALTON, from England, and his wife, *Mary Santford*.]

Cruger Walton graduated at Rutger's College, New Brunswick, N. J., was a lawyer, member of the legislature, &c., and died at Saratoga Springs, N. Y., August 29, 1861. Mrs. Martha V. Walton died July 29, 1850.

Their children were [being of the ninth generation :]
178. Mary Porter Walton, b. February 19, 1849, m. Arthur A. Camp.
179. Henry Cruger Walton, b. March 29, 1850, m. Virginia C. Jones.

[100.] PETER PORTER WIGGINS, M. A., graduated at Trinity College, Hartford, Conn., in 1855.

He married, June 12, 1860, *Sarah Emily Burhans*, daughter of *Hiram W. Burhans*, of Cairo, Greene county, N. Y., and Saratoga Springs, who was son of *John C. Burhans*, and his wife, *Clarissa Peck*, daughter of *Benjamin Peck*, of Cairo, and his wife, *Mary Buell*.

[WILLIAM BUELL, from Chesterton, Huntingdonshire, England, to Windsor, Conn., in 1635-6.

Second Generation, Samuel Buell, born in Windsor, September 2, 1641, married September 13 or 18, 1662, *Deborah Griswold*, daughter of *Edward Griswold*, of Windsor. (See Mary A. Holley, (82.)

Third Generation, Deacon *John Buell*, born at Killingworth, Conn., February 17, 1671, removed to Lebanon, Conn., and married, November 20, 1695, *Mary Loomis*, daughter of *Thomas Loomis*, of Windsor, Conn., whose wife was *Hannah Porter*, daughter of *John Porter*, (2,) and *Mary Stanley*, son of JOHN PORTER, (1,) from England.

Fourth Generation, Deacon *Peter Buell*, born May 22, 1710, at Killingworth, Conn., removed to Litchfield, Conn. He married, December 18, 1734, *Avis Collins*, born April 1, 1714, daughter of Rev. *Timothy Collins*, of Litchfield, Conn.

(JOHN COLLINS came from England, with his brother Edward Collins, in 1638, and settled in Cambridge, Mass. He married ———, *Susannah* ———, and died March 29, 1670.

Second Generation, John Collins, born ———, 1640, removed to Middletown, Conn., thence to Saybrook, Conn., and died in Guilford, in 1704. He married, June 2, 1669, *Mary Stephens*, daughter of JOHN STEPHENS, from England, who settled in Guilford, in 1646.

Third Generation, John Collins, born ———, 1670, lived in Saybrook. He married, July 23, 1691, *Anna Leete*, born August 5, 1671, daughter of *John Leete*, of Guilford, who was born (about) 1639, eldest child of WILLIAM LEETE, from England, an original settler and signer of the "planters' covenant," June 1, 1639, at New Haven, Conn., who removed to Guilford, and was deputy-governor 1658, and governor 1661 to 1665.

John Leete married, October 14, 1670, *Mary Chittenden*, daughter of WILLIAM CHITTENDEN, who came from Guilford, in the county of Sussex, England. His wife was *Joan Sheafe*, daughter of Doct. JACOB SHEAFE, of Cranbrooke, in the county of Kent, England. Her sister was wife of the noted divine, Henry

Whitfield, and Chittenden with Whitfield, came from England to Boston, Mass., in 1638.

Fourth Generation, Rev. *Timothy Collins,* born April 13, 1699, graduated at Yale College 1718. He studied medicine and became a physician, served as surgeon in the army, in the war of 1755, with the French and Indians. He had previously been pastor of the church in Litchfield, Conn., from 1723 to 1752. He married, January 16, 1723, *Elizabeth Hyde,* and died February 7, 1777.

(WILLIAM HYDE is believed to have been of the company which came from England, in 1633, with Rev. Thomas Hooker, and removed to Hartford, Conn. He removed to Norwich, Conn., where he died June 6, 1681.

Second Generation, Samuel Hyde, born in Hartford, Conn., (about) 1637, married, June —, 1659, *Jane Lee,* daughter of THOMAS LEE, who sailed from England with his family in 1641, but who died on the voyage. His widow, *Mary Lee,* and children went from Boston to Saybrook, Conn.

Third Generation, Samuel Hyde, born May —, 1665, married, December 10, 1690, *Elizabeth Calkins,* born April 18, 1673, daughter of *John Calkins,* of Norwich, Conn., who married *Sarah Royce,* daughter of ROBERT ROYCE, who came from England to Dorchester, Mass., in 1632, and removed to Norwich, and died in New London, Conn., in 1676.

John Calkins was son of HUGH CALKINS, was born at Chepstowe, on the river Wye, in Monmouthshire, England, who came to Lynn, Mass., (about) 1640, removed to Norwich, Conn., and died in 1690.

Fourth Generation, Elizabeth Hyde, baptized December 12, 1703, married Rev. *Timothy Collins.*)

Fifth Generation, Avis Collins, born April 1, 1714, married, December 18, 1734, Deacon *Peter Buell.*)

Fifth Generation, Capt. *Archelaus Buell,* born April 14, 1737, married, May 3, 1758, *Mary Landon,* of Litchfield, Conn.

Sixth Generation, Mary Buell, born April 16, 1761, married *Benjamin Peck.*

(Deacon PAUL PECK, born in the county of Essex, England, came to New England, in the ship "Defense," in 1635, with his wife, *Martha.* He removed to Hartford, Conn., in 1639, where he died December 23, 1694, aged 87.

Second Generation, Paul Peck, born ——, 1639, married *Elizabeth Baysey,* baptized August 23, 1645, daughter of JOHN BAYSEY, an early settler of Hartford, Conn.

Third Generation, Paul Peck, born ——, 1666, married *Leah Muzzey,* of Hartford, Conn., a descendant of *Benjamin Muzzey,* of Boston, Mass., whose wife *Alice Dexter,* was daughter of RICHARD DEXTER, who with his wife *Bridget,* came from England, in 1638, and settled in Charlestown, Mass.

Fourth Generation, Benjamin Peck, born —— 1715, married, October 12, 1755,

Mary Frisbie, a descendant of *John Frisbie*, of Branford, Conn., whose wife *Ruth* was a daughter of *John Bowers*, of New Haven, Conn.

(GEORGE BOWERS came from England to Plymouth, Mass., in 1639, with his wife, *Barbara*, who died March 25, 1644. He died in 1656.

Second Generation, John Bowers, born in England, (about) 1630, was a school teacher at Plymouth, Mass. He removed to New Haven, Conn., in 1653, on the invitation of Governor Eaton, and became a prominent teacher at that place, and afterwards the first minister at Derby, Conn. His wife, *Bridget*, was a daughter of ANTHONY THOMPSON, who came from England with Governor Theophilus Eaton and others, and settled in New Haven, Conn., in 1639.

Fifth Generation, Benjamin Peck, born in Litchfield, Conn., December 28, 1755, married *Mary Buell*.)

Sixth Generation, Clarissa Peck, born ———, married *John C. Burhans*.

Seventh Generation, Hiram W. Burhans, born June 9, 1806, married January 2, 1833, *Margaret Miller*.

(JOHN CHADEAYNE came from Rochelle, France, to New York, (about) 1730, with his wife, whose maiden name was *Judith Tillyou*. They were Huguenots, fleeing from persecution. They settled at Duck Creek, Kent county, Delaware.

Second Generation, Daniel Chadeayne, born in Rochelle, France, (about) 1720, came with his parents. He married *Elizabeth Secor*, of New York city, and removed to the vicinity of Sing Sing, N. Y.

Third Generation, Katherine Chadeayne, born December 20, 1745, married *John Pine*. They lived near Bedford, Westchester county, N. Y.

Fourth Generation, Phebe Pine, born October 30, 1770, married March 5, 1801, *John Miller*. They lived in New York city.

Fifth Generation, Margaret Miller, born March 3, 1803, married *Hiram W. Burhans*.)

Eighth Generation, Sarah Emily Burhans, born March 14, 1837, married *Peter Porter Wiggins*.]

Their children were [being of the ninth generation :]

180. Peter Vail Porter Wiggins, b. March 27, 1861.
181. Wallace Burhans Wiggins, b. August 23, 1864.
182. Frederick Augustus Wiggins, b. June 9, 1866.
183. Margaret Emily Wiggins, b. September 6, 1868.

[105.] ELIZABETH BURRALL, married, July 9, 1834, *Edmund Belden*, of Canaan, Conn. He died April 23, 1872.

[Edmund Belden was probably a descendant of RICHARD BELDEN, who came from England and settled in Weathersfield, Conn., in 1640. His son, *Daniel Belden*, born ——, 1638, married, November 10, 1670, *Elizabeth Foote*, daughter

Nathaniel Foote, Jr., of Weathersfield, who married, ——, 1646, *Elizabeth Smith*, born ——, 1627, daughter of SAMUEL SMITH, who came from Ipswich, England, in 1641, in the ship "Elizabeth," and removed to Weathersfield, where he was a representative, and died in Hadley, Mass., December, 1680.

Nathaniel Foote, Jr., born in England, was son of NATHANIEL FOOTE, who came from England to Watertown, Mass., (about) 1634, and removed to Weathersfield, Conn., in 1636, whose wife, *Elizabeth Deming*, was sister of *John Deming*. (See Doct. Joshua Porter, (47.) His sister, *Mary Foote*, married *Josiah Stoddard*, (see *Abigail Porter*, (48,) and his cousin, *Rebecca Foote*, married *Philip Smith*. (See Doct. Joshua Porter, (47.)

Their children were [being of the ninth generation:]
184. Harriette E. Belden, b. October 6, 1835.
185. Edmund Porter Belden, b. March 30, 1841.

[109.] JOHN HERMAN BIRD, graduated at Union College. He was a physician in Chicago, Ill. He married, September 2, 1851, *Frances E. Blaney*, and died in Sioux City, Iowa, March 3, 1871.

[*Daniel Blaney*, born at Port Penn, Newcastle county, Del., (about) 1755, was a descendant of EDWARD BLANEY, who came from England, in 1632, in the ship "Bonaventure," to James City, Virginia. He married *Hester Du Shayne*, (or Du Chene,) a descendant of a Huguenot family who were early settlers in Delaware. Their son, *Cornelius Du Shayne Blaney*, born at Port Penn, in 1790, was clerk of the court of chancery, and died in 1846. His wife was a descendant of a Swedish family, whose name was *Stedham*. Their daughter, *Frances E. Blaney*, married Doct. *John H. Bird*.]

Their children were [being of the ninth generation:]
186. Elizabeth Blaney Bird, b. October 19, 1852.
187. Grace Bird, b. March 22, 1854, died July 12, 1854.
188. William Noble Davis Bird, b. August 20, 1858.

[112.] WILLIAM AUGUSTUS BIRD, educated at Union College. He married, October 18, 1852, *Mary M. Miller*. Residence, Buffalo, N. Y.

Their children were [being of the ninth generation:]
189. Joanna Davis Bird, b. September 10, 1853.
190. Wells Miller Bird, b. June 26, 1855.
191. Porter Augustus Bird, b. February 17, 1859.
192. Walter Griffin Bird, b. May 9, 1861, d. June 26, 1862.
193. William Augustus Bird, b. July 2, 1865.
194. Grace Maria Bird, b. March 30, 1870, d. August 17, 1870.
195. Elizabeth Griffin Bird, b. August 21, 1873.

[115.] SARAH FREDERIKA PORTER, married, Sept. 9, 1863, *Stephen E. Burrall.* Resided in New York city. He died August 31, 1868.

[WILLIAM BURRALL came from England (about) 1715. He was a chemist and metallurgist, and was engaged at the copper mines in Simsbury, Conn. He married *Joanna*, daughter of *Jonas Westover*, of Simsbury. He went to Jamaica, W. I., to open a mine on that Island, where he died.

Second Generation, Col. *Charles Burrall,* born February 11, 1720, was, in August, 1776, appointed to the command of a regiment, and with it participated in the battles of Long Island, Ticonderoga, Crown Point and Saratoga. He died October 7, 1803. He married, December 25, 1747, *Abigail Kellogg.*

(JOSEPH KELLOGG came from England and settled at Farmington, Conn., previous to 1640. He married as a second wife, May 9, 1667, *Abigail Terry*, born September 27, 1646, daughter of STEPHEN TERRY, from England to Dorchester, Mass., 1630, Windsor, Conn., and Hadley, Mass., where he died September —, 1668. Joseph Kellogg died 1707-8.

Second Generation, John Kellogg, born December 23, 1656, married, December 23, 1680, *Sarah Moody,* born ——, 1660, daughter of *Samuel Moody,* who married *Sarah Deming,* daughter of John Deming, from England to Weathersfield, Conn., in 1635, whose wife was *Honor Treat,* daughter of RICHARD TREAT. (See Doct. Joshua Porter, (47.)

Samuel Moody, of Hartford, Conn., who removed to Hadley, Mass., was son of JOHN MOODY, who came from England to Roxbury, Mass., in 1635, with his wife, *Sarah,* and removed to Hartford, Conn. He was son of *George Moody,* of Moulton, county of Essex, England.

Third Generation, Joseph Kellogg, born November 6, 1685, removed to South Hadley. He married, March 15, 1711, *Abigail Smith,.*

(SAMUEL SMITH, came from England with his wife, *Elizabeth.* (See Doct. Joshua Porter, (47.)

Second Generation, Chileab Smith, born April 1, 1636, married, October 2, 1661, *Hannah Hitchcock,* born (about) 1640, daughter of *Luke Hitchcock,* of Weathersfield, Conn.

Third Generation, Ebenezer Smith, born July 11, 1668, married, October —, 1691, *Abigail Broughton,* daughter of *George Broughton,* whose wife was *Abigail Reyner,* daughter of Rev. JOHN REYNER. (See Henry P. Andrews, (95.)

Fourth Generation, Abigail Smith, born October 10, 1692, married *Joseph Kellogg.*

Fifth Generation, Abigail Kellogg, born ———, 1721, married Col. *Charles Burrall,* ———).

Third Generation, Ovid Burrall, born ———, 1761, married *Lucy Welles.*

THOMAS WELLES was one of the first settlers of Hartford, Conn., in 1635-6;

magistrate in 1637 ; deputy governor and governor, and died at Weathersfield, Conn., January 14, 1649.

Second Generation, Samuel Welles, born in England, in 1624, married *Elizabeth Hollister*, daughter of *John Hollister*, who came from England to Weymouth, Mass., and removed to Weathersfield, Conn., in 1644, and whose wife was *Joanna Treat*, daughter of RICHARD TREAT, who came from England and settled in Weathersfield. (See Doct. Joshua Porter, (47.)

Third Generation, Samuel Welles, born April 13, 1660, married, July 20, 1683, *Ruth Royce*, born April 18, 1669, daughter of *Jonathan Royce*, of New London, Conn., who married, June 1, 1660, *Deborah Calkins*, born at Gloucester, Mass., March 18, 1645, daughter of HUGH CALKINS, who with his wife, *Anna*, came from Wales to Marshfield, Mass., in 1640 ; removed to Gloucester, and thence to New London, Conn., and died at Norwich. Conn., in 1690, aged 90.

Fourth Generation, Thaddeus Welles, born March 27, 1695, married *Elizabeth Cowles*, daughter of Deacon *Timothy Cowles*, of East Hartford, Conn., whose wife, *Hannah Pitkin*, born ———, 1677, was daughter of WILLIAM PITKIN, of Hartford, Conn., attorney and treasurer of the colony, whose wife was *Hannah Goodwin*, daughter of OZIAS GOODWIN, one of the first settlers of Hartford, Conn., in 1636.

Fifth Generation, Lucy Welles, born ———, married *Ovid Burrall*.)

Sixth Generation, Frederick A. Burrall, born August 29, 1795, in Canaan, Conn., married *Mary J. Bowles*.

(JOHN BOWLES, came from England to Roxbury, Mass., in 1639. He was ruling elder in the church, and died in 1680. He married April 2, 1650, *Elizabeth Heath*, born in England, in 1630, who came with her father, ISAAC HEATH, in the ship "Hopewell," from England, in 1636, and settled at Roxbury, Mass.

Second Generation, John Bowles, baptized July 17, 1653, graduated at Harvard College in 1671, and married, November 16, 1681, *Sarah Eliot*.

(JOHN ELIOT, born at Nazing, county of Essex, England, in 1600, educated at Cambridge, graduated at Jesus College in 1619. He came to Boston, Mass., in the ship "Lion," November 2, 1631. Pastor of church 1632. He married *Anna Mountfort*, to whom he was betrothed in England, and who came out to meet him the next year. (September 12, 1632.) He was the famous "Apostle to the Indians," and died May 20, 1690. She died March 22, 1687.

Second Generation, John Eliot, born August 31, 1636, graduated at Harvard College 1656. He was the first minister at Newton, Mass., 1664. He married *Sarah Willett*, born May 4, 1643, daughter of *Thomas Willett*. (See Jane H. Porter, (120.)

Third Generation, Sarah Eliot, born ———, married *John Bowles*.

Third Generation, John Bowles, born March —, 1685, graduated at Harvard

College 1702. He married, ——, *Lydia Checkley*, born March 31, 1690, daughter of Capt. SAMUEL CHECKLEY, born in Daventry, Northamptonshire, England, who came to New England, August 3, 1670, and settled in Boston. He married, ——, 1680, *Mary Scottowe*, born May 11, 1656, daughter of JOSHUA SCOTTOWE, a a merchant in Boston, from England.

Fourth Generation, Joshua Bowles, born ——, 1722, married *Mary Hartt*, daughter of *Ralph Hartt*, of Boston, Mass.

Fifth Generation, Ralph Hartt Bowles, born ——, 1757, was a captain in the War of the Revolution. He died in Machias, Maine, September —, 1813. He married *Hannah Crocker*, daughter of Rev. *Josiah Crocker*, of Taunton, Mass.

(Rev. *Josiah Crocker* was a descendant of *Josiah Crocker*, Sr., born September 19, 1647, who married, October 22, 1668, *Meletiah Hinckley*, born November 26, 1648, daughter of *Thomas Hinckley*, governor of Massachusetts, 1681 to 1692, who married, December 4, 1641, *Mary Richards*, daughter of THOMAS RICHARDS, who came from England, in the ship "Mary and John," in 1630, and removed to Dedham, Mass. Her sister, *Alice Richards*, married Rev. *William Adams*. (See Henry P. Andrews, (95.)

Gov. *Thomas Hinckley*, came from Tenterden, in the county of Kent, England, in the ship "Hercules," from London, in 1635, with his father, SAMUEL HINCKLEY. He settled in Scituate, Mass., and removed to Barnstable, Mass., where he died October 31, 1662.

Josiah Crocker, Sr., was son of WILLIAM CROCKER, who came from England, in 1634, with his wife, *Alice*, and settled in Barnstable Mass.

Sixth Generation, Mary J. Bowles, born ——, married *F. A. Burrall*.)

Seventh Generation, Stephen E. Burrall, born March 17, 1826, married, September —, 1863, *Sarah Frederika Porter*.]

Their children were [being of the ninth generation :]
196. Augustus P. Burrall, b. January 18, 1865.
197. Stephen E. Burrall, b. ——, 1867.

[117.] JULIA MATHEWS PORTER married, September 18, 1867, *John H. Osborne*, of Auburn, N. Y.

Their children were [being of the ninth generation :]
198. Albert Porter Osborne, b. November 16, 1873, d. March 10, 1875.
199. Ruth Osborne, b. January 22, 1877.

[118.] ALBERT AUGUSTUS PORTER, graduated at Amherst College. He married, September 11, 1862, *Julia E. Jeffrey*, born in Canandaigua, N. Y., daughter of *Alexander Jeffrey*, from Edinburgh, Scotland, and *Delia Granger*, of Canandaigua, whose father was *John A. Granger*.

Their children were [being of the ninth generation :]
200. Alexander Jeffrey Porter b. June 29, 1863.
201. Albert Howell Porter, Jr., b. April 19, 1866.
202. Bessie Rochester Porter, b. July 20, 1869.
203. Julia Mathews Porter, b. March 6, 1871.
204. Augustus Granger Porter, b. June 23, 1876.
205. Charlotte Ross Porter, b. January 23, 1878.

[120.] JANE HOWELL PORTER, married, October 18, 1865, *Arthur Robinson*, born in New Haven, Conn., January 21, 1823.

[JOHN STRONG, from England. (See A. H. Porter, (69.)

Second Generation, Thomas Strong, born (about) 1633, married, December 5, 1660, *Mary Hewett*, baptized August 2, 1640, daughter of Rev. *Ephraim Hewett*.

(Rev. EPHRAIM HEWETT (or Huet) had been a minister at Wraxhall, near Kenilworth, in Warwickshire, England. He was proceeded against by Archbishop Laud, for non-conformity, ("neglect of ceremonial," in 1638. He came to New England in 1639, and removed to Windsor, Conn., August 17 of the same year, and became colleague of Rev. John Warham. He died September 4, 1644. His daughter *Mary* married *Thomas Strong*.)

Third Generation, Asahel Strong, born November 14, 1668, in Northampton, Mass., married, June 11, 1689, *Margaret Hart*.

(STEPHEN HART, born in Braintree, county of Essex, England, (about) 1605, came to New England (about) 1632, and settled first in Cambridge, Mass. He was one of the company that came with Rev. Thomas Hooker to Hartford, Conn., in 1636, and made the settlement at that place.

Second Generation, Thomas Hart. born ——, 1643, married *Ruth Hawkins*, born October 24, 1649, daughter of *Anthony Hawkins*, who came from England, and removed to Windsor, Conn., and whose wife was *Isabel Brown*, daughter of PETER BROWN, who came from England, in the ship "Mayflower," in 1620. He lived in Duxbury, Mass., and died in 1633.

Third Generation, Margaret Hart, born ——, 1673, married, June 11, 1689, *Asahel Strong*.)

Fourth Generation, Capt. *Asahel Strong*, born October 13, 1702, lived in Farmington, Conn., he married, January 28, 1729, *Ruth Hooker*, born April 16, 1708, daughter of *John Hooker*, and his wife, *Abigail Stanley*, born July 25, 1669, daughter of JOHN STANLEY, of Farmington, Conn., who was (probably) brother of THOMAS STANLEY, whose daughters, *Mary* and *Anna*, married *John Porter* (2) and *Samuel Porter* (6.)

That *John Stanley*, of Farmington, married, April 20, 1663, *Sarah Fletcher*, born ——, 1641, daughter of John Fletcher, of Weathersfield, Conn., whose wife was *Mary Ward*, daughter of "widow" *Joyce Ward*, whose husband probably had died before the family came to New England.

(Rev. THOMAS HOOKER, born in Markfield, Leicestershire, England, (about) 1586, graduated at Emanuel College, Cambridge, England, B. A. 1608, M. A. 1611, was a minister at Chelmsford, county of Essex, England. He became a "Puritan," was ejected from his living, and went to Rotterdam, Holland. He came thence, in the ship "Griffin," in 1633, with Rev. John Cotton, Rev. Samuel Stone and others, to New England, and removed in 1636 to Hartford, Connecticut, where he died July 7, 1647.

Second Generation, Rev. Samuel Hooker, born (about) 1630, was ordained in 1661, minister at Hartford, Connecticut, successor of his brother-in-law, Rev. John Newton. He married at Plymouth, Massachusetts, September 22, 1658, *Mary Willett*.

(THOMAS WILLETT, when a youth, joined the Puritan Church in England, and went to Leyden, Holland, in 1629. He came thence in the ship "Lion," in June, 1632, to Plymouth, Mass. He married, July 6, 1636, *Mary Brown*, daughter of JOHN BROWN, who had been of the church in Leyden, in 1620, and came thence, in their company, to Plymouth, Mass., and settled at Duxbury, Mass., where he was a magistrate, commissioner for the "United Colonies," etc.

When the English colonists took New York from the Dutch, "Major Thomas Willett, with John Winthrop and George Wyllys, of Connecticut, and William Clarke and John Pynchon, of Massachusetts, went from Gravesend, L. I., to the city wharf, with a flag." (Broadhead's Hist. N. Y.)

Thomas Willett became, in 1665, the first Mayor of New York city. He died in Swanzey, Mass., August 3, 1674.

Second Generation, Mary Willett, born November 10, 1637, married Samuel Hooker.)

Third Generation, John Hooker, born February 20, 1665, married ——, 1687. *Abigail Stanley*, born July 25, 1669, daughter of *John Stanley*, of Farmington, Conn., who married December 15, 1645, *Sarah Scott*, born in England ——, 1620, who came with her father, THOMAS SCOTT, from Ipswich, England, April 1, 1634, in the ship "Elizabeth," Capt. William Andrews, and removed to Hartford, Conn., in 1637.

John Stanley, born in England, was son of JOHN STANLEY, Sr., who died on the passage from England in 1634, and who was brother of THOMAS STANLEY, whose daughter *Anna* married *Samuel Porter* (6.)

Fourth Generation, Ruth Hooker, born April 16, 1708, married Capt. *Asahel Strong*.

Fifth Generation, Ruth Strong, born September 3, 1739, married February 21, 1760, Col. *Ichabod Norton*.

(THOMAS NORTON came from England, and was an early settler at Guilford, Conn., one of the signers of the first compact, June 1, 1639. His wife's name was *Grace*.

Second Generation, Thomas Norton, born (about) 1640, married May 8, 1671, *Elizabeth Mason*.

JOHN MASON, Major-General, came from England in the company with Rev. John Warham to Dorchester, Mass., in 1630, and was among the first settlers of Windsor, Conn., whence he removed in 1637 to Saybrook, Conn. Captain in 1635, and chief in command in the Pequot war in 1637, Deputy Governor, Major-General and Commissioner for the New England Colonies 1647 to 1661. (See Mary Porter (61.) He married July —, 1639, *Anne Peck*, and died at Norwich, Conn., January 30, 1672, aged 72.

(Rev. ROBERT PECK, born at Beccles, county of Suffolk, England, graduated at Magdalen College, Oxford, England, in 1599. He was a minister at Hingham, county of Norfolk, England. He came to New England in the ship "Diligent, in 1638, with his wife and children, *Robert* and *Anne*, and settled in Hingham, Mass. On the dissolution of the "Long Parliament" he embarked for England October 27, 1641, with wife, and went back to his old residence, where he died, 1656. His daughter, *Anne*, remained, and married Capt. *John Mason*.)

Second Generation, Elizabeth Mason, born August —, 1654, married May 8, 1671, *Thomas Norton*.

Sixth Generation, Elizabeth Norton, born January 13, 1761, married August 10, 1790, Rev. *William Robinson*.

(WILLIAM ROBINSON came from England in 1635, and lived in Dorchester, Mass. Member of the "Ancient and Honorable Artillery Company" in 1643. He died June 5, 1668, having been "torn to pieces and slain in his mill."

Second Generation, Samuel Robinson, born May 14, 1640, lived in Dorchester, Mass., selectman, etc. He died September 16, 1718. He married *Mary Baker*, born April 27, 1643, daughter of *Richard Baker*, of Dorchester, Mass., and his wife, *Faith*, daughter of HENRY WITHINGTON, one of the six founders of the church in Dorchester, August 20, 1636.

Third Generation, Rev. *John Robinson*, born ——, 1672, ordained at Duxbury, Mass., November 18, 1702, married January 31, 1705-6, *Hannah Wiswall*, born February 22, 1682, daughter of his predecessor in the ministry at Duxbury, the Rev. *Ichabod Wiswall*.

(THOMAS WISWALL came from England (about) 1633 to Dorchester, Mass. Removed to Cambridge, Mass., in 1635, where he was ruling elder of the church of which Rev. John Eliot was minister. He died December 6, 1683.

Second Generation, Ichabod Wiswall, born ——, 1637, Harvard College, 1654, was ordained minister at Duxbury, Mass., in 1676. He married *Priscilla Peabody* (originally "Pabodie,") daughter of *William Peabody*, of Duxbury, Mass., who married December 26, 1644, *Elizabeth Alden*, eldest daughter of Capt. JOHN ALDEN, who came in the ship "Mayflower," in 1620, aged 22 years, and whose wife was *Priscilla*, daughter of WILLIAM MULLINS, who came in the same ship.

Third Generation, Hannah Wiswall, born February 22, 1682, married Rev. *John Robinson.*

Fourth Generation, Ichabod Robinson, born December 12, 1720, married January 16, 1752, *Lydia Brown,* born in Lebanon, Conn., March 19, 1720, daughter of *Ebenezer Brown,* born June 15, 1685, who married February 25, 1714, *Sarah Hyde,* born December 20, 1696, daughter of *Samuel Hyde,* born in Norwich, Conn., May —, 1665, who married December 10, 1690, *Elizabeth Calkins,* born April 18, 1673, daughter of *John Calkins,* who married *Sarah Royce,* daughter of *Robert Royce,* of New London, Conn. (See P. P. Wiggins, (100.)

(*Samuel Hyde* was son of *Samuel Hyde,* born —, 1637, who married June -, 1659, JANE LEE, sister of *Thomas Lee,* who came from England in February, 1634, in the ship "Hopewell," and settled in Lyme, Conn., in 1641. *Samuel Hyde,* Sr., was son of WILLIAM HYDE, from England, who settled at Norwich, Conn.)

Ebenezer Brown, born June 15, 1685, was son of JOHN BROWN, born in Swanzey, Bristol county, Mass., September, 1650, an "Assistant" of the Plymouth colony, who married November 8, 1672, *Anne Mason,* born June —, 1650, daughter of Major *John Mason,* before named, her sister, *Elizabeth Mason,* having married *Thomas Norton.*

Fifth Generation, Rev. *William Robinson,* born in Lebanon, Conn., August 15, 1754, graduate of Yale College, 1773, pastor of Congregational Church at Southington, Conn., married, as before stated, *Elizabeth Norton.*

Sixth Generation, Charles Robinson, born February 10, 1801, Yale College, 1821, a lawyer in New Haven, Conn., married March 13, 1828, *Nancy M. Mulford,* born November 28, 1800, daughter of *Hervey Mulford,* of New Haven, Conn.

(WILLIAM MULFORD came from Devonshire, England, and was an early settler at Southampton, Long Island, N. Y., in 1645, and died in March, 1687.

Second Generation, Thomas Mulford, born (about) 1650, married, 1686, *Mary Conckling,* daughter of *Jeremiah Conckling,* whose wife was *Mary Gardiner,* daughter of *Lion Gardiner,* first proprietor of Gardiner's Island. (See *Mary Porter,* 61.)

Jeremiah Conckling was son of ANANIAS CONCKLING, who came from Nottinghamshire, England, to Salem, Mass., in 1637, and removed to Long Island.

Third Generation, Thomas Mulford, born ——, 1688, married June 19, 1712, *Mercy Bell.*

(*Jonathan Bell,* only son of *Francis Bell.* of Stamford, Conn., in 1641, and his wife *Rebecca,* married ——, 1672, *Susannah Pierson,* born December 10, 1652, daughter of Rev. *Abraham Pierson,* of Branford, Conn., who was born in Yorkshire, England, graduate of Trinity College, Cambridge, England, A. B. 1632, who came to New England in 1640. He was minister of the church gathered at Lynn, Mass., in 1640, to settle at Southampton, L. I. He removed to Branford, Conn., in 1647, and thence with a part of his congregation to Newark, N. J., in 1667, where he died November 8, 1732.)

Fourth Generation, Barnabas Mulford baptized June 3, 1716, removed to Branford, Conn., where he married *Hannah Pettee*, daughter of *Edward Pettee*, of Branford ; she died ——, 1781 ; he died November, 1792.

Fifth Generation, Barnabas Mulford born February 13, 1745, married November 10, 1771, *Mehitabel Gorham*, daughter of *Timothy Gorham*, a descendant of Capt. JOHN GORHAM, born in Benefield, Northamptonshire, England, where he was baptized January 28, 1621, and who married in 1643 *Desire Howland*, daughter of JOHN HOWLAND, of Plymouth, Mass., who came in the ship "Mayflower" in 1620, and whose wife was *Elizabeth Tilley*, who came with her father, *John Tilley*, in the "Mayflower" in 1620.

Sixth Generation, Hervey Mulford, born July 7, 1777, married March 29, 1797, *Nancy Bradley*, born September 29, 1778, daughter of Capt. *Abraham Bradley*, born June 13, 1741, a merchant in New Haven, Conn., who married January 23, 1760, *Amy Hemmingway*, born May 26, 1743, daughter of *John Hemmingway*, of New Haven, who married November 9, 1738, *Mary Tuttle*, born December 22, 1720, daughter of *Joseph Tuttle*, of New Haven, a descendant of WILLIAM TUTTLE, who came from England in the ship "Planter" in April, 1635, aged 26 years, with his wife *Elizabeth*, and removed in 1639 to New Haven, Conn.

(RALPH HEMMINGWAY came from England to Roxbury, Mass., in 1633, where he married July 5, 1634, *Elizabeth Hewes*, who came from England in 1633 in the ship "Griffin," with her brother, JOSHUA HEWES, and who removed to Wickford, R. I., in 1662, where he was a merchant, and died in 1677-8.

Second Generation, Samuel Hemmingway, born January —, 1636, married, 1662, *Sarah Cooper*, born September 21, 1645, daughter of JOHN COOPER, who came from England in the ship "Hopewell" in April, 1635, with his wife, *Wibroe*, and removed to New Haven, Conn.

Third Generation, Abraham Hemmingway, born. December 3, 1677, married November 11, 1713, *Sarah Talmadge*, daughter (probably) of ENOS TALMADGE, of New Haven, Conn., and his wife, *Hannah Yale*, born July 6, 1664, daughter of *Thomas Yale*, whose wife was *Mary Turner*, daughter of Capt. NATHANIEL TURNER, who came from England in the fleet with Winthrop in 1630, who served in the war with the Pequots in 1637, and removed in 1638 to New Haven, Conn.

Capt. Turner sailed for England in 1646 in that ship never heard from afterwards, until "her apparition was seen in the air." (See Appendix "G."

Thomas Yale, born in Wales, was son of DAVID YALE, whose wife was *Anne Morton*, daughter of THOMAS MORTON, Bishop of Chester, and who, after the death of *Yale*, married *Theophilus Eaton*. (See Abigail P. Stoddard (62.)

Fourth Generation, Elizabeth Hemmingway, born ——, 1716, married July 10, 1740, *Zebulon Bradley*, son of *Samuel Bradley*, who married January 7, 1717, *Sarah Robinson*, daughter (probably) of *Jacob Robinson*, of New Haven, Conn., who married in 1690 *Sarah Hitchcock*, born October 6, 1669, daughter of *Eliakim*

Hitchcock, of New Haven, Conn., son of MATTHEW HITCHCOCK, who came from England in the ship "Susan and Ellen" in 1635, settled in New Haven in 1639, and died in 1669.

Samuel Bradley was son of ISAAC BRADLEY, who settled in Branford, Conn., in 1667, and removed to New Haven, Conn., in 1683.)

Seventh Generation, Arthur Robinson, born January 21, 1843, married Jane H. Porter.]

Their children were [being of the ninth generation :]
206. Arthur Porter Robinson, b. February 14, 1867, d. April 1, 1868.
207. Charles Robinson, b. April 30, 1869.
208. Julia Osborn Robinson, b. November 17, 1871.
209. Cornelia Grace Robinson, b. November 21, 1876.
210. Jane Porter Robinson, b. July 1, 1881.

[123.] JANE HOWELL TOWNSEND married October 24, 1866, *Edward S. Wheeler.*

Their children were [being of the ninth generation :]
211. Townsend Wheeler, b. September 24, 1867, d. May 21, 1871.
212. Elizabeth Townsend Wheeler, b. July 27, 1873.
213. Frank Storer Wheeler, b. December 24, 1876.
214. Marion W. Wheeler, b. June 8, 1880.

[125.] PETER AUGUSTUS PORTER graduated at Yale College in 1874. He married February 13, 1877, *Alice Adele Taylor.*

[RICHARD TAYLOR came from England and settled at Yarmouth, Mass., in 1643, where he married ——, 1646, *Ruth Burgess,* daughter of THOMAS BURGESS, who came from England in the ship "John and Dorothy," Capt. William Andrews, in May, 1637, and settled at Lynn, Mass., removing thence to Sandwich, Mass., where he was a representative in 1646 to 1649. He died August 1, 1703; Mrs. Ruth Taylor died June 22, 1693.

Second Generation, John Taylor, born ——, 1649, married December 15, 1674, *Sarah Mathews,* born ——, 1649, daughter of JAMES MATHEWS, who came from England to Charlestown, Mass., in 1634, and removed to Yarmouth, Mass., in 1643, where he died.

Third Generation, John Taylor, born ——, 1678, married ——.

Fourth Generation, John Taylor, born ——, 1720, married ——.

Fifth Generation, William Taylor, born ——, 1755, was a captain in the war of the revolution. He married *Abigail Case.*

(JOHN CASE came from England and settled in New London, Conn., in 1656, whence he removed to Windsor, Conn., and thence in 1669 to Simsbury, Conn. He was a representative, etc., and married in 1657 *Sarah Spencer.*

(WILLIAM SPENCER came from England with his brother Thomas to Cambridge, Mass., in 1631, and in 1634 was a member of the committee of the people which led to the formation of the General Court or House of Representatives; a member of the Ancient and Honorable Artillery Company. He removed to Hartford, Conn., in 1639, and died in 1640.

Second Generation, Sarah Spencer, born about 1637, married —, 1657, *John Case*.

Second Generation, John Case, born November 5, 1662, married ——, 1693, *Sarah Holcombe*, born June 23, 1668, daughter of *Joshua Holcombe*, of Windsor, Conn., who married June 4, 1663, *Ruth Sherwood*, daughter of Thomas Sherwood, of Stratford, Conn.

Third Generation, Daniel Case, born March 7, 1695-6, married May 17, 1719, *Penelope Buttolph*, born October 1, 1699, daughter of *David Buttolph*. Daniel Case died May 28, 1733; Mrs. Penelope Case died June 27, 1746.

Fourth Generation, Ezekiel Case, born September 30, 1731, married August 2, 1763, *Lucy Cornish*, daughter of Capt, *James Cornish*, son of *James Cornish*, of Simsbury, Conn., who was son of *James Cornish* from England to Saybrook, Conn., and Northampton, Mass.

Fifth Generation, Abigail Case, born November 15, 1763, married *William Taylor*.

Sixth Generation, Virgil Taylor, born — —, 1791, married *Electa* ——.

Seventh Generation, Virgil C. Taylor, born in Hartford, Conn., ——, 1817.

Eighth Generation, Alice A. Taylor, married *Peter A. Porter*.

(WILLIAM CABELL (see Col. *Peter A. Porter* (75), born at Warminster in Wiltshire, England, at the western extremity of Salisbury plain, about 1640, was descended from an ancient family of that name, whose residence was at Frome-Selwood, in Somersetshire. He was a dissenter from the English church, and was buried at Warminster December 25, 1704.

Second Generation, Nicholas Cabell, baptized at Warminster May 29, 1667, married November 15, 1697, at Frome-Selwood, *Rachel Hooper*. He died July 30, 1730; Mrs. Rachel Cabell died October ——, 1737.

Third Generation, William Cabell, born March 9, 1699, at Warminster, England; emigrated to Virginia. He married about 1720-25, *Elizabeth Burks*, daughter of *Samuel Burks*, a planter of Virginia. William Cabell died at Warminster, Va., April 12, 1774.

Fourth Generation, Col. *Joseph Cabell*, born September 8, 1732, in Goochland county, Va.; was sheriff and justice of Albemarle county. He represented the counties of Amherst and Buckingham over twenty years in the House of Burgesses and General Assembly, and was a member of the convention of 1775 and 1776. He commanded a regiment in the war of the revolution, and was present at the surrender of Yorktown. One company of this regiment was formed of the students of *William and Mary's College*, among whom was his son Joseph Cabell. He married *Mary Hopkins*, born January , 1735, daughter of Doct. *Arthur Hopkins*, and resided at Winton, Amherst county, Va., removing to Variety Shades in Buckingham county, and thence to Sion Hill, in the latter county, where he died March 1, 1798. Mrs. Mary Cabell died July 12, 1811.

Fifth Generation, Mary Hopkins Cabell, born , married June 28, 1785, *John Breckinridge*, son of *Robert Breckinridge* and *Lætitia Preston*. (See Gen. Peter B. Porter (54).

Sixth Generation, Rev. *John Breckinridge*, born , married , *Margaret Miller*, daughter of Rev. Dr. Miller, of Princeton, N. J.

Seventh Generation, Mary Cabell Preston Breckinridge, born , married Col. *Peter A. Porter* (75).

Eighth Generation, Peter Augustus Porter, born October 10, 1853, married *Alice Adele Taylor*, ——.]

[Their children were [being of the ninth generation :]

215. Peter Augustus Porter, b. November 16, 1877.
216. Cabell Breckinridge Porter, b. April 8, 1881.

[130.] HARRIETT LOUISE HOLLEY married September 24, 1851, *John Tillottson Clark*, of Portage City, Wisconsin.

[Lieut. WILLIAM CLARK came from England to Dorchester, Mass., about 1636, with his wife *Sarah*. He removed in 1659 to Northampton, Mass., where he was a selectman, and a lieutenant in "King Philip's War." He died July 18, 1690, aged 81. His wife died September 6, 1675.

Second Generation, Capt. *William Clark*, born July 3, 1656, married July 15, 1680, *Hannah Strong*.

(Elder JOHN STRONG (see Albert H. Porter (69) came from Taunton, Somersetshire, England, with Rev. John Warham and others, and removed to Windsor, Conn., in 1635, and thence to Northampton, Mass., in 1639, where he died November 28, 1676.

Second Generation, Hannah Strong, born May 30, 1659, married Capt. *William Clark*.

Third Generation, Jonathan Clark, born May 13, 1688, married January 6, 1713-14, *Hannah Smalley*, a descendant of JOHN SMALLEY, who came from England in the ship "Francis and James" in 1632 with Edward Winslow, and settled in Barnstable, Mass.

Fourth Generation, Jonathan Clark, born November 1, 1715, married January 10, 1735, *Soria Dewey*, a descendant of THOMAS DEWEY, who came from Sandwich, county of Kent, England, to Dorchester, Mass., in 1633, removed to Windsor, Conn., with Rev. John Warham in 1635, where he married March 22, 1639,

"Widow Frances Clark." He was cornet of the "troop of horse," and died April 27, 1648.

Fifth Generation, Lemuel Clark, born August 8, 1753, married ——, 1772, *Ruth Baldwin.*

(JOHN BALDWIN came from England in the ship "Martin" in 1638, and settled in Guilford, Conn. He married April 12, 1653, *Hannah Birchard,* born in England in 1633, daughter of THOMAS BIRCHARD, who came in the ship "Truelove" from London, England, in 1635, and settled in Roxbury, Mass., removing thence to Guilford, Conn.

Second Generation, John Baldwin, born December 5, 1654, married ——, 1680, *Experience Abell,* daughter of ROBERT ABELL, who came from England in the fleet with John Winthrop in 1630, and settled in Rehoboth, Mass.

Third Generation, John Baldwin, born ——, 1680, married January 31, 1716, *Abigail Baldwin,* (his cousin, probably,) born ——, 1694, daughter of *Thomas Baldwin,* of Norwich, Conn., who married ——, 1692, *Abigail Lay,* daughter of *John Lay,* of Lyme, Conn.

(JOHN LAY, born in England in 1633, lived in Lyme, Conn. He was wounded in the "great swamp fight" with the Pequots December 19, 1675, and died November 13, 1696. He was son of JOHN LAY, who came from England with wife, *Abigail,* settled at Saybrook, Conn., in 1648.

Fourth Generation, Benjamin Baldwin, born April 2, 1727, married September 27, 1750, *Ruth Porter.*)

(JOHN PORTER, with wife, *Rose,* from England.

Second Generation, Samuel Porter, born in England, married *Anna Stanley.*

Third Generation, John Porter, born December 12, 1666, married April 3, 1690, *Mary Butler.*

RICHARD BUTLER came from Braintree, county of Essex, England, to Cambridge, Mass., in 1632. He removed to Hartford, Conn., in 1640, where he was a representative, and died August 6, 1684.

Second Generation, Thomas Butler, born in England, married *Sarah Stone,* daughter of Rev. *Samuel Stone.*

Rev. SAMUEL STONE, born in Hertford, county of Herts, England, (about 20 miles from London,) graduated at Emanuel College, Oxford, England, in 1620: A. B. 1623: A. M. 1627. He came to New England in 1633 with Revs. John Cotton and Thomas Hooker in the ship "Griffin," arriving at Boston, Mass., September 4, 1633. He went with Hooker to Cambridge, Mass., in October of the same year, as teacher of the church of which Hooker was pastor; and on May 14, 1636, he removed with Hooker and that company to Hartford, Conn. He was chaplain of the troops in the Pequot war of 1637, under Capt. John Mason, and died July 20, 1663.

Third Generation. Mary Butler. born ——, 1670, married *John Porter.*

Fourth Generation, John Porter, born October 3, 1694, married November 27, 1727, *Sarah Heaton*, daughter of *James Heaton*, of New Haven, Conn., who married ——, 1662, *Sarah Streete*, daughter of Rev. NICHOLAS STREETE, who came from England to Taunton, Mass., and was teacher of the church. He removed to New Haven, Conn., where he died April 22, 1674.

James Heaton, born about 1640, was son of NATHANIEL HEATON, who came from England with wife, *Elizabeth*, to Boston, Mass., in 1634.

Fifth Generation, Ruth Porter, born ——, 1633, married Benjamin Baldwin.)

Sixth Generation, William Clark, born September 22, 1777, in Lebanon, Conn., married ——, 1807, *Sophronia Tillotson*. He died in Parma, N. Y., ——, 1852. Mrs. Sophronia Clark died in Wolcott, N. Y., February —, 1848.

(JOHN TILLOTSON came from England in the ship "James" from Southampton, England, arriving at Boston, Mass., June 3, 1635. He was a descendant of Archbishop Tillotson, of England.

Second Generation, John Tillotson, born (about) 1620, married July 14, 1648, *Dorcas Coleman*, who came from Marlborough, in Wiltshire, England, with her brother, Thomas Coleman, in the ship "James" to Boston, Mass., June 3, 1635.

Third Generation, John Tillotson, born February 25, 1651, married November 25, 1680, *Mary Morris*, daughter of JOHN MORRIS, who came from England, and settled in Hartford, Conn., in 1640.

Fourth Generation, John Tillotson, born (about) 1683, married ——.

Fifth Generation, John Tillotson, born (about) 1725, married *Mary Norton*, a descendant of THOMAS NORTON, who, with wife *Grace*, came from Guilford, county of Surrey, England, and in 1639 was one of the founders of Guilford, Conn., (see Mary Porter (61,) and died in 1648.

Sixth Generation, John Tillotson, born ——, 1756, at Farmington, Conn., married ——, 1782, *Elizabeth Brockway*, born ——, 1760, a descendant of WALTER BROCKWAY, who came from England and settled at Lyme, Conn., in 1659. John Tillotson died in Genoa, N. Y., 1826.

Seventh Generation, Sophronia Tillotson, born October 7, 1785, in Farmington, Conn., married at Genoa, N. Y., ——, 1806, *William Clark*. He died at Parma, Monroe county, N. Y., ——, 1852.

Eighth Generation, John Tillotson Clark, born April 16, 1821, at Wolcott, (now Huron), Wayne county, N. Y., married *Harriett Louise Holley* ——.

Their children were [being of the ninth generation :]

217. Mary Holley Clark. b February 17, 1853.
218. Elizabeth S. Clark. b January 7, 1855.
219. John Tillotson Clark, b. May 9, 1856; d. November 9, 1863.
220. Helen Louise Clark. b. November 4, 1857.
221. Julia Kirkland Clark, b. January 7, 1860.
222. Sarah Amelia Clark. b. August 14, 1861.
223. William Henry Clark. b. July 21, 1863.

74

[134.] JULIA E. HOLLEY, married October 12, 1869, *Charles Henry Roys*, of Lyons, N. Y.

Their children were [being of the ninth generation :]
224. Mary Louise Roys, b. May 10, 1873.
225. Charles Kirkland Roys, b. August 15, 1875.
226. John Holley Roys, b. April 9, 1877.

[135.] JOHN MILTON HOLLEY married October 12, 1869, at Niles, Mich., ANNA ORILLA KING ; their residence, La Crosse, Wis.

Their children were [being of the ninth generation :]
227. John Milton Holley, b. July 6, 1874.

[136.] ALEXANDER LYMAN HOLLEY, born July 20, 1832, graduated in the scientific course at Brown University in 1853, and studied practical mechanics at the Corliss Engine Works of Providence, R. I. He was early distinguished as a mechanical engineer and metallurgist, and wrote and edited several works on that and kindred subjects. Mr. Holley was, however, chiefly known by his introduction of the Bessamer steel manufacture in this country, and had superintended the construction of most of the large works, adding many improvements to the process, and had come to be regarded as one of the principal authorities on the metallurgy of iron and steel in this country. He married December 11, 1855, *Mary H. Slade*. He died at his residence in Brooklyn, L. I., January 29, 1882.

Their children were [being of the ninth generation :]
228. Gertrude Holley. b. October 28, 1832.
229. Lucy Holley, b. December 15, 1863.
230. Alexander H. Holley, b. ——, 1866, d. in infancy.
231. Alice Holley, b. January 20, 1869, d. May 3, 1873.

[139.] JOHN COFFING HOLLEY married October 22, 1862, *Lucinda R. Sterling*, daughter of *George W. Sterling*, of Poughkeepsie, N. Y.

—[JOHN PORTER (1), from England, with wife ROSE.

Second Generation, John Porter, born in England in 1618, married ——, 1650, *Mary Stanley* (sister of Anna Stanley, who married his brother, Samuel Porter), daughter of THOMAS STANLEY, who came from London, England, in the ship "Planter" in 1635 to Dorchester, Mass. Thence he removed to Hartford, Conn., with the first settlers in 1636, and again to Hadley, Mass., in 1659, where he died January 30, 1663.

Third Generation, Hannah Porter, born June 1, 1662, married January 12, 1680, *Thomas Loomis*, of Windsor, Conn., who came from England with his father, JOSEPH LOOMIS, from Bristol, England, and removed to Windsor, Conn., in 1638, where he died ――, 1658.

Fourth Generation, Mary Loomis, born October 2, 1680, married November 20, 1695, *John Buell*.

(WILLIAM BUELL, born in Chesterton, Huntingdonshire, England, in 1610, came to New England in 1630, and settled at Windsor, Conn. He died November 23, 1681. His wife, *Mary Buell*, died September 24, 1684.

Second Generation, Samuel Buell, born September 2, 1641, married November 13, 1662, *Deborah Griswold*, born June 28, 1646, daughter of EDWARD GRISWOLD, who was born at Kenilworth, Warwickshire, England, in 1607, who came to New England in 1639 with his brother, Matthew Griswold, and accompanied Rev. Ephraim Hewett in the settlement of Windsor in 1639.

Third Generation, John Buell, born February 17, 1672, married *Mary Loomis*.

Fourth Generation, Solomon Buell, born August 30, 1715, married January 19, 1738, *Eunice Griswold*.

(EDWARD GRISWOLD, before named, married in England *Margaret* ―――. He removed from Windsor to Simsbury Conn., in 1663, and thence to Killingworth, Conn., where he died August 3, 1691. His wife, Margaret, died August 23, 1670.

Second Generation, George Griswold, born about 1634, married October 3, 1655, *Mary Holcombe*, daughter of THOMAS HOLCOMBE, from England to Dorchester, Mass., who removed to Windsor, Conn., in 1635, and died September, 7, 1657.

Third Generation, John Griswold, born September 17, 1668, married November 22, 1705, *Abigail Gaylord*. He died June 13, 1738.

(JOHN PORTER, from England, with wife ROSE, before named.

Second Generation, Anna Porter, born in England, married February 24, 1644, *William Gaylord*, born in England, son of WILLIAM GAYLORD, who was deacon of the first church gathered in Plymouth, England, in March, 1630, and who came to New England in the ship "Mary and John" in 1630, and removed to Windsor, Conn , in 1639. He was a representative until 1664, and died July 20, 1673, aged 88 years.

―*Third Generation, Nathaniel Gaylord*, born September 3, 1656, married October 17, 1678, *Abigail Bissell*, born November 23, 1658, daughter of *Thomas Bissell*, who married October 11, 1655, *Abigail Moore*, born ――, 1639, daughter of JOHN MOORE, who came from England in the ship "Mary and John" to Dorchester, Mass., in 1630, and removed with Rev. John Warham to Windsor, Conn. He was a deacon in the church, and died September 16, 1677.

― *Thomas Bissell*, born in England, was son of JOHN BISSELL, who came from England and removed with Rev. Ephraim Hewett to Windsor in 1639, and died October 3, 1677, aged 85 years. Thomas Bissell died July 31, 1688.

Fourth Generation, Abigail Gaylord, born March 13, 1683, married November 22, 1705, *John Griswold.*

Fifth Generation, Eunice Griswold, born ——, 1720, married January 19, 1738, *Solomon Buell.*

Sixth Generation, Dorcas Buell, born July 14, 1742, married ——, — —, *John Canfield.*

(THOMAS CANFIELD, with wife PHEBE, came from England, and was an early settler at Milford, Conn., where he died in 1687.

Second Generation, Jeremiah Canfield, born about 1680, removed to New Milford, Conn., where he was an original purchaser in 1706. He married *Judith Mallory*, born September 27, 1687, daughter of *Peter Mallory*, of New Haven, Conn., who married May 27, 1673, *Elizabeth Trowbridge*, born October 12, 1660, daughter of *James Trowbridge*, of New Haven, Conn., who married December 30, 1659, *Margaret Atherton*, daughter of HUMPHREY ATHERTON, who came from Preston in Lincolnshire, England, to Dorchester, Mass., in 1638, and was captain of the "Ancient and Honorable Artillery Company." He succeeded Robert Sedgwick as major-general of the colonial forces in 1656, and was killed by being thrown from his horse at a review September 17, 1661.

James Trowbridge, born in England, was a son of THOMAS TROWBRIDGE, who was born at Combe-St. Nicholas, Taunton, Somersetshire, England, who came to Dorchester, Mass., in 1637.

Peter Mallory, born July 29, 1653, was son of PETER MALLORY, from England, one of the signers of the original covenant at New Haven, Conn., in 1644.

Third Generation, Jeremiah Canfield, born ——, removed to New Milford, Conn., where he was an original settler in 1706.

Fourth Generation, Samuel Canfield, born ——, was a judge of the county court, etc., and lived in New Milford, Conn.

Fifth Generation, Col. Samuel Canfield, born ——, married *Elizabeth Judson.*

(JOHN PORTER, from England, with wife ROSE, before named.

Second Generation, Sarah Porter, born in England ——, 1622, married October 24, 1644, Capt. *Joseph Judson*, born in England in 1619, son of WILLIAM JUDSON, who came from England to Concord, Mass., in 1635, with wife, GRACE, and family. He removed to Hartford, Conn., in 1639, and died in New Haven, Conn., July 29, 1662. Mrs. Grace Judson died September 29, 1659.

Capt. Joseph Judson was a soldier of high repute in "King Philip's war." He removed to Woodbury, Conn., and died October 8, 1690. Mrs Sarah (Porter) Judson died March 16, 1696.

Third Generation, John Judson, born December 10, 1647, married as his second wife February 5, 1690, *Mary Orton*, daughter of *Thomas Orton*, of Windsor, Conn., who married June 16, 1641, *Margaret Pell*, daughter of THOMAS PELL, who came from England in the ship "Hopewell" in 1635, and removed to Saybrook, Conn.

He served under Capt. John Mason in the Pequot war. His wife was LUCY, widow of Francis Brewster, who was lost in the ship whose "apparition was seen in the air." (See Augusta Porter (50) and Appendix "G.")

Fourth Generation, Isaac Judson, born June 1, 1700, married November 29, 1727, *Elizabeth Hawley,* daughter of *Joseph Hawley,* whose wife was *Rebecca Stoddard,* born ——, 1686, daughter of Rev. *Solomon Stoddard,* of Northampton, Mass.

Joseph Hawley, born ——, 1682, was son of *Joseph Hawley,* born June 7, 1654, who married September 24, 1676, *Lydia Marshall,* born February 18, 1655, daughter of Capt. *Samuel Marshall,* son of THOMAS MARSHALL, who came from England in 1634 to Dorchester, Mass. *Samuel Marshall* married May 6, 1652, *Mary Wilton,* daughter of DAVID WILTON, who came from England in 1632, and removed to Windsor, Conn., in 1635-36, and was a representative in 1646 to 1656, lieutenant in "King Philip's war," and died in Windsor February 5, 1678.

Joseph Hawley, Sr., was son of THOMAS HAWLEY, from England to Roxbury, Mass., where he married February 2, 1652, *Dorothea Harbalet,* then the widow of Thomas Lamb.

(Rev. *Salomon Stoddard,* born October 4, 1643, gradnated at Harvard College in 1662. He was pastor of the church at Northampton, Mass. He married March 8, 1670, *Esther Warham,* born December 8, 1644, daughter of Rev. JOHN WARHAM, of Windsor, Conn., who had graduated at Oxford University, England, and was rector of the church at Exeter in Devonshire, England. He became a Puritan, and came to New England in the ship "Mary and John" in 1630 to Dorchester, Mass., and removed to Windsor, Conn., in 1630, where he died April 1, 1670.

Rev. *Solomon Stoddard* was son of ANTHONY STODDARD, who came from England to Dorchester, Mass., in 1639. He was a representative and a member of the "Ancient and Honorable Artillery Company." He married *Mary Downing,* daughter of EMANUEL DOWNING, a barrister of the Inner Temple, London, England, who came to New England in 1638 with his wife, *Lucy Winthrop,* daughter of ADAM WINTHROP, of Edwardstone, near Groton, county of Suffolk, England, and sister of Gov. *John Winthrop,* of Massachusetts. (See Harriett L. Holley (130.)

Samuel Marshall was one of the five captains who led the famous charge upon the Pequots in the Narragansett fort December 19, 1675, "where he fell at the head of his company."

Fifth Generation, Elizabeth Judson, born September 13, 1732, married Col. *Samuel Canfield,* of New Milford, Conn., ——.

Sixth Generation, John Canfield, born ——, graduate of Yale college. He married ——, *Dorcas Buell.*

(WILLIAM BUELL, born at Chesterton, Huntingdonshire, England. (See ante.)

Second Generation, Samuel Buell, born September 2, 1641, married November 13, 1662, *Deborah Griswold,* born June 28, 1646, daughter of EDWARD GRISWOLD, who came from Kenilworth, Warwickshire, England, with his wife MARGARET to

New England in 1639, in company with Rev. Ephraim Hewett, and removed to Windsor, Conn. He went thence to Killingworth, Conn., where he died. Mrs. Margaret Griswold died August 23, 1670.

Third Generation, John Buell, born February 17, 1671, married November 20, 1695, *Mary Loomis*, born October 2, 1680, daughter of *Thomas Loomis*, of Windsor, who married January 2, 1680, *Hannah Porter*, born June 1, 1662, daughter of *John Porter* (2) and his wife, *Mary Stanley*.

Thomas Loomis, born March 7, 1656, was son of JOSEPH LOOMIS, who came from England in 1638 and settled in Windsor, Conn., and died ——, 1658.

Fourth Generation, Solomon Buell, born August 30, 1715, married January 19, 1737, *Eunice Griswold*, born ——, 1720, daughter of *Matthew Griswold*, of Windsor, who married June 6, 1709, *Mary Phelps*.

(GEORGE PHELPS came from England to Dorchester, Mass., in 1635. He removed with Rev. John Warham and that company to Windsor. His wife was *Philura Randall*, daughter of PHILIP RANDALL, who came from England to Dorchester, Mass., in 1634, removed to Windsor, and died July 9, 1678, in Westfield, Mass.

Second Generation, Joseph Phelps, born June 24, 1647, married June 26, 1673, *Mary Porter*, born July 17, 1653, daughter of *John Porter* (2) and his wife, *Mary Stanley*, and sister of *Hannah Porter*, who married *Thomas Loomis*, before mentioned.

Mary Stanley and Anna Stanley, who married *John Porter* (2) and *Samuel Porter* (6), were daughters of THOMAS STANLEY, who came from London, England, in 1634, in the ship "Planter," and removed to Hartford, Conn., on its settlement in 1635.

Third Generation, Mary Phelps, born June 13, 1674, married June 6, 1709, *Matthew Griswold*. (See Mary Anne Holley (82).)

(EDWARD GRISWOLD, from England, before mentioned.

Second Generation, Joseph Griswold, born March 2, 1647, lived in Windsor, Conn. He married July 14, 1670, *Mary Gaylord*, born March 19, 1650, daughter of *Walter Gaylord*, of Windsor, Conn., who married April —, 1648, *Mary Stebbins*, daughter of ROLAND STEBBINS, who came from Ipswich, county of Suffolk, England, with his wife Sarah in the ship "Francis" in 1634 to Roxbury, Mass., and removed thence to Springfield, Mass., in June, 1635. His wife, Mrs. Sarah Stebbins, died October 4, 1649. He removed to Northampton, Mass., where he died December 14, 1671.

Walter Gaylord, born in England, was brother of *William Gaylord*, who married *Anna Porter* (5). They were sons of WILLIAM GAYLORD, who was chosen a deacon of the emigrating church at Plymouth, England, in March, 1630, and who came to New England in the ship "Mary and John," arriving May 30, 1630, and removed to Windsor, Conn., October —, 1635, where he died July 20, 1673, aged 88 years.

Third Generation, Matthew Griswold, born February 25, 1686, married June 6, 1709, *Mary Phelps*.

Fourth Generation, Eunice Griswold, born ——, 1720, married January 19, 1737, *Solomon Buell*.

Fifth Generation, Dorcas Buell, born July 14, 1742, married *John Canfield*.

Seventh Generation, Alma Canfield, born — , married *Elisha Sterling*, who was born at Lyme, Conn., ———, 1765, son of Capt. *William Sterling* and his wife, *Jemima Sill*.

(JOHN SILL came from Lyme-Regis, Dorsetshire, England, in 1637, to Cambridge, Mass., with his wife *Joanna* and children. He died about 1652.

Second Generation, Capt. *Joseph Sill*, born in England in 1636, married, first, December 5, 1660, *Jemima Belcher*, born April 5, 1642, daughter of ANDREW BELCHER, who came from England in 1636 and settled at Sudbury, Mass., in 1639. He was a member of the "Ancient and Honorable Artillery Company" in 1642. He married October 1, 1639, *Elizabeth Danforth*, born in England in 1618, daughter of NICHOLAS DANFORTH, who came from Framlingham, county of Suffolk, England, to New England in 1634, and settled at Cambridge, Mass. Mrs. Jemima Sill died about 1670.

Capt. Joseph Sill was distinguished in the "war with King Philip," and at its close removed to Lyme, Conn., where he married, second, February 12, 1677, *Sarah Clark*, daughter of GEORGE CLARK, who came from England in 1636, and settled in Milford, Conn. She was then the widow of Reginald Marvyn ("Lyme's famous captain.") Capt. Joseph Sill died August 6, 1696.

Third Generation, *Joseph Sill*, born January 6, 1678, married ———, 1705, *Phebe Lord*.

THOMAS LORD, born in England in 1583, came to New England in the ship "Elizabeth and Anne," with wife *Dorothy*, in May, 1635, and settled in Newtown, Mass., removing to Hartford, Conn.

Second Generation, William Lord, born in England in 1623, married about 1642 *Dorothy* ———, and died May 17, 1678.

Third Generation, Richard Lord, born May ——, 1647, in Saybrook, Conn., married ———, 1682, *Elizabeth Hyde*. He lived in Lyme, Conn., and died April 27, 1727. Mrs. Elizabeth Lord died July 22, 1736.

(WILLIAM HYDE came from England about 1635, and was an early settler at Hartford, Conn., whence he removed to Saybrook, Conn., and thence to Norwich, Conn., where he died in 1681.

Second Generation, Samuel Hyde, born in Hartford, Conn., about 1637, married June ——, 1659, *Jane Lee*, daughter of THOMAS LEE, who came from England in 1640 with wife *Phebe* and children, but who died on the passage, the survivors settling in Saybrook.

Third Generation, Elizabeth Hyde, born August ——, 1660, in Norwich, Conn., married ———, 1682, *Richard Lord*.

Fourth Generation, Phebe Lord, born about 1686, married *Joseph Sill*.

Fourth and Fifth Generations, Thomas Sill, born August 25, 1717, married ——, 1742, *Jemima Dudley*, a descendant of *Joseph Dudley*, of Guilford, Conn., who married October 8, 1670, *Anne Robinson*, daughter of *Thomas Robinson*, of Guilford.

(Joseph Dudley was son of WILLIAM DUDLEY, who came from Ockley, county of Surrey, England, with wife *Jane*, in company with Rev. Henry Whitfield, Col. George Fenwick and others to New Haven, Conn., in 1639, in the first ship with passengers to that place. (See Mary Porter (61.)

Fifth Generation, Jemima Sill, born ——, 1745, married *William Sterling*.

Sixth Generation, Elisha Sterling, born ——, 1768, graduate of Yale College, 1787. He was a lawyer in Salisbury, Conn., colonel in the war of 1812. He married *Alma Canfield*.

Seventh Generation, George W. Sterling, born December 13, 1812, married *Ruth A. Chapin*.

(SAMUEL CHAPIN came from England with wife *Cicley* to Roxbury, Mass., in 1632. He removed in 1642 to Springfield, Mass., and thence in 1660 to Westfield, Mass., where he was an original proprietor, and died November 11, 1675.

Second Generation, Japhet Chapin, born October 15, 1642, removed to Milford, Conn., where he married July 22, 1664, *Abilene Coley*, born ——, 1643, daughter of SAMUEL COLEY, who came from England and settled at Milford in 1639, where he married in 1640 *Anna Prudden*, daughter of *James Prudden*, who came from Herefordshire, England, with his brother, Rev. Peter Prudden, who had been a popular preacher in that locality. They came in company with Rev. John Davenporte, Gov. Theophilus Eaton, William Andrews and others, and settled in New Haven, Conn., in 1638. (See Mary Porter (61.)

Third Generation, Ebenezer Chapin, born July 26, 1677, married ——, *Hannah Bliss*, born November 16, 1678, daughter of *John Bliss*, of Northampton, Mass., who married October 7, 1677, *Patience Burt*, born August 18, 1645, daughter of HENRY BURT, who came from England to Roxbury, Mass., in 1630, and removed to Springfield, Mass., in 1640, where he died April 30, 1662. His wife, Mrs. *Ulalie Burt*, died August 29, 1690.

Ebenezer Chapin died in Enfield, Conn., December 13, 1772.

Fourth Generation, Charles Chapin, born ——, 1720, married —— ——.

Fifth Generation, Phinehas Chapin, born February 16, 1757, married May 14, 1783, *Love Hurd*.

(JOHN HURD came from England and removed to Stratford, Conn., where he was a representative in 1649 to 1657, and died ——, 1681. He married December 15, 1662, *Sarah Thompson*, born April 1, 1642, daughter of JOHN THOMPSON, who came with his brothers, Anthony and William, with their families, in company with Gov. Theophilus Eaton, Rev. John Davenporte, William Andrews and others, from Coventry, Warwickshire, England, embarking at London on the ship "Hector," arriving at Boston, Mass., June 26, 1637. They removed thence to New Haven, Conn., where they signed the compact (or constitution for the colony) June 4, 1639. (See Mary P. Walton (178.)

John Thompson died in East Haven, Conn., December 11, 1674.

Second Generation, Benjamin Hurd, born February 16, 1666, married , 1692, *Sarah Walker.*

(ROBERT WALKER came from Manchester, England, to New England about 1632. He was one of the founders of the "Old South Church" in Boston, and died May 29, 1687, aged 80.

Second Generation, Joseph Walker, born July 19, 1646, married November 14, 1667, *Abigail Prudden*, born ——, 1647, daughter of Rev. *Peter Prudden*, before named.

Third Generation, Sarah Walker, born January 23, 1670, married *Benjamin Hurd* ——.)

Third Generation, Nathan Hurd, born July — —, 1694, married November 7, 1718, *Eunice Hinman.*

(EDWARD HINMAN came from England and settled at Stratford, Conn., previous to 1650. He married *Hannah Stiles*, daughter of FRANCIS STILES, who was born at Ampthill, Bedfordshire, England, August 1, 1602, who came from London in the ship "Christian" in 1635 to Dorchester, Mass., where "he sat down a short time." He removed in 1636 to Windsor, Conn. Edward Hinman died November 26, 1681.

Second Generation, Benjamin Hinman, born February ——, 1662, married at Woodbury, Conn., July 12, 1684, *Elizabeth Lamb*, daughter of *Samuel Lamb*, who came with his father, THOMAS LAMB, in the fleet with Winthrop in 1630.

Third Generation, Eunice Hinman, born May ——, 1696, married *Nathan Hurd* ——.

Fourth Generation, Gideon Hurd, born August 22, 1724, married May 20, 1752, *Sarah Graham.*

(Rev. JOHN GRAHAM, born in Edinburgh, Scotland, in 1694, was of the family of Graham of Montrose. He graduated at the University of Glasgow and Theological Institute of Edinburgh, Scotland, and came to New England in 1718 and married *Abigail Chauncey.*

(CHARLES CHAUNCEY, baptized November 5, 1592, son of George Chauncey, of Yardleigh, Herefordshire, England, graduated at Trinity College, Cambridge. England, A. M. 1624, and married *Catherine Eyre*, daughter of *Robert Eyre*, of Wiltshire, England. He was vicar of Ware, Herefordshire, from which he was ejected by Archbishob Laud in 1634. He came to Plymouth, Mass., in 1637, where he officiated as assistant to Rev. John Reyner. (See Henry P. Andrews (95.) He succeeded in 1654 Henry Dunster as president of Harvard University at Cambridge, Mass., where he died February 19, 1672, aged 80.

Second Generation, Rev. *Nathaniel Chauncey,* born ——, 1639, at Plymouth, Mass., graduated at Harvard University in 1661. He settled in the ministry at Hatfield, Mass., and married November 12, 1673, *Abigail Strong,* born ——, 1645, daughter of Elder JOHN STRONG, of Windsor, Conn., and Northampton, Mass. (See A. H. Porter (69.)

Third Generation, Nathaniel Chauncey, born September 26, 1681, graduated at Yale College in 1702, and settled at Durham, Conn. He married October 12, 1708, *Sarah Judson.*

(WILLIAM JUDSON came from England to Concord, Mass., in 1635. He removed to Stratford, Conn., and died in New Haven, Conn., in 1662. His wife, *Grace,* died September 29, 1659.

Second Generation, Joseph Judson, born in England, married October 24, 1644, *Sarah Porter* (4), daughter of JOHN PORTER (1), who came from England with wife, ROSE, and settled at Windsor, Conn.

Third Generation, James Judson, born September 24, 1650, married August 13, 1680, *Rebecca Welles.*

(THOMAS WELLES came from England previous to 1635 and settled at Swampscott, Mass., removing in 1636 to Hartford, Conn. He was a magistrate in 1637, Deputy Governor and Governor, and died June 23, 1654.

Second Generation, Thomas Welles, born in England about 1630, married June 23, 1654, *Anna Tuttle,* born in England, daughter of RICHARD TUTTLE, who came from England with wife, *Anna,* and family, in the ship "Planter" to Boston, Mass., in 1635 from London, England.

Third Generation, Rebecca Welles, born April 18, 1655, married August 13, 1680, *James Judson.*

Fourth Generation, Sarah Judson, born February 16, 1683, married October 12, 1708, Rev. *Nathaniel Chauncey.*

(CHARLES CHAUNCEY, born in England ——, 1592, son of *George Chauncey,* of Herefordshire, England, married *Katherine Eyre,* daughter of *Robert Eyre,* of Wiltshire. Charles Chauncey came to New England in 1638 and settled at Scituate, Mass. He had graduated at Trinity College, Oxford, England, A. M. 1624. In 1654 he succeeded Dunster as president of Harvard College, where he continued until his death, February 19, 1672, in his 80th year.

Second Generation, Nathaniel Chauncey, born in Plymouth, Mass., ——, 1639, graduated at Harvard College in 1661. He settled in the ministry at Hatfield, Mass., where he married November 12, 1673, *Abigail Strong,* born ——, 1645, daughter of Elder JOHN STRONG, of Windsor, Conn., and Northampton, Mass. (See Albert H. Porter (69.)

Third Generation, Nathaniel Chauncey, born September 26, 1681, married October 12, 1708, *Sarah Judson.*

Fifth Generation, Abigail Chauncey, born October 2, 1717, married Rev. *John Graham*. He settled in the ministry at Exeter, N. H., removing in 1722 to Stafford, Conn., and thence in 1732 to the pastorate of the church in Woodbury, Conn., where he died December ——, 1774, in his 81st year. His daughter, *Sarah Graham*, born March 18, 1735, married May 20, 1752, *Gideon Hurd*.

Fifth Generation, Love Hurd, born September 9, 1759, married *Phinehas Chapin*. He died in Salisbury, Conn., February 12, 1816. Mrs. Love Chapin died in Kent, Conn., April 15, 1844, aged 85.

Sixth Generation, Phinehas Chapin, born March 7, 1789, married March 1, 1809, *Lucinda Martin*, daughter of *Seth Martin*, who married June 6, 1788, *Mary Gordon*.

(ALEXANDER GORDON came from Scotland with wife *Jane*, arriving at Boston, Mass., November 2, 1719. He removed to Voluntown, Conn., and thence to Woodbury, Conn., where he died July 27, 1774, aged 104 years.

Second Generation, Robert Gordon, born March 14, 1730, married *Jeane Kasson*, daughter of WILLIAM KASSON, who came from Belfast, Ireland, to Boston, Mass., in 1722, removed to Bethlehem, Conn., and died July 5, 1791. William Kasson married *Elizabeth McKay*, and died ——, 1760.

Third Generation, Mary Gordon, born November 5, 1759, married June 6, 1788, *Seth Martin*, a descendant of *William Martin*, of Woodbury, Conn., who married *Abigail Curtis*, daughter of *Jonathan Curtis*, of Stratford, Conn., and his wife *Abigail Thompson*, daughter of JOHN THOMPSON, who came from England and settled at New Haven, Conn.

(WILLIAM CURTIS, born in Hatton, Warwickshire, England, embarked with wife *Elizabeth* and children in the ship "Lion" June 22, 1632, with Rev. John Eliot and others, and arrived at Scituate, Mass., December 16, 1632. He removed to Roxbury, Mass., where he (probably) died. His widow and children removed to Stratford, Conn., where she died in 1658.

Second Generation, William Curtis, born in England, lived in Stratford, and married about 1640 *Sarah* ——. He died in Stratford December 21, 1702.

Third Generation, Jonathan Curtis, born February 1, 1644, married *Abigail Thompson*, born May 1, 1646, daughter of *John Thompson*.

(Her sister, Sarah Thompson, born April ——, 1642, married *John Hurd*. (See *ante*.)

Fourth Generation, Abigail Curtis, born October 17, 1671, married *Seth Martin*.

Jonathan Curtis' brother, *Zechariah Curtis*, born November 15, 1659, married *Hannah Porter*, daughter of *Nathaniel Porter* (11). Another brother, *Josiah Curtis*, born August 1, 1662, married *Abigail Judson*, daughter of *Joseph Judson*, whose wife was *Sarah Porter* (4). A third brother, *Ebenezer Curtis*, born February 10, 1664, married *Ruth Porter*, daughter of *Nathaniel Porter* (11).

Fourth Generation, Lucinda Martin, born about 1792, married *Phinehas Chapin*.

Seventh Generation, Ruth A. Chapin, born ——, married *George W. Sterling*.

84

Eighth Generation, Lucinda R. Sterling, born July 4, 1842, married *John C. Holley.*

Their children were [being of the ninth generation :]
232. Alma Sterling Holley, b. May 9, 1864.
233. John Cofting Holley, b. ——; died in infancy.

John M. Holley died November 3, 1865.

[141.] MARIA COFFING HOLLEY married June 7, 1865, *William B. Rudd,* a descendant of *Nathaniel Rudd,* whose wife was *Waity Hopkins,* daughter of *Samuel Hopkins,* of Milford, Conn., who married at New Haven, Conn., December 5, 1667, *Hannah Turner,* daughter of Capt. NATHANIEL TURNER.

Capt. Nathaniel Turner came in the fleet with JOHN WINTHROP in 1630 and settled at Lynn, Mass. He was a representative in the first General Court in Massachusetts in 1634, and served in the Pequot war in 1637. He removed in 1638 to New Haven, Conn., and in 1640 was one of the purchasers of Stamford, Conn. He sailed for England in January, 1646, in that ill-fated bark, never heard from, "until her apparition was seen in the air." (See Augusta Porter (50) and Appendix (G.)

Nathaniel Rudd was a descendant of *Nathaniel Rudd, Sr.*, who married April 16, 1685, *Mary Post,* born ——, 1662, daughter of *John Post,* of Saybrook, Conn., born in 1627, who came from England with his father, STEPHEN POST, in 1634, who removed to Hartford, Conn. John Post married March ——, 1652, *Hester Hyde,* daughter of WILLIAM HYDE, from England, who settled in Hartford, Conn., in 1636, removed to Saybrook, Conn., and died in Norwich, Conn., Jan. 6, 1681.

Nathaniel Rudd, Sr., born about 1654, was son of JONATHAN RUDD, who came from England in the fleet with Winthrop in July, 1635, and removed to Saybrook, Conn., in 1646, and thence to Hartford, Conn., in 1651, and died in 1658.

[Their children were [being of the ninth generation :]
234. Maria Holley Rudd, b. February 23, 1866 ; d. March 21, 1866.
235. Alexander Holley Rudd, b. March 8, 1867.
236. Fanny Rudd, b. May 5, 1869.
237. William Beardslee Rudd, b. June 18, 1870 ; d. September 8, 1870.
238. George Robert Rudd, b. November 9, 1872 ; d. March 11, 1877.
239. Malcolm Day Rudd, b. April 3, 1877.
240. Charles Edward Rudd, b. January 2, 1881.

[142.] WILLIAM HOLLEY BURRALL graduated at the Rensselaer Institute, Troy, N. Y., in 1851 ; chief engineer of Cairo and Fulton railroad in 1851 ; civil engineer and bridge builder in Springfield, Mass. ; unmarried.

[143.] JOHN MILTON BURRALL married November 19, 1872, *Mary H. Dickinson*, at Fort Reid, Florida, daughter of *John Dickinson*, of Richmond, Va. He died at sea May 8, 1880, while on the passage from Florida to New York.

Their children were [being of the ninth generation :]
241. William D. Burrall, b. February ——, 1876.
242. John D. Burrall, b. February 20, 1880.

[145.] SARAH BOSTWICK BURRALL married at Lakeville, Litchfield county, Conn., December 26, 1861, *Henry H. Anderson*, counselor-at-law of New York city, son of *Rufus Anderson*, and his wife, *Eliza Hill*.

Their children were [being of the ninth generation :]
243. Henry Burrall Anderson, b. January 2, 1863.
244. William Burrall Anderson, b. December 2, 1864.
245. Chandler Parsons Anderson, b. September 5, 1868.
246. Harriett Holley Anderson, b. July 17, 1870; d. August 28, 1870.

[148.] PORTER STODDARD BURRALL married June 12, 1873, *Anna E. Croom*, daughter of *George W. Croom*, and his wife, *Julia M. Church*, both of Atlanta, Georgia. They have no children.

[154.] MARY A. ROBBINS married October 6, 1858, *Alonzo W. Church*, born in Athens, Georgia, son of —— *Church*, president of the University of Georgia.

Their children were [being of the ninth generation :]
247. Samuel R. Church, b. December 24, 1863.
248. John R. Church, b. November 13, 1865.
249. James R. Church, b. October 11, 1866.
250. Sarah R. Church, b. January 24, 1868.
251. Mary R. Church, b. June 29, 1869.
252. Alonzo W. Church, b. December 31, 1870.
253. William W. Church, b. December 17, 1874.

[156.] MILTON HOLLEY ROBBINS married April 16, 1863, *Anne Eliza Bostwick*.

[ARTHUR BOSTWICK came from the county of Chester (or Cheshire), England, and settled in Stratford, Conn., about 1645.

Second Generation. John Bostwick, born in England, married *Mary Brinsmeade*, born July 24, 1640, daughter of *Daniel Brinsmeade*, who came with his father, JOHN BRINSMEADE, from England to Charlestown, Mass., in 1637, and removed to Stratford, Conn., in 1646, where he died ——, 1673. "leaving a good estate to his widow, Mary."

Third Generation, Zechariah Bostwick, born July 25, 1669, married ——, *Susannah* ——.

Fourth Generation, Benjamin Bostwick, born ——, 1710, married ——.

Fifth Generation, Benjamin Bostwick, born ——, 1740, married *Anna Smith*.

(SAMUEL SMITH came from England with wife *Elizabeth* to Watertown, Mass., in the ship "Elizabeth" from Ipswich, England, Capt. William Andrews, master, in April, 1634. (See Doct. Joshua Porter (47). He removed to Weathersfield, Conn., and was a representative from 1641 to 1653. In 1659 he removed to Hadley, Mass., where he died in 1680, aged 78. His wife *Elizabeth* died March 16, 1686, aged 84 years.

Second Generation, Chileab Smith, born ——, 1636, married October 2, 1661, *Hannah Hitchcock*, daughter of *Luke Hitchcock*, an early settler of Weathersfield, Conn.

Chileab Smith died in Hadley, Mass., March 7, 1731, aged 95 years.

Third Generation, Luke Smith, born April 16, 1666, married ——, 1690, *Mary Crowe*, born February 5, 1672, daughter of *Samuel Crowe*, who married May 17, 1671, *Hannah Lewis*, born ——, 1652, daughter of WILLIAM LEWIS, of Farmington, Conn., who married ——, 1644, *Mary Hopkins*, daughter of WILLIAM HOPKINS, who came from England with wife *Mary* and settled in Stratford, Conn., in 1640.

(WILLIAM LEWIS, born in England, came with his parents, WILLIAM and AMY LEWIS, in the ship "Lion," arriving at Boston, Mass., September 16, 1632. He removed in 1636 to Hartford, Conn., and thence to Hadley, Mass., on the settlement of that place in 1659. He was a representative, and removed to Farmington. Conn., where he died August 2, 1683.

(Samuel Crowe was son of JOHN CROWE, who came from England and settled in Hartford, Conn., where he was one of the original proprietors. (See Sally P. Holley (81.) He was one of the largest land proprietors in Connecticut. He married *Elizabeth Goodwin*, only child of WILLIAM GOODWIN, who came from England in the ship "Lion," arriving at Boston, Mass., September 16, 1632, and settled at Cambridge, Mass., where he was a deputy in the first general court of Massachusetts in 1634. He removed with Hooker and Stone to Hartford, Conn., in May, 1636, and was a ruling elder in the church at Hartford, as also at Hadley, Mass., whither he removed with a large part of the congregation in 1659. He removed again in 1670 to Farmington, Conn., and died March 11, 1673. His wife, Mrs. *Susannah Goodwin*, died May 17, 1676. (See Moses Lyman (159.) Samuel Crowe was killed in the "Fall's fight" with the Pequots May ——, 1676.

Fourth Generation, Joseph Smith, born September 18, 1708, married May 24, 1739, *Miriam Church*. He died July   , 1797; she died ——, 1791.

(RICHARD CHURCH, from England. (See Geo. W. Holley (80.)

Second Generation, Samuel Church, born about 1636, married *Mary Churchill*, born March 24, 1639, daughter of JOSIAH CHURCHILL, who came from England to Watertown, Mass., in 1634, and removed to Weathersfield, Conn., where he married in 1638 *Elizabeth Foote*, daughter of NATHANIEL FOOTE, who came from England with wife *Elizabeth* and settled in Watertown, Mass., about 1633, and removed to Weathersfield, Conn., in 1636, where he was a representative, and died in 1644. (See Doct. Joshua Porter (47.)

Third Generation, Benjamin Church, born September 1, 1680, married January 30, 1709, *Miriam Horey*.

(DANIEL HOVEY came from England and settled at Ipswich, Mass., in 1637. He married in 1640 *Rebecca Andrews*, daughter of ROBERT ANDREWS, who came from England in 1632 with his wife *Elizabeth*, and settled in Ipswich, where he was the keeper of the "ordinary" (inn).

Second Generation, Lieut *Thomas Horey*, born ——, 1648, settled in Hadley. He married November ——, 1677, *Sarah Cooke*, born January 31, 1662, daughter of Capt. *Aaron Cooke*, of Hadley, who married May 30, 1661, *Sarah Westwood*, daughter of WILLIAM WESTWOOD, who, with his wife *Bridget*, came from England in the ship "Francis" in April, 1634, and removed in 1636 with Rev. Thomas Hooker to Hartford, Conn. He was a member of the first general court at Hartford and Hadley, Mass., to which place he removed, and where he died, April 9, 1669, aged 63. His wife, *Bridget*, died ——, 1644.

(Capt. *Aaron Cooke*, born February 21, 1640, was son of AARON COOKE, who came from England to Dorchester, Mass., in 1630, and removed to Windsor, Conn., in 1636. He was, with JOHN PORTER (1), a member of the first troop of horse raised in Connecticut, and was in command of Major John Mason. He married *Joanna Denslow*, daughter of NICHOLAS DENSLOW, who came from England in the ship "Mary and John" in 1630 to Dorchester, Mass., and removed to Windsor, Conn.

Second Generation, Miriam Horey, born ——, 1689, married *Benjamin Church*.

Fourth Generation. Miriam Church, born May 12, 1712, married May 24, 1739, *Joseph Smith*.

Fifth Generation, Anna Smith, born ——, 1746, married *Benjamin Bostwick*, son of *Zechariah Bostwick*, of Stratford, Conn., who was born July 25, 1669. Zechariah Bostwick was son of ARTHUR BOSTWICK, who came from Cheshire, England, and settled in Stratford, Conn., about 1650. Benjamin Bostwick removed to New Milford, Conn. He was a captain in the war of the revolution.

Sixth Generation. Rufus Bostwick, born February 15, 1786, married ——.

Seventh Generation, Robert Bostwick, born April 7, 1811, married ——.

Eighth Generation, Anna E. Bostwick, born March 29, 1840, married *Milton H. Robbins*.

Their children were [being of the ninth generation :]

254. Mary E. Robbins, b. October 4, 1865.
255. Samuel B. Robbins, b. October 15, 1867.
256. Milton H. Robbins, b. January 17, 1871.

[159.] MOSES LYMAN graduated at Brown University in 1858. He married, first, December 31, 1863, *Ellen A. Douglas*.

[WILLIAM DOUGLAS came from England to Boston, Mass., in 1640, with wife, *Anna*. She was daughter of *Thomas Maybell*, of Ringstead, Northamptonshire, England. William Douglas removed to New London, Conn., where he died in July, 1682, aged 71.

Second Generation, William Douglas, born April 1, 1645, married December 18, 1667, *Abiah Hough*, born September 16, 1648, daughter of WILLIAM HOUGH, who came from Cheshire, England, in 1640, and married October 28, 1645, *Sarah Caulkins*, daughter of HUGH CALKINS, who came from England in 1639 and settled at Lynn, Mass., removing to Gloucester, and thence to Norwich, Conn., where he died in 1690, aged 90. William Hough died August 10, 1683. (See P. P. Wiggins (100.)

Third Generation, William Douglas, born February 19, 1672, in New London, Conn., married *Sarah Proctor*, born January 28, 1677, daughter, probably, of *John Proctor*, whose wife was *Elizabeth Bassett*, daughter of *John Bassett*, of New Haven, Conn.

John Proctor, born in 1632, was son of *John Proctor*, who came from London, England, in the ship "Susan and Ellen" in 1635, with his wife *Martha* and children, and settled in Ipswich, Mass.

William Douglas removed to Plainfield, Conn., and in 1705 was one of the founders of the first church, of which he was the first deacon. He died August 10, 1747.

Fourth Generation, Asa Douglas, born December 11, 1715, married ——, 1737, *Rebecca Wheeler*, born August 28, 1718, a descendant of THOMAS WHEELER, who came from England and settled in Fairfield, Conn.

Capt. Asa Douglas removed to Canaan, Litchfield county, Conn., in 1746, and thence in 1766 to Jericho, Mass. (now Stephentown, Columbia county, N. Y.) The house he then built was in the war of the revolution used as a jail, and is now (in 1882) in good repair. He died November 12, 1792.

Fifth Generation, William Douglas, born August 22, 1743, in Plainfield, Conn., married *Hannah Cole*, born December ——, 1744, daughter of *Samuel Cole*, of Farmington, Conn., who was son of *John Cole*, of Hartford, Conn. William

Douglas was a captain in the war of the revolution. He died December 29, 1811. Mrs. Hannah Douglas died December 24, 1795.

Sixth Generation, William Douglas, born January 1, 1768, in Stephentown, N. Y., married in 1798 *Margaret Hunter.*

(ROBERT CAMPBELL, born in Argyleshire, Scotland, in 1673, was of a family which removed to the county of Ulster, Ireland. With his wife *Janet* he came to New England, and in 1719 settled in Voluntown, Windham county, Conn., where, with other "Scotch-Irish" families (Douglas, Dixon, Edmonds, Gibson, Houston, Hunter, Wylie, etc.), they established the first Presbyterian church. Robert Campbell died February 14, 1725, aged 52 years.

Second Generation, Doct. *John Campbell,* born in county Ulster, Ireland, about 1690, came with his parents to New London, Conn., and removed to Voluntown, where he married November 19, 1719, *Agnes Allen.* He was the first physician in the town, and died in 1773 or '74.

(EDWARD ALLEN came from Scotland in 1636 to Ipswich, Mass. He married *Sarah Kimball,* daughter of RICHARD KIMBALL, who came from Ipswich, England, in the ship "Elizabeth" to Watertown, Mass., in 1634, with his wife *Ursula.* They removed to Suffield, Conn., where he died in 1675. Mrs. Sarah Allen died June 12, 1696.

Second Generation, John Allen, born about 1656, married February 22, 1681, *Elizabeth Prichard,* daughter of *William Prichard,* of Suffield, Conn., who was son of WILLIAM PRICHARD, who came from England and settled at Lynn, Mass., in 1645, thence removing to Ipswich in 1648, and afterwards one of the first settlers of Brookfield, Fairfield county, Conn.

Third Generation, Agnes Allen, born ——, 1692, married November 19, 1719, Doct. *John Campbell.*

Third Generation, Sarah Campbell, born July 31, 1722, married December 9, 1742, *John Wylie,* son of JOHN WYLIE and his wife, *Agnes Parke,* who came from county Antrim, Ireland, in transitu from Scotland, and settled in Voluntown, where he died December 26, 1781. Mrs. Agnes Wylie died in New Lebanon, Columbia county, N. Y., January 28, 1807, at the residence of her daughter.

Fourth Generation, Agnes Wylie, born July 26, 1754, married ——, 1773, *Andrew Hunter,* a descendant of *William Hunter,* of Springfield, Mass., and his wife *Priscilla,* who was, probably, son of ROBERT HUNTER, from England, with wife *Mary,* who settled in Ipswich, Mass., in 1640.

Andrew Hunter settled in New Lebanon, Columbia county, N. Y.

Fifth Generation, Margaret Hunter, born December 17, 1776, married ——, 1798, *William Douglas.* William Douglas died in Stephentown, N. Y., December 13, 1821. Mrs. Margaret Douglas died November 8, 1833.

Seventh Generation, Edwin A. Douglas, born March 3, 1804, married February 6, 1834. *Harriett C. Dexter.*

(THOMAS DEXTER came from England in the fleet with John Winthrop in 1630 and settled at Lynn, Mass. He removed to Barnstable, Mass., where he died in 1677.

Second Generation, William Dexter, born about 1632, married July ----, 1653, *Sarah Vincent,* daughter of *John Vincent,* of Lynn, Mass. He removed to Rochester, Mass., where he died about 1690.

Third Generation, Benjamin Dexter, born February 6, 1670, married in Rochester, Mass., ----, 1696, ---- ----, daughter of Rev. *Samuel Arnold,* son of SAMUEL ARNOLD, of Sandwich, Mass., 1643, and Yarmouth, who came from England. Benjamin Dexter died in 1734.

Fourth Generation, Seth Dexter, born October 3, 1713, married in 1742 *Elizabeth* ----.

Fifth Generation, Seth Dexter, born December 26, 1743, married December 18, 1768, *Deborah Haskell,* born at Dartmouth, Mass., July 26, 1743, a descendant, probably, of WILLIAM HASKELL, who came from England and settled at Gloucester, Mass., in 1642, and who married November 6, 1643, *Mary Tybbott,* daughter of *Walter Tybbott,* of Gloucester, Mass.

Seth Dexter removed to Pine Meadow, Litchfield county, Conn., where he died August 1, 1797. Mrs. Deborah Dexter died February 14, 1830, aged 87.

Sixth Generation, Seth Dexter, born December 22, 1776, married May 5, 1803, *Sylvia Gaylord.*

— (WILLIAM GAYLORD, a deacon of the church gathered at Plymouth, England, in March, 1630, came in the ship "Mary and John," arriving at Dorchester, Mass., May 30, 1635. He removed to Windsor, Conn., where he died July 20, 1673, aged 88 years.

— *Second Generation, William Gaylord,* born in England about 1620, married February 24, 1644, *Anna Porter* (5), daughter of JOHN PORTER (1) and his wife, *Rose.* William Gaylord died Dec. 14, 1656. Mrs. Anna Gaylord died ----, 1654.

—*Third Generation, Nathaniel Gaylord,* born September 3, 1656, married October 7, 1673, *Abigail Bissell,* born November 23, 1658, daughter of *Thomas Bissell,* of Windsor, Conn., who married October 11, 1655, *Abigail Moore,* born in 1639, daughter of JOHN MOORE, who came from England in the ship "Mary and John" to Dorchester, Mass., in 1630. He was a deacon in the church, and removed with Rev. John Warham to Windsor, Conn., where he died September 18, 1677.

—Thomas Bissell, born in England, was son of JOHN BISSELL, who came from Somersetshire, England, to Plymouth, Mass., and removed with Rev. Ephraim Hewett to Windsor, Conn., August 17, 1639, where he died October 3, 1677, aged 88 years.

Fourth Generation, Nathaniel Gaylord, born November 23, 1681, married January 7, 1707, his cousin, *Elizabeth Gaylord,* born April 18, 1682, daughter of *William Gaylord, Jr.,* born in England, son of WILLIAM GAYLORD from England.

William Gaylord, Jr., married December 21, 1671, *Ruth Crowe*, born ——, 1652, daughter of JOHN CROWE, who came from England to Charlestown, Mass., in 1635, and removed to Hartford, Conn., in 1636, where he was an original proprietor, and married *Elizabeth Goodwin*, only child of WILLIAM GOODWIN, who came from England in the ship "Lion" September 16, 1632, and was a representative in the first general court in Massachusetts in 1634.

William Goodwin removed in 1636 with Rev. Thomas Hooker and that company to Hartford, Conn., and thence in 1659 to Hadley, Mass. He was ruling elder of the church, and died March 11, 1673. His widow, Mrs. Susannah Goodwin, died May 17, 1676. (See Sally P. Holley (81) and Milton H. Robbins (156.)

Fifth Generation, Eliakim Gaylord, born December 4, 1707, married —— , 1743, *Elizabeth Hayden*.

(WILLIAM HAYDEN came from England in the ship "Mary and John" to Dorchester, Mass., in 1630. He served with Capt. John Mason in the Pequot war in 1630. His residence was in Hartford, Conn., whence he removed in 1643 to Windsor, and died in Killingworth, Conn., September 27, 1699. His wife died in Windsor July 17, 1655.

Second Generation. Daniel Hayden, born September 2, 1610, married November 16, 1664, *Hannah Wilcoxson*, daughter of WILLIAM WILCOXSON, who came from England in the ship "Planter" from London in 1635 to Dorchester, Mass., with wife *Margaret*, and removed to Hartford, and thence to Stratford, Conn., where he died in 1652. Daniel Hayden died March 22, 1714. Mrs. Hannah Hayden died April 19, 1722.

Third Generation, William Hayden, born January 1, 1675, married January 21, 1702, *Elizabeth Gibbes*.

(GILES GIBBES came from England in the ship "Mary and John" in 1630 and removed to Windsor, Conn. He was a selectman, and died May 21, 1641. His wife, Mrs. Katherine Gibbes, died October 24, 1660.

Second Generation, Samuel Gibbes, born ——, 1636, married April 15, 1664, *Hepzibah Deble*, born December 25, 1642, daughter of *Thomas Deble*, of Windsor, who came from England with his father, ROBERT DEBLE (or Dibble), to Dorchester, Mass., in 1634, and settled in Windsor, Conn., removing thence to Simsbury, Conn.

Third Generation, Elizabeth Gibbes, born January 30, 1668, married *William Hayden*.

Fourth Generation, Elizabeth Hayden, born April 24, 1712, married ——, 1743, *Eliakim Gaylord*.

Sixth Generation, Eleazar Gaylord, born May 14, 1753, married ——, 1780, *Sylvia Clark*, a descendant of DANIEL CLARK, who came from England in company with Rev. Ephraim Hewett August 17, 1639, and settled in Windsor, Conn.

Daniel Clark was a magistrate and secretary of the colony from 1658 to 1664;

representative from 1657 to 1661 ; captain of the "troop of horse." He married June 30, 1644, *Mary Newberry*, daughter of THOMAS NEWBERRY, who was born in Exeter, Devonshire, England, and came in the ship "Mary and John" to Dorchester, Mass., in May, 1630. He had a large farm at Squantum, and lands at Neponsett, and in 1635 was appointed to oversee the works at the castle. He was early engaged in the Connecticut emigration, but died in 1636. His widow, *Jane*, with their children, however, removed there.

Seventh Generation, Sylvia Gaylord, born September 8, 1787, married May 5, 1808, *Seth Dexter*.

Eighth Generation, Harriett Clarke Dexter, born April 5, 1809, married February 6, 1834, *Edwin A. Douglas*. He died at Mauch Chunk, Pa., Dec. 3, 1859.

Ninth Generation, Ellen Augusta Douglas, born ——, married December 31, 1863, *Moses Lyman*.

[Their children were [being of the ninth generation :]

257. Moses Lyman, b. July 17, 1865.
258. Isabel Douglass Lyman, b. March 21, 1867.
259. Harriett Dexter Lyman, b. July 27, 1870 ; d. August 7, 1871.

Mrs. Ellen A. Lyman died August 17, 1871.

Moses Lyman married, second, March 6, 1873, *Sarah H. Beebe.*

(JOHN PORTER (1), from England, with wife *Rose.*

Second Generation, Nathaniel Porter, born February 29, 1640, married ——, 1664, *Anna Groves*, born ——, 1664, daughter of PHILIP GROVES, who came from England in 1636 and settled in Hartford, Conn., where he was a representative. He removed to Stratford, Conn., and was a "noted captain in King Philip's war." He died in Stratford, Conn., January —, 1680.

Third Generation, Ruth Porter, born November 22, 1669, married ——, 1690, *Ebenezer Curtis.*

(WILLIAM CURTIS embarked at London, England, June 22, 1632, on the ship "Lion," with wife *Elizabeth* and their children, landing at Scituate, Mass., December 16, 1632 ; removed to Roxbury, Mass., where he died. His wife *Sarah*, with children, removed to Stratford, Conn., where she died in 1658. (See Sally P. Holley (81.)

Second Generation, Capt. *William Curtis*, born in England, married ——. He died in Stratford, Conn., December 21, 1702.

Third Generation, Ebenezer Curtis, born July 10, 1657, married *Ruth Porter;* his brother, *Zechariah Curtis*, born November 30, 1659, married *Hannah Porter:* his brother, *Josiah Curtis*, born August 1, 1662, married *Abigail Judson*, born October 17, 1669, daughter of *Joseph Judson*, whose wife was *Sarah Porter* (4).

Fourth Generation, Ephraim Curtis, born September 27, 1693, married December 20, 1720, *Hannah Burroughs*, daughter (probably) of *John Burroughs*, of

New London, Conn., who married December 14, 1670, *Mary Culver*, daughter of *John Culver*, of New London, Conn.

Fifth Generation, Ruth Curtis, born October 27, 1723, in Stratford Conn., married ——, 1749, *James Beebe*, a descendant of *Nathaniel Beebe*, son of *Samuel Beebe*, of New London, Conn., who married *Mary Keeney*, born about 1638, daughter of *William Keeney*, of New London, Conn., who, with wife *Agnes*, came from England and settled in New London in 1651.

Sarah H. Beebe, a descendant of *James Beebe*, married March 2, 1673, *Moses Lyman*.

Their children were [being of the ninth generation :]

260. Margaret Lyman, b. July 24, 1874; d. November 25, 1875.
261. Lucy Beebe Lyman. b. June 18, 1875; d. April 1, 1876.
262. Mary Alice Lyman, b. July 8, 1877.
263. Samuel Lyman, b. July 2, 1879.

[160.] MARY LYMAN married in Goshen, Conn., June 15, 1865, *Philip Wells*. He died in Amenia, Duchess county, N. Y., January 28, 1872. She married, second, August 5, 1877, Rev. *Lyman Phelps*. There were no children by either marriage.

[161.] ALICE LYMAN married October 24, 1872, *John T. Sawyer*, of Waverly, Tioga county, N. Y.

Their child [being of the ninth generation :]
264. Ellen Sawyer b. May 12, 1874.

[164.] ULYSSES S. GRANT graduated at West Point Military Academy in 1843. He served throughout the Mexican war; was brevetted captain "for gallant services." He married August —, 1848, *Julia Boggs Dent*, daughter of *Frederick Dent*, a merchant of St. Louis, Mo., and his wife, *Ellen Wrenshall*.

Capt. U. S. Grant resigned his commission in the army in 1854. At the commencement of the civil war he was appointed colonel of the 21st Illinois volunteers and brigadier-general August 7, 1861. He served in the campaign in Tennessee at *Fort Donelson*, etc., and was promoted to major-general. Battles of *Corinth, Shiloh* (or Pittsburgh Landing), *Siege of Vicksburgh, Chattanooga;* promoted to lieutenant-general; battles of the *Wilderness, Spottsylvania, North Anna, Cold Harbor, Siege of Richmond, Five Forks,* etc. ; President of the United States 1868–76.

Their children were [being of the ninth generation :]

265. Frederick D. Grant, b. May 30, 1850; married Ida M. Honore.
266. Ulysses S. Grant, b. July 22, 1852.
267. Ellen W. Grant, b. July 4, 1855; married Algernon C. F. Sartoris.
268. Jesse Root Grant, b. February 6, 1858; married Lizzie Chapman.

[178.] MARY PORTER WALTON married at Saratoga Springs, N. Y., August 28, 1878, *Arthur A. Camp*, M. D., son of Rev. *Norman W. Camp*, whose wife was *Matilda Hopkins*, daughter of Rt. Rev. *John H. Hopkins*, bishop of Vermont.

(Rev. Norman W. Camp was probably a descendant of *Daniel Camp*, who married *Mary Whittlesey*.

(JOHN WHITTLESEY came from England about 1650 and settled in Saybrook, Conn. He married June 26, 1664, *Ruth Dudley*, born April 20, 1645, daughter of WILLIAM DUDLEY, who came from Ockley, county of Surrey, England, in 1638, and settled at Guilford, Conn. (See Mary Porter (61.)

John Whittlesey died April 15, 1704. Mrs. Ruth Whittlesey died September 29, 1714.

Second Generation, Eliphalet Whittlesey, born September 11, 1665, married December 1, 1702, *Mary Pratt*, born May 24, 1677, daughter of *John Pratt*, of Saybrook, Conn., who married August 10, 1676, *Mary Andrews*, daughter of EDWARD ANDREWS, who came from England and settled in Hartford, Conn., in 1655.

Third Generation, Eliphalet Whittlesey, born May 10, 1714, married December 16, 1736, *Dorothy Kellogg*, born ——, 1717, daughter of *Martin Kellogg*, of Newington, Conn.

(JOSEPH KELLOGG. (See Abigail P. Stoddard (62).

Second Generation, Martin Kellogg, born October 1, 1660, married December 10, 1684, *Anna Hinsdale*, born February 22, 1666, daughter of *Samuel Hinsdale*, whose wife was *Mehitabel Johnston*, daughter of *Humphrey Johnston*, born in England, son of JOHN JOHNSTON, who came from England in the fleet with John Winthrop, with wife *Margery*, and was a representative in the first general court in 1634; a member of the ancient and honorable artillery company in 1638. He lived in Roxbury, Mass., where he died September 30, 1659.

Samuel Hinsdale lived in Hadley, Mass. He removed to Deerfield, Mass., where he was killed by the Indians September 8, 1675. He was born March 5, 1642, son of ROBERT HINSDALE, who came from England to Dedham, Mass., about 1636.

Third Generation, Dorothy Kellogg, born ——, 1717, married *Eliphalet Whittlesey*.

Fourth Generation, Martin Whittlesey, born October 5, 1737, married *Sarah*

Deming, a descendant, probably, of *John Deming*, of Weathersfield, Conn. (See Doct. Joshua Porter (47.)

Martin Whittlesey lived in New Preston, Conn., served in the war of the revolution, and died in 1800.

Fifth Generation, Mary Whittlesey, born December ——, 1767, married *Daniel Camp*, a descendant of NICHOLAS CAMP, who came from Nazing, county of Essex, England, in the ship "Lion" in 1631 with Rev. John Eliot, the "apostle to the Indians," who was son of Roger Eliot and Catherine Camp, of Nazing, England.

Nicholas Camp was an early settler of Milford, Conn., in 1639. He married *Catherine Thompson*, daughter of ANTHONY THOMPSON, who came from England in 1637 with Gov. Theophilus Eaton, and removed to New Haven, Conn., in 1639.

Their children were [being of the tenth generation :]

269. Arthur Walton Camp, b. September 3, 1879.
270. Ethel Camp, b. November 25, 1880.

[179.] HENRY CRUGER WALTON married July 15, 1879, in Philadelphia, Pa., *Virginia Clay Jones*, daughter of Maj. *John Richter Jones*, whose wife was *Anne E. Clay*.

Major J. R. Jones was an officer of the Union army, and was killed in North Carolina May 23, 1863.

(ROBERT CLAY, of Bridge House, Chesterfield, in Derbyshire, England, was an officer of the English army. He married *Hannah Slater*.

Second Generation, Robert Clay, of Bridge House, born ——, 1668 (baptized at Chesterfield December 9, 1688), came to Delaware and married December 16, 1710, *Anne Curtis*, born November 15, 1690, daughter of *Winlolock Curtis*, of Kent county, Delaware. Robert Clay was lost at sea in 1717. Mrs. Anne Clay died May 5, 1747.

Third Generation, Slater Clay, born November 2, 1711, married February 12, 1740, *Anne Curtis*, daughter of *Joseph Curtis*, and died February ——, 1767.

Fourth Generation, Curtis Clay, born April 9, 1747, married September ——, 1766, *Margaret Wood*. He died September 11, 1809.

Fifth Generation, Joseph Clay, born ——, 1768, married ——, 1805, *Mary Ashmeade*. He died ——, 1811. Mrs. Mary Clay died February 10, 1871, aged 89 years.

Sixth Generation, Anne Eliza Clay, born July 26, 1810, married, first, *Anthony Lausatt*; second, Maj. *John Richter Jones*.

Seventh Generation, Virginia Clay Jones, born ——, married July 15, 1879, *Henry Cruger Walton*.

Their only child [being of the tenth generation :]

271. Matilda C. Walton, b. June 1, 1881.

Henry C. Walton died at Saratoga Springs July 19, 1881.

ADDENDA.

[Page 20, *et seq.*]

Gen. Peter B. Porter married *Lætitia Preston Breckinridge*, born June 13, 1786. She was then the widow of Col. *Alfred Grayson*, of Virginia, their only child having been *John Breckinridge Grayson*, who graduated at the Military Academy, West Point, and became a colonel in the United States army, and afterwards a brigadier-general in the Confederate army, and died about 1865.

Mrs. Lætitia (Breckinridge-Grayson) Porter died in Buffalo, N. Y., September 1, 1831.

Gen. Peter B. Porter died at Niagara Falls, N. Y., March 20, 1844.

[Page 43.]

A. H. Holley (78) married, third, November 11, 1856, *Sarah C. Day*, daughter of Hon. *Thomas Day*, of Hartford, Conn., who was a descendant of *Thomas Day*, of Springfield, Mass., who married October 27, 1659, *Sarah Cooper*, daughter of Lieut. THOMAS COOPER, who came from England in the ship "Christian" in 1635, and removed to Springfield, Mass., in 1641. He was killed by the Indians October 5, 1675.

Thomas Day was son of ROBERT DAY, who came from England in the ship "Elizabeth" in 1634, from Ipswich, England, and settled at Cambridge, Mass., removing thence with Hooker and that company in 1636 to Hartford, Conn. His wife, *Editha*, was a sister of EDWARD STEBBINS, from England, to Cambridge, Mass., in 1633, who removed to Hartford, Conn., and died in 1663.

Hon. Thomas Day married *Sarah Coit*.

(JOHN COIT came from England with wife *Mary* to Dorchester, Mass., in 1636. He removed to New London, Conn., in 1651, and died April 25, 1659.

Second Generation, *Joseph Coit*, born in England, married July 13, 1667, *Martha Harris*, born ———, 1648, daughter of WILLIAM HARRIS, who came from England to Charlestown, Mass., in 1642, with wife *Edith*, and removed to Weathersfield, Conn., and died May 27, 1704.

Third Generation, Rev. *Joseph Coit*, born April 4, 1673, graduated at Harvard college in 1697; minister at Norwich and Plainfield, Conn. He married September 18, 1705, *Experience Wheeler*, born May 21, 1685, daughter of *Isaac Wheeler*, of Stonington, Conn., who married January 10, 1668, *Martha Parke*, born ——, 1646, daughter of *Thomas Parke*, of Weathersfield, Conn., who was son of ROBERT PARKE, who came from England and settled at Weathersfield, Conn., in 1639, removing in 1649 to New London, Conn. (See Eunice Porter, 49.)

Fourth Generation, Samuel Coit, born ——, 1708, settled in North Preston, Conn. He removed to Griswold, Conn. He was colonel of militia, judge, etc. He married in 1730 *Sarah Spaulding*, daughter of *Benjamin Spaulding*, of Plainfield, Conn., and died October 4, 1792, aged 84.

Fifth Generation, Wheeler Coit, born February 24, 1738, married December 26, 1765, *Mehitabel Lester*, daughter of *Timothy Lester*, of Preston, Conn., a descendant of ANDREW LESTER, from England, to Gloucester, Mass., in 1643, with wife *Barbara*, and removed to New London, Conn.

Sixth Generation, Sarah Coit, born September 27, 1786, married Hon. *Thomas Day*, of Hartford, Conn.

Seventh Generation, Sarah Coit Day, born September 23, 1813, married Hon. A. H. *Holley*.

APPENDIX.

(A.)

The principal planters of Massachusetts, says Chalmers, were English country gentlemen, of no inconsiderable fortunes; of enlarged understandings, improved by liberal education; of extreme ambition, concealed under the appearance of religious humility.

The leading emigrants to Massachusetts were of that brotherhood of men who, by force of social consideration, as well as intelligence and resolute patriotism, moulded the public opinion and action of England in the first half of the sixteenth century. While the larger part stayed at home to found, as it proved, the short lived English republic, another part devoted themselves at once to the erection of free institutions in this distant wilderness.

In an important sense the associates of the *Massachusetts Company* were builders of the British as well as the New England commonwealth. Some ten or twelve served in the Long Parliament. Of the four commoners of that Parliament, distinguished by Lord Clarendon, as first in influence, *Vane* had been governor of the company, and *Hampden*, *Pym* and *Fiennes* (all patentees of Connecticut) were consulted upon its affairs, as also the *Earl of Warwick*, and those excellent persons, *Lord Say-and-Sele* and *Lord Brooke*, both of whom at one time proposed to emigrate.

The company's meetings placed *Winthrop* and his colleagues in relations with numerous persons destined to act busy parts in the stirring times that were approaching; *Brereton* and *Hewson* (afterwards two of the parliamentary major-generals); with *Philip Nye*, who helped Sir Henry Vane to "cozen" the Scottish Presbyterian commissioners; with *Samuel Vassall;* with *John Venn*, who, at the head of six thousand citizens, beset the House of Lords during the trial of Lord Strafford, and who King Charles, after the battle of Edge-Hill, excluded from his offer of pardon; with *Owen Rowe*, the fire-brand of the city; with *Thomas Andrews*, the Lord Mayor of London, who proclaimed the abolition of royalty, and others of equal distinction.

(B.)

Wood's history of Long Island contains the following record. Rev. *John Youngs*, of Southold, had been minister of St. Margaret's church in Suffolk, England. He came with his wife *Joan* and six children to America. They would have come to Salem, Mass., in the ship "Mary Anne" from Great Yarmouth, England, which sailed in May, 1637, as is seen in the records at Westminster, on the margin of which is noted:

"*This man was forbyden passage by the commissioners, and went not from Yarmouth.*"

Perhaps the scrivener had no idea of a *negative pregnant*, as the lawyers say, but may have supposed that the power of the great archbishop, the impervious and foolish *Laud*, could forever restrain the migration. As the whole complication of ecclesiastical authority was overthrown the year after, the Puritan's desire was then, if not earlier, gratified.

One report places him at New Haven, Conn., 1638 to 1640. We make him to come to New Haven with part of his church in 1640, and to begin the settlement of Southold in October of that year. He died in Southold, 1672, aged 74 years.

His eldest son, *John Youngs*, was born in England in 1623. He lived in Southold, and in 1680 was sheriff of the whole insular territory, then called "Yorkshire." During the controversy with the Dutch at Manhattan he was a delegate to that place to effect a settlement. In 1681, at a court of assize, the court appointed "Capt. *John Youngs* high sheriff, a gentleman of family and education, and of known ability," to draft a petition to the Duke of York, for the privilege of an assembly (which was granted in 1683). He was a member of that council from 1683 to 1697, and colonel of the Suffolk militia until his death in 1698. With John Howell and John Mulford he was also a judge of the county of "Yorkshire."

(C.)

Sketch of the life of Col. Joshua Porter (26), written by himself:

Salisbury, August ye 2nd, 1820.

"I now being in ye 91st year of my age, sit down to write a short history of my life.

"I was born in Lebanon, county of Windham, State of Connecticut, on ye 26th day of June, A. D. 1730, of respectable parents. My father was a country merchant, and in ye year 1739, being in Boston, transacting his business, taking up goods, etc., he there sickened and died, being about thirty-five years old, leaving a widow and 4 children, 2 sons and 2 daughters, viz., Nathaniel and Joshua, Mehitabel and Eunice. I am now ye only surviving one of ye children. My father, at his death, left a decent property, and after ye estate being settled it was divided among his heirs, my brother being ye oldest son took two shares. My mother lived a widow about five years and then married. I then being fourteen years old chose a guardian, to wit, my great uncle, *Peter Buell*, Esq., of Coventry, with whom I lived about five years, and worked at the farming business. My brother having had college education took his first degree September, 1749, I being at commencement. I then determined to lay out ye small patrimony left to me by my father in getting an education. My brother settling at New Haven, I immediately repaired there, and studied under my brother, and ye next September I was examined and admitted a member of college, and in September, 1755, I was graduated, soon after which I was invited to go to Newbern, North Carolina, to keep a family school, and accordingly I went, and there remained towards a year. I then returned to Lebanon, where mother lived, and soon after I went again to Coventry, and studied physic and surgery with a Doct. Josiah Rose, and after I judged I was able to commence ye practice of physic, I returned once more to Lebanon and there begun practice, but being there old practitioners my business was small. In November, 1757, hearing of ye death of Doct. *Solomon Williams*, of Salisbury, Conn., and there being no physician in the town, I was advised to settle there. Accordingly I went, about ye latter end of ye month, and soon went into full practice, which I followed for about forty years from ye time I went there. I boarded with one Mr. John Earle, (a respectable member of society,) until May, 1759, and in March of same year I purchased about three acres of land, with a small dwelling house and a small barn standing thereon, including a small orchard. For ye premises I gave £60 lawful money.

On ye 14th day of May, 1759, I married *Abigail Buell*, daughter of my aforesaid guardian, with whom I lived with ye greatest harmony, and connubial state until ye 7th day of October, 1797, at which time she died, and by whom I had six children, viz.: Joshua, Abigail, Eunice, Augustus, Peter B., and Sally.

On ye 31st day of December, 1799, I married Jerusha Fitch, widow of Hezekiah Fitch, Esq., deceased, daughter of Col. Burr, of Fairfield, with whom I lived until February, 1808, at which time she died. In August following I married Lucy, widow of Samuel Dutcher, with whom I lived until August, 1814, at which time she died. She was daughter of Col. John Ashley, of Sheffield, Mass.

In June, 1761, I purchased of Daniel Morris his dwelling house and one acre of land, lying at the forking of ye road leading from ye meeting-house, and thirty-eight acres on ye east side of ye road, for which I gave £494 lawful money; and in May, 1763, I purchased of Daniel Morris one hundred and seventeen acres of land, ye remaining part of his farm, for which I gave him £190 lawful money. In 1777 I purchased of Elijah Bennett 82 acres of land, for which I gave him £242 lawful money. Since purchasing this land I have carried on considerable farming business, some years having sold grain, wheat, rye, corn, etc., and carried on the making of potash, for several years, at ye same time keeping a handsome stock on my farm.

In ye year 1766 (July) I was innoculated with the small pox, and in ye fall after Mr. Amos Bird, of Salisbury, set up a house in ye oblong, in which I innoculated a number of persons, having purchased ye skill of Dr. Burard, of Elizabethtown, in ye Jerseys, since which time I have innoculated a number with great success, and some considerable profit.

As to my political and public life it is as follows: Two years after I came into Salisbury I was chosen as a lister, to which office I was annually appointed for three years going. A few years after I was appointed one of ye selectmen of ye town, which office I sustained about twenty years. In September, 1765, I was chosen a representative to attend the general assembly in October ye same year, since which time I think I have been a member of ye assembly rising of forty sessions being almost annually chosen during ye revolutionary war.

In ye year 1777 I was appointed justice of ye peace for ye county of Litchfield, and in ye year 1778 I was appointed justice of quorum for ye county, which I held until ye year 1791, when I was appointed judge of ye court, which office I held until ye year 1808; and in ye year 1774 I was appointed judge of probate for ye district of Sharon, which office I held until ye year 1812, being thirty-seven years. In ye year 1774 I was appointed lieutenant-colonel of ye 17th regiment of militia of ye State of Connecticut, which office I sustained a number of years during ye revolutionary war, during which time I commanded a regiment at Peekskill, six weeks at ye town of Danbury, being burnt, and likewise commanded a regiment at the capture of Gen. Burgoyne and army, and was in ye battles in ye year 1777.

(D.)

The battle of Lexington was fought on Wednesday, April 19, 1775, and the news reached Berkshire county on Friday, about noon.

Before sunrise on Saturday the Berkshire regiment was on its way to Boston, completely equipped in arms, and, generally, in uniform.

On its arrival in Cambridge the regiment was found so much too large for one command that it was divided, Col. *John Fellows*, of Sheffield, Mass., commanding one, and Col. *Patterson* the other. The former was stationed in Charlestown, and built "Fort No. 3," and on the 17th of June, at the battle of Bunker Hill, was in the command of Gen. Ward.

After the evacuation of Boston Col. Fellows' regiment was ordered to New York, and thence joined the army under *Washington* at Newton, Pa., and in 1776 was engaged in the battles of White Plains, Monmouth, etc.; and at the battles of Saratoga in 1777 Col. Fellows commanded a brigade, and was in active service to the close of the war.

(E.)

Col. *William A. Bird*, of Buffalo, N. Y., communicates the following:

"On the 23d June, 1812, only the fifth day after war was declared (with England), my brother was killed by an 18 lb. shot from the frigate 'Belvidere,' the particulars of which were communicated by *Commodore Rodgers* on his arrival in Boston in October following.

"At the commencement of the action on board the 'President,' frigate, a ball (an 18 pdr.) from the 'Belvidere' came over the waist cloths of the 'President,' and such was its force that it actually cut off, without throwing them down, the muzzles of several of the muskets (left there by the marines), from six to eight inches in length, killed one marine, took off the wrist of one midshipman (Mr. Montgomery), killed another, (Mr. Bird), together with the quarter gunner, and finally lodged upon the deck, and was taken below by the narrator of this and shown the third lieutenant (Mr. Dallas), who took it in his hand and wrote on it with chalk: '*Cousin— I have received your present and return it,*'—clapped it in the gun himself and fired the piece. It is a remarkable fact, that it actually killed several of the officers and men on the 'Belvidere,' and finally lodged in the cabin of that vessel, where it was afterwards hung up as a globe during the war."
(See John Herman Bird (63), Midshipman U. S. Navy.)

(F.)

Col. *Albert Pawling* was a native of Duchess county, N. Y., son of Col. *Levi Pawling*, an officer of the American army.

Col. Albert Pawling joined the army as second lieutenant in a regiment commanded by Col. James Clinton, and went to Canada, where he served under Gen. Montgomery in the fatal expedition of 1776. In that year he was appointed a brigade-major under Gen. George Clinton, and served as such until 1777, when he was made a major in one of the sixteen additional regiments, under Col. William Malcolm.

Under a mistaken view of the situation, in 1779, Major Pawling sent in his resignation, which the following letter from Washington could not induce him to recall:

"Headquarters, Middlebrook, 2d March, 1779.

"Sir—In your letter of 25th ult. you seem to have misconceived the intention of Congress, upon which is founded your application for leave to resign.

"It is not their purpose to reduce Col. Malcolm's regiment. This will be incorporated with Col. Spencer's, and as you are the only major in the two regiments of course you will be continued.

"After considering the just claims which the country has on good officers, I am persuaded you will suspend your application.

"I am, sir,
"Your most humble serv't,
"GEO: WASHINGTON.

"To Major Albert Pawling."

Col. Pawling afterwards served as colonel of a regiment of Swiss for the defence of the New York frontier.

"Pawling avenue," in Troy, the city of his adoption, perpetuates his memory. (See Judge N. B. Sylvester's History of Rensselaer County.)

(G.)

Allusion having been made to the "ship in the air," it may be of interest to insert here the following:

The people of New Haven, having built a ship, freighted and dispatched it for England with a cargo of their products.

They sailed in January, 1647, and were obliged to cut their way out of the harbor through the ice. They were never heard of after.

According to the belief at the period, the apparition of this ship was seen in the air after she had foundered, with all on board. Rev. Cotton Mather having heard of the circumstance wrote his friend, Rev. James Pierpont, and received the following reply:

"Rev. and Dear Sir—

"In compliance with your desires, I now give you the relation of that *apparition of a ship in the air*, which I have received from the most credible, judicious and curious surviving observers of it.

"In the year 1647, besides much other lading, a far more rich treasure of passengers (five or six of which were persons of chief note and worth in New Haven) put themselves on board a new ship, built at Rhode Island, of about 150 tons, but so walty* that the master (Lamberton) often said that she would prove their grave.

"In the month of January, cutting their way through much ice, in which they were accompanied by the Rev. Mr. Davenport, besides many other friends, with many fears, as well as prayers and tears, they set sail. Mr. Davenport, in prayer, with an observable emphasis, used these words:

"'Lord, if it be thy pleasure to bury these our friends in the bottom of the sea, they are thine, save them.'"

"The spring following no tidings of these friends arrived with the ships from England. New Haven's heart began to fail her. This put the good people

* Walty, from Waeltan, Anglo Saxon, to roll over. In seamau's parlance, "crank."

on much prayer, both public and private, that the Lord would (if it was his pleasure) let them hear what he had done with their dear friends, and prepare them with a suitable submission to His Holy Will.

"In June next ensuing a great thunder storm arose out of the northwest; after which, the hemisphere being serene, about an hour before sunset, a ship of like dimensions with the aforesaid, with her canvass and colors abroad, though the wind northerly, appeared in the air, coming up from our harbor's mouth, which lyes southward from the town, seemingly with her sails filled under a fresh gale, holding her course north, and continuing under observation, sailing against the wind for the space of half an hour.

"Many were drawn to behold this great work of God; yea, the very children cryed out, 'there's a brave ship.' At length, crouding up as far as there is usually water sufficient for such a vessel, and so near some of the spectators, as they imagined, a man might hurl a stone on board her; her maintop seemed to be blown off, but left hanging in the shrouds; then her mizzen-top; then all her masting seemed blown away by the board. Quickly after the hulk brought unto a careen, she overset, and so vanished into a smoky cloud, which in some time dissipated, leaving, as everywhere else, a clear air.

"The admiring spectators could distinguish the several colors of each part, the principal rigging, and such proportions as caused not only the generality of persons to say, 'this was the mould of their ship, and this was her tragick end;' but Mr. Davenport also in public declared to the effect 'that God had condescended, for the quieting of their afflicted spirits, this extraordinary account of His sovereign disposal of those for whom so many fervent prayers were made continually.

"Thus I am, Sir, your humble servant,

"JAMES PIERPONT."

[Rev. James Pierpont married Abigail Davenport, grand-daughter of Rev. *John Davenport*, of New Haven, mentioned in above extract.]

(H.)

"It was not long before the Massachusetts colony was become a Hive overstocked with Bees, and many of the new Inhabitants entertained thoughts of swarming into Plantations extended further into the country.

"The fame of the Connecticut river — a long, fresh, rich river, as, indeed, the Indian name 'Connecticut' is Indian for 'Long river'— made it a little *Nilus* in the expectation of the good people about the Massachusetts Bay. Whereupon many of the Planters belonging to the towns of Cambridge, Dorchester, Watertown and Roxbury took up Resolutions to move a hundred miles for a further settlement upon this famous River.

"Reader! come with me now to behold some Worthy and Learned and Genteel Persons going to be buried alive in the Banks of the Connecticut. * * * * So there was a great remove of good people thither.

"On this remove they that went from *Cambridge* became a Church on a spot of Ground now called *Hartford;* they that went from *Dorchester* became a Church at Windsor; they that went from *Watertown* sat down at *Weathersfield*, and they that left *Roxbury* were in-Churched higher up the River at *Springfield*, at a place which was afterwards found within the lines of the Massachusetts charter." This was in 1635. (Extract from "Mather's Antiquities.")

(I.)

The following is a list of settlers at Windsor, Conn., who accompanied Rev. Ephraim Huet in 1639:

Roger Ludlow,	Joseph Loomis,	John Loomis,
John Porter,	William Hill,	James Marshall,
John Taylor,	Eltweed Pomeroy,	William Heffard,
Aaron Cooke,	Elias Parkman,	Thomas Stoughton,
William Hayden,	George Phelps,	Return Strong,
John Hillyer,	Thomas Barber,	Nicholas Palmer,
Thomas Buckland,	Isaac Sheldon,	Robert Watson,
Stephen Terrey,	Bray Rossiter,	William Hulbert,
Thomas Dewey,	Owyn Tudor,	Roger Williams,
John Mason,	Richard Oldage,	Thomas Bascombe,
Matthew Allyn,	Nicholas Denslowe,	Thomas Thornton.
Henry Stiles,	William Phelps,	

Of another party were

Samuel Phelps,	Thomas Holcombe,	Peter Tilton,
William Gaylord,	Humphrey Pinney,	Richard Vore,
Matthew Grant,	Bigod Eggleston,	Thomas Ford,
John Bissell,	John Whitefield,	Walter Fylar,
Daniel Clark,	Nathan Gillette,	Abraham Randall,
Henry Wolcott,	John Moore,	Thomas Deble.
	Edward Griswold,	

(J.)

The following sketch of Judge *Augustus Porter* (50) was prepared by his son, Albert H. Porter (69), of Niagara Falls, N. Y., who says in that connection:

"It is very imperfect, and only glances at some of the more important events in his long, active and useful life, and his connection with, and the prominent part he bore, in the early history of Western New York, Ohio and the great lakes.

"AUGUSTUS PORTER was born in Salisbury, Conn., January 18, 1769, the second son of Doctor (and Colonel) *Joshua Porter*, in a family of three sons and three daughters. He received a common English education, including a course of mathematical instruction, and was well qualified for the business he had chosen — that of land surveying — and also for the successful application of water-power, and kindred enterprises, requiring mechanical skill, in which he was for many years engaged.

"In the spring of 1789, at the age of twenty years, he left his native State for Ontario (then Montgomery) county, in the State of New York, as a well qualified surveyor, at first to survey lands in which his father held an interest, and afterwards in the same capacity in the employment of the original purchasers of the lands of Western New York from the State of Massachusetts. He was an assistant surveyor to Andrew Ellicott, surveyor-general of the United States, in running the line from Pennsylvania to Lake Ontario, as also of all the lands lying west of Seneca lake, first sold by the State of Massachusetts to Phelps and Gorham, and afterwards to Robert Morris, the great financier of the war of the Revolution.

"In 1796 Mr. Porter was employed by the Connecticut Land Company as chief surveyor, with a large corps of assistants and other men, to make a survey of the lands on the south shore of Lake Erie, being the reservation made by the State of Connecticut from the grant made by the United States of western territory, called the "Western Reserve," the boundaries of which were described by latitude and longitude, no survey having at that time been made, and the portion covered by Lake Erie not known. No settlements had been made on this territory. It was still an unbroken wilderness, a large portion of which was in possession of unfriendly tribes of Indians.

"Mr. Porter made a traverse of the lake, from the east to the west bounds of the territory, to enable him to estimate the quantity of land within the boundaries not covered by the lake.

"A large number of townships were surveyed during that and the following year preparatory to their settlement.

"He also surveyed and laid out the town at the mouth of the Cuyahoga river, which received the name of Cleveland in compliment to Gen. Cleveland, the managing agent of the company.

"In 1797-98 Mr. Porter was engaged in behalf of Robert Morris in laying down the boundaries of the lands lying west of Genesee river, purchased of the State of Massachusetts, and to which he had obtained the Indian title, and also in delineating the boundaries of a large portion of the Indian lands which had been sold by Mr. Morris to the Holland Land Company.

"In 1802 he was elected a member of Assembly from Ontario county. He continued to reside at Canandaigua until 1806, when he removed his family to Niagara Falls, N. Y., where he was the first permanent settler, and with which he was identified during the remainder of his life.

"In 1805 Augustus Porter, in connection with his brother, Peter B. Porter, and Benjamin Barton, purchased of the State of New York a large quantity of land in the State reservation along the Niagara river, including the water-power and lands adjacent to the falls.

"In connection with his associates he immediately commenced building mills and making other improvements. They also built a number of vessels on lakes Erie and Ontario, and with suitable means for transportation around the falls and on the river were the chief forwarders between Oswego and the upper lakes previous to the war of 1812.

"Their vessels were taken by the United States and used for public purposes during the war.

"On its conclusion the business was resumed, and continued until the completion of the Erie canal, when transportation westward, by way of the Niagara river, was abandoned.

"In 1808 the county of Niagara, then including Erie county, was organized, of which Buffalo was the county seat, and Augustus Porter appointed first judge, serving in that office for several years.

"The dwellings, mills and other buildings at the falls were burned by the enemy in 1813, and the inhabitants all fled from the frontier.

"On the return of peace in 1815 Mr. Porter was engaged for some time in rebuilding his houses and mills, and in making other improvements. He was his own engineer in constructing the bridge across the rapids to Goat island, a work at that time deemed very dangerous and difficult.

"At an early day he fixed on a plan for an extended use of the great water-power at Niagara Falls, and with this in view retained an exclusive ownership of the land necessary for that purpose. His heirs have since caused this plan to be carried out, by extensive grants of land and water-power of immense value, now fully developed.

"In 1821 Judge Porter was elected a member of the convention for revising the Constitution of the State of New York.

"In 1825 he took an active part in the construction of Black Rock harbor, and in 1836 was among the most liberal and efficient contributors to the Buffalo and Niagara Falls railroad.

"The latter years of his life were chiefly devoted to his private business, in the cultivation of his lands, and in various local improvements, with his characteristic energy, his mental faculties unimpaired, to the time of his decease in 1849, in the 81st year of his age.

"He was a man of untiring industry, sterling integrity and sound religious principles — the peer of the best men of a class for which Western New York was early distinguished, and of which he had been a resident for sixty years, witnessing and participating in its advance from the condition of Indian hunting grounds to that of cultivated fields, pleasant homes and thriving villages and cities, inhabited by a numerous population, enjoying the blessings of a Christian cultivation."

Peter Buel Porter (51), page 20.

[From current Journals of the Day.]

The last mail from the west brings tidings of the death of Gen. Peter B. Porter. He expired at his residence at Niagara Falls on Wednesday evening.

Gen. Porter has been distinguished in our annals in civic and martial life; and there are few among us to whom the meed of talents, bravery and patriotism, will be more freely awarded.

He was appointed in 1811, with Gouverneur Morris, Stephen Van Rensselaer, De Witt Clinton, William North, Simeon De Witt, Thomas Eddy, Robert R. Livingston and Robert Fulton, the first commissioners in relation to inland navigation — being the incipient step that led in the sequel to the noble works of art and improvement which have contributed so largely (whatever excesses may have been committed) to the glory and the prosperity of the State.

Their labors were suspended, however, by the war of 1812; and for these civic duties Gen. Porter exchanged the privations and dangers of the frontier campaigns. Residing then at Black Rock, he was in the midst of the most eventful and stirring of the border scenes. He rallied the hastily-gathered volunteers, who repelled the first invasion of that place in midsummer, 1813, and shared, at the head of his corps, with intrepidity and skill, in those brilliant and memorable affairs of the succeeding year, the battles of Chippewa and Bridgewater, and the sortie of Fort Erie.

At the close of the war he was appointed Secretary of State in place of Jacob Rutsen Van Rensselaer, but he declined the appointment, having been elected to Congress the previous year. Near the close of his congressional term he was appointed commissioner under the British treaty to run the boundary line between the United States and Canada. In 1817 he was the antagonist candidate to De Witt Clinton in the democratic caucus held for the nomination for Governor, and at the election received a few votes cast by politicians in the city of New York, who refused to acquiesce in the nomination of Mr. Clinton.

In the political controversies of his time Gen. Porter was a prominent participator until his retirement from public life with Mr. Adams in 1829. Under that administration, and for the last year of it, he discharged the duties of Secretary of War. He was warmly attached to Mr. Clay, and was related to him by the marriage of his second wife.

A frontier resident during the last forty years; possessed of large estates on the border; he is identified with the history of Western New York, and with its gigantic progress in the great elements of social and physical development.

As a public man he was sagacious, shrewd and able, though to ordinary observers, in latter years, the impression was one of heaviness, approaching to dullness. In his military career he was distinguished by high qualities of command, and by undoubted coolness and courage.

Since 1838 he has occupied his new and elegant residence at the Falls—in the midst, as it were, of the scenes that have become classic ground to every American, and in the presence and within the perpetual roar of the great cataract.

Gen. Porter died, the Buffalo *Commercial Advertiser* states, in the 71st year of his age.

COL. PETER AUGUSTUS PORTER (75), page 37.

To the Editor of the New York Times:

In a recent issue of the *Times* the late Peter B. Porter, recently deceased at Niagara Falls, is mentioned as a son of the late Gen. Peter B. Porter, the distinguished soldier of the war of 1812, and in 1828 Secretary of War under President Adams. He was not a son of the general, but of his brother, Judge Augustus Porter. "Among the earliest of the pioneers in Western New York were two brothers, Augustus and Peter B. Porter, sons of Dr. Joshua Porter, of Salisbury, Conn." (F. S. Cozzens' eulogy before the Century Club on the Life and Services of Col. Peter A. Porter.) The lustre of military services alone was wanting to the elder brother, but in the narrower sphere of his home—that "Western New York," of which he had been one of the "pioneers," and among the most energetic and useful, the work of converting it from a wilderness to what it now is, Judge Porter was scarcely less eminent than his distinguished brother. He died full of years and honors in (I think) 1848—a few years after his younger brother. The excellent and distinguished gentleman recently deceased—the younger son of Judge Porter—bore the general's name of Peter Buel; but it would be a wrong to the memory of the only son of Gen. Porter to forget that he fell on the battle-field of Cold Harbor, an illustrious example of that devotion to duty of which our civil war furnished so many beautiful exemplars. Born to a fortune, educated in the first learned institutions of Europe and America, endowed by nature with beauty of person and brilliancy of intellect, which eminently fitted him for social enjoyment and distinction, surrounded by everything that could make life enviable, he deliberately renounced all these for the service of his country in her hour of need. Before leaving his home, "feeling to its full extent the probability that he might not return from the path of duty on which he had entered," he solemnly recorded, in his "last will and testament," his motives in the following words :

"I can say with truth that I have entered on the course of danger with no ambitious aspirations, nor with the idea that I am fitted by nature or experience to be of any important service to the government; but in obedience to the call of duty, demanding every citizen to contribute what he could in means, labor or life to sustain the government of his country — a sacrifice made the more willingly by me when I consider how singularly benefited I have been by the institutions of the land, and that up to this time all the blessings of life have been showered upon me beyond what usually falls to the lot of man."

Soon after he had entered the military service, and while in command of his regiment at Fort McHenry, he was nominated for Secretary of State of New York. In declining this appointment he gives, besides the original motives which brought him into the field, the following reason : "I left home in command of a regiment composed mainly of the sons of friends and neighbors, committed to my care. I can hardly ask for my discharge while theirs cannot be granted."

He fell on the 3d of June, 1864, pierced by six bullets, while leading his regiment up to the enemy's works at Cold Harbor.

Believing that the memory of such a life and death should be cherished ; that the State and city of New York, which (each separately) made public acknowledgment of the eminent services of the father, should be proud, too, of the son, I have sketched these lines, drawing most of the details from the eloquent "eulogy," already referred to. It is worthy of remark, that, in the mother of the wife of Dr. Joshua Porter (Abigail Buell), Col. Porter had, with the general (now President of the United States) who commanded our armies on the battlefield where he fell, a common maternal ancestor. B.

Aboriginal Names of some of the Localities mentioned in this Record.

Boston	Massachusetts	Shawmut.
Branford	Connecticut	Tetoket.
Cambridge	Massachusetts	Menotomy.
Charlestown	Massachusetts	Mishawan.
Deerfield	Massachusetts	Pocumtuc.
Derby	Connecticut	Paugassett.
Dorchester	Massachusetts	Mattapan.
Duxbury	Massachusetts	Mattakeesett.
Durham	Connecticut	Coginchaug.
Easthampton	Massachusetts	Paskhomuc.

East Windsor	Connecticut	Scantic.
Farmington	Connecticut	Tunxis.
Great Barrington	Massachusetts	Housatonic.
Guilford	Connecticut	Menunketuc.
Hartford	Connecticut	Suckiaug.
Hadley	Massachusetts	Norwottuc.
Killingworth	Connecticut	Hamonassett.
Lebanon	Connecticut	Poquechanneeg.
Litchfield	Connecticut	Bantam.
Lyme	Connecticut	Nehantic.
Longmeadow	Massachusetts	Masacksic.
Lynn	Massachusetts	Saugus.
Milton	Massachusetts	Uncataquissett.
Mansfield	Connecticut	Naubesetuc.
Medford	Massachusetts	Mystic.
Middletown	Connecticut	Mattabesett.
Milford	Connecticut	Wepauwaug.
New Milford	Connecticut	Weantinogue.
New Haven	Connecticut	Quinnipiac.
New London	Connecticut	Naumeaug.
Northfield	Massachusetts	Squakheaug.
Northampton	Massachusetts	Nonotuc.
Newton	Massachusetts	Nonantum.
Pittsfield	Massachusetts	Pontoosuc.
Plainfield	Massachusetts	Quinnebaug.
Rochester	Massachusetts	Seipican.
Salisbury	Connecticut	Wetaugnc.
Saybrook	Connecticut	Pautapoag.
Sharon	Connecticut	Mashapoag.
Sheffield	Massachusetts	Staytooc.
Salem	Massachusetts	Naumkeag.
Simsbury	Connecticut	Massacoe.
Stamford	Connecticut	Rippowams.
Stonington	Connecticut	Pawcatuc.
Stratford	Connecticut	Oronoacke.
Southold, L. I.	New York	Yennycott.
Stockbridge	Massachusetts	Muhhekanew.
Springfield	Massachusetts	Agawam.
Watertown	Massachusetts	Pygussett.
Weathersfield	Connecticut	Pyquiaug.
Westfield	Massachusetts	Waronoko.
Westbrook	Connecticut	Pochaug.
Windsor	Connecticut	Matteneaug.
Woodbury	Connecticut	Pomeraug.
Worcester	Massachusetts	Quinsigamond.
Waterbury	Connecticut	Mattatuc.

INDEXES.

I.—INDEX OF PORTER NAMES.

Abigail, 9, 13, 14.
Albert A., 36, 63.
Albert Howell, 20, 34, 36, 64.
Alexander Jeffrey, 64.
Anna, 2, 75, 78, 90.
Augusta, 11, 24, 27.
Augustus, 9, 17, 19, 20.
Augustus Granger, 64.
Augustus Seymour, 9, 27, 33, 54.

Bessie Rochester, 64.

Cabell Breckinridge, 71.
Charles Leonard, 6.
Charlotte Ross, 64.

Eleazer, 16.
Elizabeth L., 22.
Emily W., 6.
Eunice, 4, 9, 14, 16.
Experience, 3, 16.

Frederick Augustus, 12.

George Morris, 38.

Hannah, 3, 16, 52, 57, 75, 78, 83, 92.

Henry Chester, 6.
Hezekiah, 3.

Ichabod, 3.

James, 2.
Jane Augusta, 34.
Jane H. (Mrs.), 20.
Jane Howell, 36, 34.
Jane Seymour, 20, 36, 37.
Jerusha, 16.
JOHN, 1, 2, 7, 31, 41, 44, 47, 57, 72, 74, 75, 76, 82, 87, 90, 92.
John, 2, 3, 6, 41, 44, 52, 57, 64, 72, 73, 74, 78.
John F., 12.
Joshua (Col.), 4, 6, 8, 9.
Joshua (Dr.), 9, 11, 12, 13.
Joseph, 3.
Julia M., 36, 63, 64.

Lætitia E., 38.
Lavinia (Mrs.), 19.
Lavinia E., 20.

Mary, 2, 7, 78.
Mary Breckinridge, 38.
Mary S., 13, 27, 29, 30.
Mehitabel, 3, 4, 5.

Minerva, 12.

Nathaniel, 3, 4, 6, 44, 83, 92.
Nathaniel Buel, 3, 4.
Nathaniel W., 20.

Peter Augustus, 22, 37, 38, 69, 71.
Peter Buel, 9, 19, 20, 22, 33, 97.

Rebecca, 2.
ROSE, 23, 44, 72, 74, 75, 76, 82, 90, 92.
Ruth, 72, 73, 83, 92.

Sally, 9, 22.
Samuel, 2, 3, 16, 64, 65, 72, 74, 78.
Samuel Mansfield, 34.
Sarah, 2, 16, 44, 45, 47, 76, 82, 83, 92.
Sarah A. (Mrs.), 34.
Sarah Fredericka, 34, 61, 63
Sophia, 6.

Thomas, 3.
Thomas S., 3.

Vincent, M., 36.

II.—INDEX OF OTHER NAMES.

ABEEL,
  Johannes, 36.
  Katrina, 35.
  Magdalen, 56.
ABELL,
  Experience, 72.
  Robert, 72.
ADAMS,
  Alice, 49.
  Anna, 13, 14.
  Elijah (Dr.), 55.

ADAMS,
  Jeremiah, 14.
  John, 9.
  Maria L., 29, 55.
  William, 55.
  William (Rev.) 49, 55, 63
ALDEN,
  Elizabeth, 66.
  John (Capt.), 66.
ALLEN,
  Agnes, 89.

ALLEN,
  Edward, 89.
  Elizabeth, 45.
  John, 89.
  Matthew, 2.
  Thomas, 45.
ANDERSON,
  Chandler Parsons, 85.
  Harriet Holley, 85.
  Henry Burrall, 85.
  Henry H., 44, 85.

ANDERSON,
  Rufus, 85.
  William Burrall, 85.
ANDREWS,
  Ashbel, 28, 29.
  Charles Adams, 56.
  Edward, 94.
  Henry Porter, 29, 55.
  Harry Seymour, 56.
  Henry W., 13, 27, 29.
  Maria L., 56.
  Mary, 94.
  Rebecca, 87.
  Robert, 87.
  Samuel, 27.
  William, 27, 28, 29, 32.
ARNOLD,
  Samuel (Rev.), 90.
ASHLEY,
  David, 11.
  John (Col.), 9.
  Lucy, 9.
  Mary, 11.
  Robert, 11.
ASHMEADE,
  Mary, 95.
ASTWOOD,
  John, 42.
ATHERTON,
  Humphrey, 76.
  Margaret, 76.
ATWOOD,
  Herman, 15.
  Jonathan, 15.
  Mary, 15.
  Thomas (Dr.), 15.

BABCOCK,
  Thankful, 3.
BACKUS,
  Sarah, 39.
  William, 39.
BAKER,
  Faith, 66.
  Mary, 66.
  Richard, 66.
BALDWIN,
  Abigail, 42, 72.
  Benjamin, 72.
  John, 42, 72.
  Joseph, 26.
  Mary, 26.
  Ruth, 72.
  Samuel, 42.
  Sarah, 42.
  Sylvester, 42.
  Thomas, 72.
BARNARD,
  Abigail, 11.
  Abner, 26.
  Anna McHenry, 55.
  Augustus Porter, 55.
  Bartholomew, 5, 18.

BARNARD,
  Ebenezer, 25, 26.
  Frederick A. P. (Rev.), 27, 53.
  Francis, 5, 18, 24.
  Jane Brand, 55.
  John, 11, 24.
  John G., 27, 54, 55.
  John Hall, 55.
  Joseph, 25, 34.
  Phœbe, 11.
  Robt. F. 11, 24, 27, 54, 55
  Sally (Mrs.), 27.
  Sarah, 18.
  Sarah G., 27, 34, 53.
  Sylvester (Dr.), 26, 27.
  William Frederick, 55.
BATES,
  James, 25.
  Mary, 25.
BAYSEY,
  Elizabeth, 46, 58.
  John, 46, 58.
BEEBE,
  James, 50, 93.
  Lucy, 50.
  Mary, 50.
  Nathaniel, 93.
  Samuel, 93.
  Sarah H., 92, 93.
BELL,
  Francis, 67.
  Jonathan, 67.
  Mary, 67.
  Rebecca, 67.
BEACH,
  Adna, 42, 43.
  Hannah, 42.
BECKLEY,
  Sarah, 44.
  Richard, 44.
BELCHER,
  Andrew, 79.
  Catharine, 27.
  Dorothy, 26.
  Gregory, 27.
  Jeremiah, 79.
  Josiah, 26, 27.
BEEKMAN,
  Gerard, 56.
  Maria, 56.
BELDEN,
  Daniel, 59.
  Edmund P., 60.
  Edmund S., 33, 59.
  Harriet E., 60.
  Richard, 59.
BENTON,
  Jesse, 21.
  Thomas H., 21.
BIDWELL,
  Anna, 51.
  John, 51.

BIRCHARD,
  Hannah, 72.
  Sarah, 5, 18.
  Thomas, 6, 18, 72.
BIRD,
  Clarence, 16.
  Elizabeth B., 60.
  Elizabeth Griffin, 60.
  Grace, 60.
  Grace Eunice, 33.
  Grace Maria, 60.
  James, 14.
  Joanna Davis, 60.
  John, 9, 14, 15, 16.
  John Herman, 16, 33, 60
  Maria, 16.
  Maria Davis, 33.
  Porter Augustus, 60.
  Seth (Dr.), 15.
  Thomas, 14, 15.
  Walter Griffin, 60.
  Wells Miller, 60.
  William A., 16, 17, 33, 60.
  Williams, N. D., 60.
BISHOP,
  Anna, 18.
  John, 18.
BISSELL,
  Abigail. 75, 90.
  John, 75, 90.
  Thomas, 75, 90.
BLAIR,
  Francis P., 21.
  Montgomery, 21.
BLANEY,
  Cornelius Duchene, 60.
  Daniel, 60.
  Edward, 60.
  Frances E., 33, 60.
BLISS,
  Hannah, 80.
BOLTWOOD,
  Robert, 50.
BOOTHE,
  Elizabeth, 7.
  Richard, 6, 7.
  William, 6, 7.
BORRODELL,
  Anna, 17.
  John, 17.
BOSTWICK,
  Anna E., 50, 85, 88.
  Arthur, 85, 87.
  Benjamin, 86, 87.
  John, 85.
  Rufus, 87.
  Robert, 87.
  Zechariah, 86, 87.
BOWERS,
  Barbara, 59.
  Bridget, 59.
  George, 59.
  John, 59.

BOWLES,
  Elizabeth, 62.
  John, 62, 63.
  Joshua, 63.
  Mary J., 63.
  Ralph Hartt, 63.
BOYD,
  Anna E. (Hall), 27, 55.
BRADFORD,
  Alice, 55.
  Anna, 32.
  Mercy, 19.
  William (Col.), 19, 35, 55, 56.
BRADLEY,
  Abraham (Capt.), 68.
  Isaac, 69.
  Nancy, 68.
  Samuel, 68, 69.
  Zebulon, 68.
BRAND,
  Jane E., 27, 54, 55.
  William, 54.
BRECKINRIDGE,
  Alexander, 21.
  John, 21, 22, 38, 71.
  Joseph C., 22.
  Lætitia, 9, 21, 27.
  Lætitia Preston, 22, 71.
  Mary A., 22.
  Mary C. P., 22, 37, 71.
  Robert (Col.), 21.
  Robert, 71.
  Robert J. (Rev.), 22.
  William L., 22.
BREWSTER,
  Amy, 35, 36.
  Jonathan, 9, 35.
  Lucy, 77.
  Nathaniel (Rev.), 35.
  William (Elder), 35.
BRINSMEADE,
  Daniel, 85.
  John, 86.
  Mary, 85.
BROCKWAY,
  Elizabeth, 73.
  Walter, 74.
BRONSON,
  Dorcas, 18, 45.
  John, 18, 45.
BROUGHTON,
  Abigail, 61.
  George, 61.
BROUWER,
  Jane, 54.
BROWN,
  Ebenezer, 66, 67.
  Isabel, 64.
  John, 3, 65, 67.
  Lydia, 66.
  Mary, 65.
  Peter, 64.

BUCKE,
  Henry, 12.
  Ruth, 12.
BUELL,
  Abel, 23.
  Abigail, 4, 6, 8, 9.
  Anna, 10, 23, 24.
  Archelaus, 58.
  Benjamin, 8.
  Deborah, 8.
  Dorcas, 76, 77, 79.
  Elizabeth, 42, 51, 53.
  Ira, 41, 53.
  John (Dea.) 41, 52, 57, 75.
  Josiah, 5.
  Mary, 58, 59, 75.
  Mehitabel, 3.
  Peter, 8, 52.
  Peter (Dea.), 57, 58.
  Peter (Capt.), 3, 6, 8, 9.
  Samuel, 3, 4, 6, 8, 23, 41, 51, 57.
  Solomon, 41, 52, 53, 75, 76, 78, 79.
  William, 4, 6, 8, 23, 41, 51, 57, 75, 77.
BURGESS,
  Ruth, 69.
  Thomas, 69.
BURHANS,
  Hiram W., 57, 59.
  John C., 59.
  Sarah E., 31, 57, 59.
BURKS,
  Elizabeth, 37, 70.
  Samuel, 37, 70.
BURR,
  Aaron, 14.
  Jerusha, 9.
BURRALL,
  Abigail, 33.
  Augustus P., 63.
  Charles, 31.
  Charles (Col.), 31, 61.
  Elizabeth, 33, 59.
  Elizabeth M., 43.
  Edward, 33.
  Frederick A., 62, 63.
  Harriet (Mrs.), 43.
  Harriet H., 44.
  John D., 85.
  John Milton, 43, 85.
  Ovid, 61, 62.
  Porter, 44.
  Porter S., 44, 85.
  Sarah Bostwick, 44, 85.
  Stephen E., 34, 61, 63.
  William D., 85.
  William, 31, 32, 61.
  William Holley, 43, 84.
  William M. 14, 31, 33, 43.
  William Porter, 22, 33, 43.

BURROUGHS,
  Hannah, 92.
  John, 92.
BURR,
  Abigail, 26.
  Henry, 26, 80.
  Patience, 80.
  Ululie, 26, 80.
BUTLER,
  Mary, 3, 13, 72.
  Richard, 18, 72.
  Samuel, 18.
  Thomas, 72.
BUTTOLPH,
  David, 70.
  Penelope, 70.
CABELL,
  Joseph, 71.
  Joseph (Col.), 38, 70.
  Mary, 37, 38.
  Mary H., 21, 38, 71.
  Nicholas, 37, 70.
  William, 37, 70.
CALKINS,
  Anna, 62.
  Deborah, 62.
  Elizabeth, 5, 58.
  Hugh, 58, 62, 88.
  John, 5, 58, 67.
  Sarah, 87.
CAMP,
  Arthur A., 57, 94.
  Arthur W., 95.
  Catharine, 95.
  Daniel, 94, 95.
  Ethel, 95.
  John, 13.
  Nicholas, 95.
  Norman W. (Rev.), 94.
  Sarah, 13.
CAMPBELL,
  Janet, 89.
  John (Dr.), 89.
  Robert, 89.
  Sarah, 89.
CANFIELD,
  Alma, 79, 80.
  Jeremiah, 76.
  John, 76, 77, 79.
  Phœbe, 76.
  Samuel, 76.
  Samuel (Col.), 76, 77.
  Sarah Porter, 76.
  Thomas, 76.
CASTLEMAN,
  David, 22.
CATLIN,
  Elizabeth, 26.
  Isabel, 26.
  John, 26.
  Joseph, 26.
  Rachel, 26.

CATLIN,
  Ruth, 26.
CASE,
  Abigail, 69, 70.
  Daniel, 70.
  Ezekiel, 70.
  John, 69, 70.
  Penelope, 70.
CHADEAYNE,
  Catharine, 50.
  Daniel, 50.
  John, 50.
CHAPIN,
  Charles, 80.
  Ebenezer, 80.
  Japhet, 80.
  Phinehas, 80, 83.
  Ruth A., 80, 83.
  Samuel, 80.
  Sicily, 80.
CHAPMAN,
  Lizzie, 94.
CHAUNCEY,
  Abigail, 81, 83.
  Charles, 81, 82.
  George, 82.
  Nathaniel, 82.
  Nathaniel (Rev.), 82.
CHECKLEY,
  Lydia, 63.
  Samuel (Capt.), 63.
CHESTER,
  Penelope, 16.
  John (Col.) 16.
CRITTENDEN,
  Mary, 57.
  William, 57, 58.
CHRISTOPHERS,
  Christopher, 29.
  Margaret, 29.
CHURCH,
  Alonzo, 50, 85.
  Alonzo W., 85.
  Anne, 44.
  Benjamin, 87.
  Caroline E., 23, 44, 47.
  Irving P., 47.
  James R., 85.
  John, 44.
  John R, 85.
  Julia M., 85.
  Mary R., 85.
  Miriam, 87.
  Nathaniel, 45, 46.
  Richard, 44, 87.
  Samuel, 44, 45, 46.
  Samuel R., 85.
  Sarah R., 85.
  William W., 85.
CHURCHILL,
  Elizabeth, 12.
  Josiah, 12, 44, 87.
  Mary, 44, 87.

CLAP,
  Barbara, 42.
  Edward, 42.
  Roger, 42.
CLARK,
  Daniel, 91.
  Elizabeth S., 73.
  Faith, 10.
  Frances, 24, 72.
  George, 79.
  Helen Louise, 73.
  John, 39.
  John T., 39, 71, 73.
  Jonathan, 71.
  Julia Kirkland, 73.
  Lemuel, 72.
  Mary Holley, 73.
  Sarah, 71, 79.
  Sarah Amelia, 73.
  Sylvia, 91.
  Tristram, 10.
  William, 73.
  William (Capt.), 71.
  William (Lieut.), 71.
  William Henry, 73.
CLAY,
  Anna E., 95.
  Curtis, 75.
  Robert, 95.
  Slater, 95.
CODDINGTON,
  William, 32.
COFFING,
  Marcia, 22, 45.
  John C., 43.
COIT,
  Mary, 97.
  John, 97.
  Joseph, 97.
  Joseph (Rev.), 97.
  Samuel, 97, 98.
  Sarah, 98.
  Wheeler, 98.
COLE,
  Anna, 36.
  Hannah, 88.
  John, 88.
  Robert, 36.
  Samuel, 88.
COLES,
  Hannah, 3.
COLEMAN,
  Dorcas, 73.
  John, 3.
  Thomas, 73.
COLEY,
  Abilene, 80.
  Samuel, 80.
COLLINS,
  Avis, 57, 58.
  Edward, 23, 51, 57.
  Elizabeth, 23.
  Henry, 23.

COLLINS,
  John, 57.
  Joseph (Rev.), 23.
  Martha, 23.
  Ruth, 41, 51.
  Sybil, 23.
  Timothy (Rev.), 57, 58.
  William, 41.
CONCKLIN,
  Ananias, 67.
  Avis, 29.
  Jeremiah, 29, 67.
  Mary, 67.
COOKE,
  Aaron (Capt.), 87.
  Joanna, 3.
  Sarah, 87.
COOPER,
  John, 68.
  Sarah, 68, 97.
  Thomas (Lieut.), 97.
  Wibroe, 68,
COREY,
  Abraham, 29.
  Mary, 29.
CORNISH,
  James, 70.
  James (Capt.), 70.
  Lucy, 70.
COWLES,
  Elizabeth, 62.
  Timothy (Dea.), 62.
COTTON,
  John (Rev.), 41, 45, 65.
CRITTENDEN,
  Thomas J., 21.
CROCKER,
  Alice, 63.
  Hannah, 63.
  Josiah, 63.
  Josiah (Rev.), 63.
  William, 63.
CROOME,
  Anna E., 44, 85.
  George W., 85.
CROWE,
  John, 47, 86, 91,
  Mary, 86.
  Ruth, 91.
  Samuel, 86, 87.
  Sarah, 47, 48.
CRUGER,
  Henry, 56.
  Matilda Caroline, 56.
  Polly, 56.
CULVER,
  Mary, 93.
  John, 93.
CURTIS,
  Abigail, 83.
  Anne, 95.
  Ebenezer, 83, 92.
  Elizabeth, 13, 48, 83, 92.

CURTIS,
  Ephraim, 92.
  Jonathan, 83, 92.
  Joseph, 95.
  Josiah, 83, 92.
  Ruth, 93.
  Sarah, 83, 92.
  Thomas, 13.
  William, 48, 83, 92
  Winlolock, 95.
  Zechariah, 83, 92.
CUSHMAN,
  Robert, 9.

DAKIN,
  Sarah, 22.
DANFORTH,
  Elizabeth, 79.
  Nicholas, 79.
DAVIS,
  Grace Noble, 33.
  Joanna, 16, 33.
  Thomas (Col.), 33.
  William, 33.
DAY,
  Editha, 97.
  Robert, 97.
  Sarah C., 22, 43, 97.
  Thomas, 43, 97, 98.
DAVENPORT,
  John (Rev.), 27, 32, 80.
DEBLE,
  Hepzibah, 91.
  Robert, 91.
  Thomas, 91.
DE LA GRANDE,
  Ralph, 1.
  William, 1.
DELANO,
  Jonathan, 9, 10.
  Susannah, 8, 9. 10.
DE LA NOYE,
  Jean, 9.
  Marie, 9.
  Philip, 9.
DEMING,
  Elizabeth, 12, 60.
  John, 12, 42, 44, 53, 60, 61, 95.
  Prudence, 41, 53.
  Rachel, 44.
  Sarah, 61, 94.
DENISON,
  George, 17.
  Sarah, 17.
  William, 17.
DENSLOW,
  Joanna, 86.
  Nicholas, 86.
DENT,
  Frederick, 93.
  Julia B., 53, 93.

DESBOROUGH,
  Esther, 7.
  James, 9.
  Samuel, 9.
DEWEY,
  Josiah, 23, 24
  Mehitabel, 23.
  Sophia, 71.
  Thomas, 24, 71.
DEXTER,
  Alice, 58.
  Bridget, 58
  Harriet C., 89, 52.
  Richard, 58.
  Seth, 90, 92.
  Thomas, 89.
  William, 89.
DICKINSON,
  Elizabeth, 46.
  Esther, 3.
  John, 85.
  Mary H., 44, 85.
  Thomas, 46.
DOTEN,
  Edward, 10.
  Hannah, 10.
  Thomas, 10.
DOUGLASS,
  Anna, 88.
  Asa, 88.
  Asa (Capt.), 88.
  Edwin A., 88.
  Ellen A., 53, 88, 92,
  Hannah (Mrs.), 89.
  Margaret (Mrs.), 89.
  William, 89.
DOWNING,
  Emmanuel, 77.
  Mary, 77.
DUCHAYNE,
  Hester, 60.
DUDLEY,
  Jane, 80.
  Jemima, 80
  Joseph, 80.
  Mary, 28.
  Ruth, 94.
  William, 28, 80, 94.
DUNSTER,
  Henry, 81.
DUTCHER,
  Samuel, 9.

EATON,
  Theophilus (Gov.), 27, 29, 32, 59, 68, 80.
EGGLESTON,
  Abigail, 44.
  Bigod, 45.
  James, 44.
ELIOT,
  John (Rev.) 39, 62, 66, 95.
  Roger, 95.

ELIOT,
  Sarah, 62.
ELLSWORTH,
  Esther, 47.
  John, 17, 48
  Josias, 48.
ENDICOTT,
  John (Rev.), 35.
  Mary, 35.
ENO,
  Sarah, 51.
  James, 51.
ENSIGN,
  David, 11, 46.
  Huldah, 11.
  James, 11, 45, 46.
  John, 45, 46.
  John (Capt.), 46.
  Lois, 45.
  Mary, 46.
  Thomas, 46.
EVETT,
  Esther, 5.
EYRE,
  Catharine, 81, 82.
  Robert, 81, 82.

FAIRBANKS,
  Grace. 49.
  Jonathan, 49.
  John, 49.
  Mary, 49.
FELLOWS,
  Anna, 11.
  Hannah, 9, 10, 12.
  John (Gen.), 8, 10.
  John (Col.), 11.
  Samuel, 11.
FILLEY,
  Anna, 6.
  Samuel, 6.
  William, 6.
FLETCHER,
  Benjamin, 35.
  John, 64.
  Sarah, 64.
FLOYD,
  John B., 21.
FOOTE,
  Elizabeth, 12, 44, 59, 87.
  Nathaniel, 12, 44, 60, 87.
  Mary, 13, 60.
  Rebecca, 60.
  Thomas M., 33.
FORD,
  Abigail, 25, 34.
  Hepzibah, 24.
  Thomas, 24, 25, 34.
FOSTER,
  Elizabeth, 25, 26.
  Hopestill, 25.
  James, 25.
  Patience, 25.

FREMONT,
  John C., 21.
FRISBIE,
  John, 59.
  Mary, 59.
  Ruth, 59.

GARDINER,
  Lyon, 29, 67.
  Mary, 29, 67.
GAYLORD,
  Abigail, 75, 76.
  Anna, 90.
  Eliakim, 91.
  Eleazur, 91.
  Elizabeth, 90.
  Joanna, 52.
  Mary, 52, 78.
  Nathaniel, 75, 90.
  Sylvia, 90, 92.
  Walter, 52, 78.
  William, 2, 75, 78, 90.
  William, Jr., 90, 91.
GIBBES,
  Catharine (Mrs.), 91.
  Elizabeth, 91.
  Giles, 91.
  Samuel, 91.
GIBSON,
  John, 56.
  Rebecca, 56.
  R. L. (Gen.), 21.
GILBERT,
  John, 30.
  Prudence, 30.
  Winifred, 30.
GILLETTE,
  Anna, 6.
  Jonathan, 6.
GLOVER,
  Hannah, 11.
  Henry, 11.
GOODWIN,
  Elizabeth, 47, 86, 91.
  Hannah, 62.
  Nathaniel, 3.
  Ozias, 62.
  Susannah, 48, 91.
  Susannah (Mrs.), 86.
  William, 28, 47, 86, 91.
GOODRICH,
  Elizabeth, 48.
  William, 48.
GORDON,
  Mary, 83.
GORHAM,
  John (Capt.), 68.
  Mehitabel, 68.
  Timothy, 68.
GRAHAM,
  John (Rev.), 81, 83.
  Sarah, 81, 83.

GRANGER,
  Delia, 63.
  John, 63.
GRANT,
  Adoniram, 8.
  Cluny, 53.
  Frederick D., 91.
  Ellen W, 94.
  Jesse R, 24, 53, 94.
  John, 24.
  Margaret, 24.
  Mary F., 53
  Martha Huntington, 8.
  Matthew, 7.
  Noah, 3, 6, 8, 9, 10, 23, 24, 53
  Orville L, 53.
  Peter, 10, 24.
  Rachel, 24.
  Roswell, 24.
  Samuel S, 53.
  Samuel, 2, 6, 7, 8.
  Solomon, 8, 10, 24.
  Solomon (Capt.), 10
  Susannah, 10, 24.
  Ulysses S, 53, 93, 94.
  Virginia, 53.
GREENHILL,
  Rebecca, 14, 46.
  Samuel, 46.
  Thomas, 46.
GRAYSON,
  Alfred (Col), 97.
  John Breckinridge, 97.
GREGSON,
  Thomas, 18.
GRISWOLD,
  Deborah, 3, 6, 8, 23, 41, 51, 52, 57. 75, 97.
  Edward, 3, 6, 8, 23, 52, 57, 75, 77, 78
  Eunice, 41, 52, 53, 75, 76, 78, 79.
  George, 75.
  John, 75, 76.
  Joseph, 52.
  Margaret, 75, 77, 78
  Mary, 52.
  Matthew, 8, 41, 51, 52, 53, 75, 78, 79.
GROSSE,
  Clement, 27.
  Edmund, 26, 27.
  Sally, 26
GROVES,
  Anna, 3, 92.
  Phillip, 9.
GUNN,
  Mehitabel, 46.
  Thomas, 46.

HALL,
  Benedict E., 55.

HALL,
  Henry (Maj.), 55.
HALLEY,
  John, 22.
HALSEY,
  Elizabeth, 20.
  Phœbe, 20.
  Thomas, 20.
HARBOTEL,
  Dorothea, 77.
HARRIS,
  Edith, 97.
  Martha, 97.
  William, 97.
HART,
  Margaret, 64
  Mary, 48.
  Stephen, 49, 64,
  Thomas, 64.
HARTT,
  Mary, 63.
  Ralph, 63.
HASKELL,
  Deborah, 90.
  William, 90.
HAWKINS,
  Anthony, 54.
  Ruth, 54.
HAWKHURST,
  Christopher, 37.
  Hannah, 37.
HAWLEY,
  Elizabeth, 7, 77.
  Joseph, 7, 77.
  Thomas, 77.
HAYDEN,
  Daniel, 40, 51, 91.
  Elizabeth, 91.
  Hannah (Mrs.), 91.
  Samuel, 40, 51.
  Sarah, 40.
  William, 40, 51, 91.
HAYNES,
  John (Rev.), 22.
HAYTE,
  Elizabeth, 27.
  Walter, 27.
HEATH,
  Elizabeth, 62.
  Isaac, 62.
HEATON,
  Elizabeth, 73.
  James, 73
  Nathaniel, 73.
  Sarah, 73.
HEMMINGWAY,
  Abram, 68.
  Amy, 68
  Eliza, 68.
  John, 68.
  Ralph, 68.
  Samuel, 68.

119

HEWES,
  Elizabeth, 68.
  Joshua, 68.
HEWETT,
  Ephraim (Rev.), 2, 8, 41,
    51, 64, 75, 78, 90.
  Mary, 64.
HILL,
  Eliza, 85.
  Joseph, 32.
  Margery, 32.
HINCKLEY,
  Meletiah, 63.
  Samuel, 63.
  Thomas, 63.
  Thomas (Gov.), 63.
HINMAN,
  Benjamin, 81.
  Edward, 81.
  Eunice, 81.
HINSDALE,
  Anna, 94.
  Robert, 94
  Samuel, 94.
HITCHCOCK,
  Eliakim, 68.
  Hannah, 61, 86.
  Luke, 61, 86.
  Matthew, 69.
  Sarah, 68.
HOLCOMBE,
  Anna, 51.
  Benajah, 51.
  Elizabeth, 48.
  Hannah, 40.
  Joshua, 40, 70.
  Mary, 75.
  Sarah, 70.
  Thomas, 48, 51, 75.
HOLGRAVE,
  John, 16.
  Martha, 16.
HOLLISTER,
  Elizabeth, 62.
  John, 62.
HOLLEY,
  Alexander H., 22, 39, 43,
    74, 97, 98.
  Alexander L., 43, 74.
  Alice, 74.
  Alma Sterling, 82.
  Edith, 47.
  Elizabeth P., 47.
  George W., 23, 43, 44, 47.
  Gertrude, 74
  Harriet, 22, 33, 43.
  Harriet L., 39, 71, 73.
  Henry K., 39.
  John, 22.
  John M., 9, 22, 38, 39,
    74, 82.
  John Coffing, 43, 74,
    82, 84.

HOLLEY,
  Julia K., 39.
  Lucy, 74.
  Luther, 22.
  Marcia (Mrs.), 43.
  Maria, 22.
  Maria C., 43, 84.
  Mary Ann, 22, 23, 50, 53.
  Mary E., 39.
  Porter, 47.
  Sally Porter, 28, 47, 50.
  Sarah, 39.
  William R., 43.
HOLTON,
  Rachel, 34.
  William, 34.
HONORE,
  Ida M., 94.
HOOGEBAUM,
  Hannah, 11.
  Pieter Meese, 11.
HOOKER,
  John, 64, 65.
  Ruth, 64, 65.
  Samuel, 65.
  Samuel (Rev.), 65
  Thomas (Rev.), 5, 18, 22,
    38, 41, 45, 46, 48, 49,
    58, 64, 65, 91.
HOOPER,
  Rachel, 37, 70.
HOPKINS,
  Arthur (Dr.), 38, 71.
  Ebenezer, 18.
  Jane, 19.
  John, 19, 45.
  John H. (Rt. Rev.), 94.
  Mary, 18, 38, 45, 71, 86.
  Matilda, 94.
  Samuel, 84.
  Stephen, 18, 19, 45.
  Waity, 84.
  William, 86.
HORTON,
  Barnabas, 4.
  Eunice, 3, 4.
  Joseph, 4.
  Joshua, 4.
HOSFORD,
  John, 52, 53.
  Sarah, 52
  William, 53.
HOSMER,
  Clemence, 16.
  Thomas, 15.
HOVEY,
  Daniel, 87.
  Miriam, 87.
  Thomas (Lieut.), 87.
HOUGH,
  Abiah, 88.
HOWARD,
  Margaret, 21.

HOWELL,
  Edward, 19.
  Henry, 19.
  Hezekiah, 19, 20.
  Jane, 19.
  Judge, 34.
  Richard 19.
HOWLAND,
  Desire, 68.
  John, 68.
HUITT,
  (See Hewett.)
HULL,
  Andrew, 43
  Catharine, 43.
HUNT,
  Jonathan, 16.
  Theoda, 15
HUNTER,
  Andrew, 89.
  Margaret, 89.
  Mary, 89.
  Priscilla, 89.
  Robert, 89.
  William, 89.
HUNTINGTON,
  Christopher, 6.
  John, 6.
  Martha, 3, 6, 8.
  Simon, 6.
HURD,
  Benjamin, 8.
  Gideon, 81, 82.
  John, 80, 83.
  Love, 80, 83.
  Nathan, 81.
HUTCHINSON,
  Elisha, 5.
HYDE,
  Bezaleel, 4, 5.
  Daniel, 5.
  Elizabeth, 58, 79.
  Eunice, 5.
  Hester, 84.
  Joshua. 5.
  Lucretia, 5.
  Mehitabel, 5.
  Nathaniel, 5.
  Oliver C., 5.
  Samuel, 5, 58, 67, 79.
  Sarah, 67.
  William, 5, 58, 67, 79, 84.

JACKSON,
  Elizabeth, 37.
  Robert, 37.
JEFFREY,
  Alexander, 63.
  Julia E., 36, 63.
JOHNSON,
  Lucretia, 5.
JOHNSTON,
  Albert Sydney, 21.

JOHNSTON,
    Humphrey, 94.
    John, 94.
    Mehitabel, 84.
JONES,
    Elizabeth, 32.
    John Richter (Maj.), 95.
    Virginia C., 57, 95.
    William, 32.
JOURDAINE,
    Stephen, 46.
    Susannah, 46.
JUDSON,
    Abigail, 83, 92.
    Elizabeth, 76, 77.
    Grace, 76, 82.
    Isaac, 77.
    James, 82.
    Joseph, 2, 47, 76, 82, 83, 92.
    Ruth, 47.
    Sarah, 82.
    William, 47, 76, 82.

KASSON,
    Jeanne, 83.
    William, 83.
KEENEY,
    Agnes, 93.
    Mary, 93.
    William, 93.
KELLEY,
    Rachel, 24
KELLOGG,
    Abigail, 31, 61.
    Dorothy, 94.
    John, 61.
    Joseph, 31, 61.
    Martin, 94.
    Stephen, 31.
KENRICK,
    Anna, 49.
    John, 49.
KIMBALL,
    Richard, 89.
    Sarah, 99.
    Ursula, 89.
KING,
    Orilla, 39, 74.
    Walter (Rev.), 6.
KIRKLAND,
    Daniel, 38.
    John, 38.
    Joseph, 39.
    Joseph (Gen.), 38.
    Mary, 22, 38, 39.

LAMB,
    Elizabeth, 81.
    Samuel, 81.
    Thomas, 77, 81.
LAMBERTON,
    Captain, 18.

LANDON,
    Mary, 58.
LANE,
    Anna, 25.
    Job, 25.
LATIMER,
    John, 12.
    Rebecca, 12.
LAWRENCE,
    George, 55.
    Judith, 55.
LAWTON,
    Elizabeth, 32.
    Thomas, 32.
LAY,
    Abigail, 72.
    John, 72.
LEE,
    David, 49.
    Jane, 5, 58, 67, 79.
    John, 48.
    Jonathan, 4, 49.
    Mary, 5, 58.
    Phœbe, 5, 79.
    Salome, 48, 49.
    Thomas, 5, 58, 67, 79.
LEISTER,
    Edward, 10.
LEETE,
    Anna, 57.
    John, 57.
    William, 57.
LEWIS,
    Amy, 86.
    Hannah, 86.
    William, 86.
LESTER,
    Andrew, 98.
    Barbara, 93.
    Mehitabel, 98.
    Timothy, 98.
LOBDELL,
    Anna, 30.
    Simon, 30.
LOOMIS,
    Joseph, 2, 75, 78.
    Mary, 41, 52, 57, 75, 78.
    Thomas, 41, 52, 57, 75, 78
LORD,
    Anna, 19.
    Dorothy, 19, 79.
    Phœbe, 79, 80.
    Richard, 79.
    Sarah, 22.
    Thomas, 17, 22, 79.
    William, 22, 79.
LOTHROP,
    Hannah, 39.
    John (Rev.), 7, 39.
    Samuel, 6, 7, 39.
LUDLOW,
    Roger, 14, 19, 25, 35.
    Sarah, 35.

LYMAN,
    Alice, 53, 93.
    Anna, 50.
    Ellen A. (Mrs.), 92.
    Erastus, 39, 42.
    Harriet Dexter, 92.
    Hepzibah, 24.
    Holley Porter, 53.
    Isabel Douglass, 92.
    Jane M., 22, 39, 43.
    John, 40, 50.
    John (Lieut), 50.
    Lucy Beebe, 93.
    Margaret, 93.
    Mary, 53, 93.
    Mary Alice, 93.
    Moses, 23, 40, 42, 50, 51, 53, 88, 92.
    Moses (Capt.), 50.
    Moses (Col.), 40, 41, 51.
    Richard, 24, 39, 50, 53.
    Samuel, 93.
    Sarah, 40.

McDOWELL,
    (Governor,) 21.
McKAY,
    Elizabeth, 83.
McMURRAY,
    Margaret, 27, 54.
MALLORY,
    Judith, 76.
    Peter, 76.
MANSFIELD,
    Gillian, 34.
    Moses, 34.
    Richard, 34.
    Sarah Augusta, 34.
MARSH,
    Dorcas, 3.
MARSHALL,
    Lydia, 77.
    Samuel, 77.
    Samuel (Capt.), 77.
    Thomas, 77.
    Thomas F., 21.
MARTIN,
    Alexander, 83.
    Jane, 83.
    Lucinda, 83.
    Mary Gordon, 83.
    Robert, 83.
    Seth, 83.
    William, 83.
MARVYN (or Marvin),
    Hannah, 25.
    Matthew, 25, 48.
    Reginald, 25, 79.
    Sarah, 48.
MASON,
    Ann, 67.
    Elizabeth, 28, 66, 67.

MASON,
  John (Capt.), 25, 28, 29, 45, 51, 66, 72, 77.
  John (Maj.), 66, 67.
MATHER,
  Anna, 14.
  Eleazer, 13.
  Eunice, 16.
  Nathan (Capt.), 8.
  Richard (Rev.), 14, 49.
MATHEWS,
  James, 36, 69.
  Julia, 20, 34, 36.
  Peter, 35.
  Sarah, 69.
  Vincent, 34, 35, 36.
  Vincent (Gen.), 36.
MAVERICK,
  John, 1.
MAY,
  Dorothy, 56.
MAYBELL,
  Thomas, 88.
MEACHAM,
  Eunice, 8
MERRILL,
  Abraham, 46.
  Nathaniel, 46.
  Prudence, 46.
METCALF,
  Elizabeth, 49.
  Jonathan, 49.
  Joseph, 49.
  Joseph (Rev.), 49.
  Michael, 49.
  Sarah, 49.
MILES,
  Hannah, 42, 43.
  Richard, 43.
  Samuel, 43.
MILLER,
  (Rev. Doctor), 71.
  John, 59.
  Margaret, 22, 37, 59, 71.
  Mary M., 33, 60.
MINOR,
  Grace, 6, 7.
  John, 7.
  Thomas, 7.
  William, 7.
MIX,
  Hannah, 18.
  Thomas, 18.
MOODY,
  George, 61.
  John, 61.
  Samuel, 61.
  Sarah, 61.
MOORE,
  Abigail, 75, 90.
  John, 75, 90.
MORGAN,
  Elizabeth, 32.
  Hannah, 30.
  James, 32.
  John (Capt.), 32.
  Miles, 30.
  Theophilus, 32.
MORRIS,
  George W., 38.
  John, 73.
  Josephine M., 38.
  Mary, 73.
MORTON,
  Anna, 32, 68.
  Thomas, 32, 68.
MOUNTFORD,
  Anna, 62.
MULFORD,
  Barnabas, 67, 68.
  Hervey, 67, 68.
  Nancy M., 67.
  Thomas, 67.
  William, 67.
MULLER,
  Jane, 11.
MULLINS,
  Priscilla, 66.
  William, 66.
MUNN,
  Benjamin, 26.
  Mary, 26.
MUZZEY,
  Benjamin, 58.
  Leah, 58.
MYGATT,
  Joseph, 41.
  Mary, 41.

NEWBERRY,
  Jane, 92.
  Mary, 92.
  Thomas, 92.
NEWELL,
  Cynthia, 46.
  Rebecca, 15.
  Seth, 46.
  Thomas, 15, 47.
NEWTON,
  John (Rev.), 65.
NOBLE,
  Abel, 33.
  Anna, 33.
  Grace, 33.
NORTON,
  Elizabeth, 66, 67.
  Grace, 28, 65, 73.
  Ichabod (Col.), 65.
  Mary, 73.
  Ruth, 28.
  Thomas, 28, 66, 67, 73.

OLMSTEAD,
  Hannah, 18.
  James, 15, 47.
OLMSTEAD,
  John, 15.
  Rebecca, 15, 17.
  Richard, 15, 47.
  Thomas, 18.
OSBORNE,
  Albert Porter, 63.
  John H., 36, 63.
  Ruth, 63.
ORTON,
  Mary, 76.
  Thomas, 76.
PALMER,
  Grace, 7.
  Walter, 7.
PARKE,
  Agnes, 89.
  Martha, 98.
  Theoda, 16.
  Robert, 16, 98.
  Thomas, 98.
  William, 16.
PARTRIDGE,
  Mary, 12.
  William, 12.
PATTON,
  Elizabeth, 21.
  James (Col.), 21.
PAWLING,
  Albert (Col.), 9, 17.
  Levi (Col.), 17.
PEABODY,
  Priscilla, 66.
  William, 66.
PECK,
  Ann, 66.
  Anna, 28.
  Benjamin, 57, 58, 59.
  Clarissa, 57, 59.
  Elizabeth, 27.
  Martha, 46, 58.
  Paul, 46, 58.
  Paul (Dea.), 58.
  Robert, 66.
  Robert (Rev.), 28, 66.
  William, 27.
PELL,
  Margaret, 76.
  Thomas, 76.
PERKINS,
  Hannah, 39.
  Jabez, 39.
  Jacob, 39.
  John, 39.
  Judith, 39.
PETTEE,
  Edward, 68.
  Hannah, 68.
PETTIBONE,
  Lauren W., 37.

PHELPS,
  Eliphalet, 5.
  George, 2, 78.
  Joseph, 52, 53, 78.
  Lyman (Rev.), 93.
  Mary, 52, 53, 78, 79.
  Timothy, 52.
  William, 52.
PIERSON,
  Abraham (Rev.), 67.
  Susannah, 67.
PINE,
  John, 59.
  Phœbe, 59.
PITKIN,
  Hannah, 62.
  William, 62.
PLUMB,
  Dorcas, 40, 50.
  John, 40, 50.
POST,
  John, 84.
  Mary, 84.
  Stephen, 84.
PRATT,
  Elizabeth, 38.
  John, 94.
  Lydia, 38.
  Mary, 94.
  William, 38.
PRESTON,
  Anne, 21.
  Harrietta, 21.
  James P. (Col.), 21.
  John, 21.
  Lætitia, 21.
  Mary W., 21.
  Sophronisha, 22.
  William, 21.
PRICHARD,
  Elizabeth, 89.
  William, 89.
PROCTOR,
  John, 85, 88.
  Martha, 88.
  Sarah, 88.
PROVOST,
  Frances C., 22.
PRUDDEN,
  Abigail, 81.
  Anna, 80.
  James, 80.
  Peter (Rev.), 80, 81.
PYNCHON,
  Amy, 10.
  John, 10, 11, 65.
  Mary, 10.
  Nicholas, 10.
  William, 10, 11, 14, 19.

RAINSFORD,
  Ranis, 26.
  Edward, 26.

RAMSEY,
  Charlotte, 9, 54.
RANDALL,
  Philura, 78.
  Philip, 78.
RAYNOR,
  Abigail, 61.
  Alice, 56.
  John (Rev.), 56, 61.
REYNER,
  Anna, 25.
  John (Rev.), 25, 81.
RICHARDS,
  Alice, 19, 55, 63.
  Mary, 63.
  Thomas, 55, 63.
ROBBINS,
  Hannah, 48.
  John, 47, 48.
  Joshua, 48.
  Joshua (Capt.), 12.
  Lucy Maria, 50.
  Mary, 12, 47.
  Mary Ann, 50.
  Mary E., 88.
  Milton Holley, 50, 85, 88.
  Sally Holley, 50, 85.
  Samuel, 48, 49, 50.
  Samuel B., 88.
  Samuel S., 23, 47. 50.
  Sarah Lucretia, 50.
ROBERTS,
  John, 14.
  Sarah, 14.
ROBINSON,
  Ann, 80.
  Arthur, 36, 64, 69.
  Arthur P., 69
  Charles, 67, 69.
  Cornelia G, 69.
  Ichabod, 67.
  Jacob, 68
  Jane Porter, 69.
  John (Rev), 35, 66, 67.
  Julia O , 69.
  Samuel, 66.
  Sarah, 68.
  Thomas, 80.
  William, 66.
  William (Rev), 67.
ROOT,
  Jesse, 53.
ROPER,
  Alice, 42.
  John, 42.
  Priscilla, 42.
ROYCE,
  Robert, 5, 58, 67.
  Sarah, 5, 58, 67.
ROYS,
  Charles H , 39, 74.
  Charles Kirkland, 74.
  John Holley, 74.

ROYS,
  Jonathan, 62.
  Mary Louise. 74.
  Ruth, 62.
RUDD,
  Alexander Holley, 84.
  Charles Edward, 84.
  Fanny, 84.
  George Robert, 84.
  Maria Holley, 84.
  Malcolm Day, 84.
  Nathaniel, 84.
  William Beardslee, 84.

SADLIER,
  Anne, 45.
  Mr (Rev.), 45.
SANFORD,
  Mary, 13.
  Robert, 13, 14.
SARTORIS,
  Algernon C. F., 94.
SAUNDERS,
  Elizabeth, 41, 52.
SAYLES,
  Catalina, 36.
SAYRE,
  Job, 20.
  Susannah, 20.
  Thomas, 20.
SAWYER,
  Ellen, 93.
  John T., 53, 93.
SCOTT,
  Sarah, 65.
  Thomas, 65.
SCOTTOWE,
  Joshua, 63.
  Mary, 63.
SECOR,
  Elizabeth, 59.
SEDGWICK,
  Ebenezer, 46.
  Joanna, 45.
  Mary, 46.
  Robert, 45, 76.
  Samuel, 45.
  William, 45.
SEYMOUR,
  John, 17, 28.
  Mary, 27, 28.
  Richard, 17, 27.
  Sarah, 18.
  Thomas, 28.
  Zechariah, 18.
SHEAFE,
  Joan, 57.
  Jacob (Dr.), 57.
SHELDON,
  Hannah, 15, 26.
  Isaac, 15, 26, 40, 50.
  Mindwell, 40, 50.

SHEPARD,
  Hannah, 46.
  John, 46.
SHERMAN,
  Elizabeth, 32.
  Peleg, 32.
  Ruth, 40, 70.
  Thomas, 40, 70.
  William, 32.
SHIPMAN,
  Rebecca, 32.
SILL
  Jemima, 79.
  John, 79.
  Joseph, 80.
  Joseph (Capt.), 79.
  Thomas, 80.
SIMPSON,
  Harriet, 24, 53.
  John, 53.
SLADE,
  Mary H., 43, 74.
SLATER,
  Hannah, 94.
SMALLEY,
  Hannah, 71.
  John, 71.
SMITH,
  Abigail, 6.
  Anna, 86, 87.
  Benjamin, 12.
  Chileab, 61, 86.
  Ebenezer, 61.
  Elizabeth, 12, 44, 60, 61, 86.
  John, 12
  Joseph, 87.
  Josiah (Capt.), 12, 13.
  Josiah Churchill, 12.
  Luke, 86.
  Philip, 60.
  Samuel, 12, 44, 60, 61, 86.
  Thankful, 9, 11, 12, 13.
SOUTHWORTH,
  Edward, 56.
SPAULDING,
  Benjamin, 98.
  Sarah, 98.
SPENCER,
  Sarah, 69.
  Thomas, 70.
  William, 70.
STANLEY,
  Abigail, 64, 65.
  Anna, { 2, 3, 4, 61.
  Hannah, } 65, 72, 74.
  John, 64, 65.
  Mary, 2, 41, 52, 57, 64, 74, 78.
  Thomas, 2, 41, 52, 57, 64, 65, 74.

STANTON,
  Abigail Porter, 16.
  Eunice (Bird), 17.
  Joshua, 9, 16, 17.
  Thomas, 17.
STARK,
  Abigail, 42, 43.
  Comfort, 42.
  Comfort (Dr.), 42.
  Elizabeth, 42.
  Ephraim, 42.
  Joseph, 42.
  Rachel, 42.
  Thomas (Dr.), 42.
STEARNS,
  Charles, 56.
  John, 55, 56.
  Maria, 55.
STEBBINS,
  Edward, 52, 97.
  Mary, 52, 78.
  Roland, 78.
  Sarah, 78.
STEELE,
  Daniel, 18, 19.
  George, 18.
  James, 18.
  John, 14.
  John, Jr , 19.
  Lavinia, 9, 17, 19.
  Lydia, 14.
  Rachel, 19.
  Samuel, 19.
  Sarah, 18.
  Timothy, 17, 18.
STEPHENS,
  John, 57.
  Mary, 57.
STERLING,
  Elisha, 79, 80.
  George W., 74, 80, 83.
  Lucinda R , 43, 74, 84
  William, 80.
  William (Capt.), 79.
STILES,
  Hannah, 81.
  Francis, 81.
STODDARD,
  Abigail P., 14, 31, 33, 43.
  Anthony, 13, 77.
  John, 13
  Joseph, 77.
  Josiah, 13, 14, 16.
  Josiah (Ensign), 14.
  Luther, 9, 13, 14, 17.
  Rebecca, 77.
  Solomon (Rev.), 13, 77.
STONE,
  Elizabeth, 41.
  Samuel (Rev.) 45, 65, 72.
  Sarah, 72.
STOUGHTON,
  Thomas, 6.

ST. JOHN,
  Mary, 27.
  Matthew, 27.
  Samuel, 27.
STRATTON,
  Elizabeth, 16.
STREETE,
  Nicholas (Rev.), 73.
  Sarah, 73.
STRONG,
  Abigail, 82.
  Asahel, 64, 65.
  Asahel (Capt.), 64.
  Hannah, 36, 71.
  Henry, 25.
  Jedediah, 49.
  John, 64
  John (Elder), 25, 34, 49, 71, 82.
  Julianna, 34, 35, 36.
  Lydia, 49.
  Nathaniel (Maj.), 35, 36.
  Richard, 25.
  Ruth, 65
  Sarah, 25, 34.
  Selah, 30, 34, 35.
  Thomas, 34, 64.
SYMMES,
  Zachary, 45.

TALMADGE,
  Enos, 68.
  Sarah, 68.
TAYLOR,
  Alice A , 38, 69, 70.
  Electa, 70.
  John, 69.
  Richard, 69.
  William, 69, 70.
  Virgil, 70.
  Virgil C , 70.
TERRILL,
  Roger, 15.
  Sarah, 15.
TERRY,
  Abigail, 30, 31, 34, 61.
  Matthew, 30.
  Ruth, 30, 34.
  Samuel, 30.
  Stephen, 31, 61.
  Thomas, 30, 34
THOMPSON,
  Abigail, 83.
  Anthony, 59, 80, 95.
  Bridget, 59.
  Catharine, 95.
  John, 80, 81, 83.
  Sarah, 80, 82.
  William, 80.
TILLEY,
  Elizabeth, 68.
  John, 68.

TILLOTSON,
   (Archbishop), 73.
   John, 73.
   Sophronia, 73.
TILLYOU,
   Judith, 59.
TITUS,
   Elizabeth, 37.
   Samuel, 37.
THRALL,
   Phillippa, 52.
   William, 52.
TOWNSEND,
   Augustus P., 37.
   Beckman H., 36.
   Daniel J., 20, 36, 37.
   Elizabeth J., 37.
   Henry, 36, 37.
   Isaac, 37.
   Jane H., 37, 69.
   John, 36.
   Lavinia P., 37.
   Peter, 37.
   Richard, 36.
TREAT,
   Honor, 42, 44, 53, 61.
   James, 12.
   Joanna, 12, 41, 62.
   Joseph, 12.
   Mary, 12.
   Richard, 12, 42, 44, 53, 61, 62.
TROWBRIDGE,
   Elizabeth, 76.
   James, 76.
   Thomas, 76.
TUDOR,
   Sarah, 2.
TURNER,
   Mary, 68.
   Nathaniel (Capt.), 18, 68, 84.
   Mary, 19.
   Rebecca, 18.
TUTTLE,
   Anna, 47, 82.
   Elizabeth, 68.
   Joseph, 68.
   Mary, 68.
   Richard, 47, 82.
   William, 68.
TYBBOTT,
   Mary, 90.
   Walter, 90.

UFFORD,
   Thomas, 15.
UNDERHILL,
   Deborah, 36.
   Helena, 36.
   John, 36.

VAILL,
   Ann, 30.

VAILL,
   Jeremiah, 30.
   Mary, 30.
   Peter, 30.
VINCENT,
   Benjamin, 90.
   John, 90.
   Sarah, 90.
   Thomas, 90.

WADSWORTH,
   Elizabeth, 5.
   James (Gen.), 31.
   Joseph, 5.
   William, 5, 28.
   Zerviah, 4, 5.
WALKER,
   Joseph, 81.
   Robert, 81.
   Sarah, 10, 81.
WALTON,
   Cruger, 31, 56.
   Henry, 56.
   Henry Cruger, 57, 95.
   Jacob, 56.
   Mary Porter, 57, 94.
   Matilda C., 95.
   William, 56.
WARD,
   Isabel, 26.
   Joyce, 64.
   Lawrence, 26.
   Mary, 64.
WARHAM,
   Esther, 13, 77.
   John (Rev.), 1, 2, 6, 13, 24, 25, 28, 31, 40, 52, 64, 65, 71, 75, 77, 90.
WARNER,
   Andrew, 15, 19, 40, 51.
   Daniel, 15, 40, 50.
   Mary, 19.
   Sarah, 15, 40, 50.
WARREN,
   Joseph, 16.
   Joseph (Gen.), 16.
   Mercy, 10.
   Nathaniel, 10.
   Richard, 10.
WATSON,
   John, 17, 28.
   Mary, 17, 28.
WATTELS,
   Abigail, 5.
WEBB,
   Richard, 22.
   Waitstill, 22.
WEBSTER,
   Abigail, 46.
   John, 16, 46.
   Mary, 16.
WELD,
   Joseph, 42.

WELD,
   Marah, 42.
WELLES,
   Esther, 47.
   John, 48.
   Joseph, 48.
   Lucy, 61, 62.
   Philip, 53, 93.
   Rebecca, 82.
   Robert, 48.
   Samuel, 62
   Samuel (Capt.), 47.
   Thaddeus, 62.
   Thomas, 47, 61, 82.
WEST,
   Mary, 8.
WESTOVER,
   Joanna, 31, 61.
   Jonas, 31, 61.
   Mary, 31.
WESTWOOD,
   Aaron, 87.
   Aaron (Capt.), 87.
   Bridget, 87.
   Sarah, 87.
   William, 48, 87.
WHEELER,
   Edward S., 37, 69.
   Elizabeth T., 69.
   Experience, 97.
   Frank Storer, 69.
   Isaac, 97.
   Marion W., 69.
   Rebecca, 88.
   Thomas, 88.
   Townsend, 69.
WHITE,
   Esther, 47.
   Daniel, 47, 48.
   John, 28.
   John (Elder), 29, 48.
   Mary, 29.
WHITFIELD,
   Henry (Rev.), 29, 57, 58, 80.
WHITING,
   John, 23.
   John (Rev.), 51.
   Joseph, 10, 11.
   Mary, 11.
   Sybil, 23.
   William, 10, 23, 51.
WHITTLESEY,
   Eliphalet, 94.
   John, 94.
   Martin, 94, 95.
   Mary, 94, 95.
   Ruth (Mrs.), 94.
WICLIFFE,
   Robert, 21.
WIGGINS,
   Augusta P., 31.
   David, 30.

WIGGINS,
    Ellen M., 31
    Frederick A , 59.
    Frederick B., 31.
    James, 29.
    John, 29, 31.
    John (Capt.), 29, 30.
    John P., 31.
    Margaret E., 59.
    Martha Vail, 31, 56.
    Mary Corey, 30.
    Mary E , 31.
    Peter Porter, 31, 57, 59.
    Peter Vail, 13, 29, 30.
    Peter Vail Porter, 59.
    Thomas, 23.
    Wallace B., 59.
    William F., 31.
WILBOR,
    Martha, 32.
    Samuel, 32.
    William, 32.
WILCOXSON,
    Hannah, 40, 51, 91.
    Margaret, 91
    William, 40, 51, 91.
WILLETT,
    Mary, 65.
    Sarah, 62.
    Thomas, 62, 65.
    Thomas (Maj.), 65.
WILLIAMS,
    Abigail, 3, 16.
    Chester (Rev.), 16.
    Deborah, 16.
    Ebenezer (Rev.), 16.
    Ebenezer (Col.), 16.

WILLIAMS,
    John (Rev.), 16.
    Martha, 16.
    Mary, 3, 6.
    Robert, 16.
    Samuel (Rev.), 16.
WILLIAMSON,
    Dericke, 29.
    Mary, 29
WILMOT,
    Benjamin, Jr., 43.
    Hannah, 43.
WILTON,
    David, 77.
    Mary, 77.
WINSLOW,
    John, 9.
WINTHROP,
    Adam, 77.
    Fitzjohn, 47.
    John, 28, 36, 44, 65, 77, 94.
    Lucy, 77.
    Margery, 94.
WISWALL,
    Hannah, 66, 67.
    Ichabod, 66.
    Ichabod (Rev.), 66.
WITHINGTON,
    Henry, 66.
WOLCOTT,
    Anna, 41, 52.
    Henry, 2, 41, 52.
WOOD,
    Margaret, 95.
WOODFORD,
    Joseph, 15.

WOODFORD,
    Mary, 15, 26, 40, 50.
    Thomas, 15, 26, 40, 50.
WOODHULL,
    Hannah, 35.
    Joanna, 20.
    Nathaniel, 35.
    Richard, 20.
WOODWARD,
    Elizabeth, 49.
    Freedom, 49.
    Henry (Dr.), 49.
WRENSHAW,
    Ellen, 93.
WRIGHT,
    Elizabeth, 37.
    Joseph, 37.
    Thomas, 37.
WYLIE,
    Agnes, 89.
    John, 89.
WYLLIS,
    Amy, 11.
    George, 10, 23, 65.

YALE,
    David, 68.
    Hannah, 68.
    Thomas, 68.
YATES,
    (Mrs.) 56.
YOUNGS,
    Elizabeth, 30.
    Eunice, 4.
    John (Col.), 4.
    John (Rev.), 4, 29, 30.

www.ingramcontent.com/pod-product-compliance
Lightning Source LLC
Chambersburg PA
CBHW031333160426
43196CB00007B/676